# Deconstruction and Criticism

# Deconstruction and Criticism

HAROLD BLOOM · PAUL DE MAN

JACQUES DERRIDA · GEOFFREY H. HARTMAN

J. HILLIS MILLER

A Continuum Book

THE SEABURY PRESS · NEW YORK

1979
The Seabury Press
815 Second Avenue
New York, N.Y. 10017

Printed in the United States of America

LIBRARY OF CONGRESS CATALOGING IN PUBLICATION DATA
Main entry under title:
Deconstruction and criticism.
(A continuum book)
CONTENTS: Bloom, H. The breaking of form.—
De Man, P. Shelley disfigured.—Derrida, J. [etc.]
Includes index.
1. Criticism—20th century. I. Bloom, Harold.
PN94.D4     801'.951     79-11860
ISBN 8164-9347-2     ISBN 0-8164-9354-5 pkb.

# Contents

# Preface

This is neither a polemical book nor a manifesto in the ordinary sense. If it wants to "manifest" anything, by means of essays that retain the style and character of each writer, it is a shared set of problems. These problems center on two issues that affect literary criticism today. One is the situation of criticism itself, what kind of maturer function it may claim—a function beyond the obviously academic or pedagogical. While teaching, criticizing, and presenting the great texts of our culture are essential tasks, to insist on the importance of literature should not entail assigning to literary criticism only a service function. Criticism is part of the world of letters, and has its own mixed philosophical and literary, reflective and figural strength. The second shared problem is precisely that of the importance—or *force*—of literature. What does that force consist in, how does it show itself? Can a theory be developed that is descriptive and explanatory enough to illuminate rather than pester works of art?

There are many ways of describing the force of literature. The priority of language to meaning is only one of these, but it plays a crucial role in these essays. It expresses what we all feel about figurative language, its excess over any assigned meaning, or, put more generally, the strength of the signifier vis-à-vis a signified (the "meaning") that tries to enclose it. Deconstruction, as it has come to be called, refuses to identify the force of literature with any concept of embodied meaning and shows how deeply such logocentric or incarnationist perspectives have influenced the way we think about art. We assume that, by the miracle of art, the "presence of the word" is equivalent to the presence of meaning. But the opposite can also be urged, that the word carries with it a certain absence or indeterminacy of meaning. Literary language foregrounds language itself as something not reducible to meaning: it opens as well as closes the disparity between symbol and idea, between written sign and assigned meaning.

Deconstructive criticism does not present itself as a novel enterprise. There is, perhaps, more of a relentless focus on certain questions, and a new rigor when it comes to the discipline of close reading. Yet to suggest that meaning and language do not coincide, and to draw from that noncoincidence a peculiar strength, is merely to restate what literature has always revealed. There is the difference, for instance, between sound and sense, which both stimulates and defeats the writer. Or the difference which remains when we try to reduce metaphorical expressions to the proper terms they have displaced. Or the difference between a text and the commentaries that elucidate it, and which accumulate as a variorum of readings that cannot all be reconciled.

Our essays move toward a theory of this difference, but because they retain the form of commentary they also move toward a theory of commentary. They expose the difficulty of locating meaning totally within one textual source. (Derrida's double analysis is an emblem of this, an expanding hendiadys, exegesis within or upon exegesis.) Each text is shown to imbed other texts by a most cunning assimilation whose form is the subject both of psychoanalytic and of purely rhetorical criticism. Everything we thought of as spirit, or meaning separable from the letter of the text, remains within an "intertextual" sphere; and it is commentary that reminds us of this curious and forgettable fact. Commentary, the oldest and most enduring literary-critical activity, has always shown that a received text means more than it says (it is "allegorical"), or that it subverts all possible meanings by its "irony"—a rhetorical or structural limit that prevents the dissolution of art into positive and exploitative truth.

If Federal Law obliged us to list the ingredients of our book, we would have to acknowledge a higher than average proportion of theory in the form of poetics and semiotics, and philosophical speculation generally. The separation of philosophy from literary study has not worked to the benefit of either. Without the pressure of philosophy on literary texts, or the reciprocal pressure of literary analysis on philosophical writing, each discipline becomes impoverished. If there is the danger of a confusion of realms, it is a danger worth experiencing. Since the era of the German Romantics, however, and of Coleridge—who was deeply influenced by the philosophical criticism coming from Germany around 1800—we have not seen a really fruitful intereaction of these "sister arts." Yet the recent revival of philosophic criticism, associated with such names as Lukács, Heidegger, Sartre, Benjamin, Blanchot, and even Richards, Burke, and Empson, is like a new dawn that should not fade into the light of common day. The important place taken in these essays by Romantic poetry is also worth noting: perhaps we have begun to understand what kind of thinking poetry is, especially Romantic poetry that was often held to be intellectually confused or idle. The emphasis on Shelley in some of the essays reflects an earlier scheme to acknowledge the importance of Romantic poetry directly, by focussing all contributions on that poet.

It should be repeated, in conclusion, that the critics amicably if not quite convincingly held together by the covers of this book differ considerably in their approach to literature and literary theory. *Caveat lector.* Derrida, de Man, and Miller are certainly boa-deconstructors, merciless and consequent, though each enjoys his own style of disclosing again and again the "abysm" of words. But Bloom and Hartman are barely deconstructionists. They even write against it on occasion. Though they understand Nietzsche when he says "the deepest pathos is still aesthetic play," they have a stake in that pathos: its persistence, its psychological provenance. For them the ethos of literature is not dissociable from its pathos, whereas for deconstructionist criticism literature is precisely that use of language which can purge pathos, which can show that it too is figurative, ironic or aesthetic.

GEOFFREY HARTMAN

# 1

## HAROLD BLOOM

# The Breaking of Form

## I

The word *meaning* goes back to a root that signifies "opinion" or "intention," and is closely related to the word *moaning*. A poem's meaning is a poem's complaint, its version of Keats' Belle Dame, who looked *as if* she loved, and made sweet moan. Poems instruct us in how they break form to bring about meaning, so as to utter a complaint, a moaning intended to be all their own. The word *form* goes back to a root meaning "to gleam" or "to sparkle," but in a poem it is not form itself that gleams or sparkles. I will try to show that the lustres of poetic meaning come rather from the breaking apart of form, from the shattering of a visionary gleam.

What is called "form" in poetry is itself a trope, a figurative substitution of the as-it-were "outside" of a poem for what the poem is supposed to represent or be "about." Etymologically, "about" means "to be on the outside of" something anyway, and so "about" in regard to poems is itself only another trope. Is there some way out of this wilderness of tropes, so that we can recover some sense of either a reader's or writer's other-than-verbal needs and desires?

All that a poem can be about, or what in a poem *is* other than trope, is the skill or faculty of invention or discovery, the heuristic gift. Invention is a matter of "places," of themes, topics, subjects, or of what Kenneth Burke rephrased as the implicit presence of forms in subject-matter, and named as "the Individuation of Forms." Burke defined form in literature as "an arousing and fulfillment of desires." The Burkean formula offered in his early *Counter-Statement* is still the best brief description we have:

> A work has form in so far as one part of it leads a reader to antici-
> pate another part, to be gratified by the sequence.　[P. 124]

I will extend Burke, in a Burkean way, by investing our grati-
fication not even in the disruption of sequence, but in our awareness, however precarious, that the sequence of parts is only another trope for form. Form, in poetry, ceases to be trope only
when it becomes topos, only when it is revealed as a place of invention. This revelation depends upon a breaking. Its best analogue is when any of us becomes aware of love just as the object
of love is irreparably lost. I will come back to the erotic analogue,
and to the making/breaking of form, but only after I explain my
own lack of interest in most aspects of what is called "form in poetry." My aim is not to demystify myself, which would bore
others and cause me despair, but to clarify what I have been trying to say about poetry and criticism in a series of books published during the last five years. By "clarify" I partly mean "extend," because I think I have been clear enough for some, and I
don't believe that I ever could be clear enough for others, since
for them "clarity" is mainly a trope for philosophical reduc-
tiveness, or for a dreary literal-mindedness that belies any deep
concern for poetry or criticism. But I also seem to have had generous readers who believe in fuller explanations than I have given.
A return to origins can benefit any enterprise, and perhaps an enterprise obsessed with origins does need to keep returning to its
initial recognitions, to its first troubles, and to its hopes for insight into the theory of poetry.

> By "theory of poetry" I mean the concept of the nature and func-
> tion of the poet and of poetry, in distinction from poetics, which
> has to do with the technique of poetical composition. This distinc-
> tion between the concepts "theory of poetry" and "poetics" is a

fruitful one for knowledge. That *de facto* the two have contacts and often pass into each other is no objection. The history of the theory of poetry coincides neither with the history of poetics nor with the history of literary criticism. The poet's conception of himself . . . or the tension between poetry and science . . . are major themes of a history of the theory of poetry, not of a history of poetics.

I have quoted this paragraph from Curtius' great book, *European Literature and the Latin Middle Ages* (Excursus VII). My own books from *The Anxiety of Influence* through my work on Wallace Stevens are all attempts to develop a theory of poetry in just this sense. The poet's conception of himself necessarily is his poem's conception of itself, in my reading, and central to this conception is the matter of the sources of the powers of poetry.

The truest sources, again necessarily, are in the powers of poems *already written,* or rather, *already read.* Dryden said of poets that "we have our lineal descents and clans as well as other families." Families, at least unhappy ones, are not all alike, except perhaps in Freud's sense of "Family Romances." What dominates Freud's notion is the child's fantasy-making power. What counts in the family romance is not, alas, what the parents actually were or did, but the child's fantastic interpretation of its parents. The child provides a myth, and this myth is close to poets' myths of the origin of their creativity, because it involves the fiction of being a changeling. A changeling-fiction is one of the stances of freedom. The changeling is free because his very existence is a disjunction, and because the mystery of his origins allows for Gnostic reversals of the natural hierarchy between parents and children.

Emerson, in his most idealizing temper, said of the poets that they were liberating gods, that they were free and made others free. I would amend this by saying that poets make themselves free, by their stances towards earlier poets, and make others free only by teaching them those stances or positions of freedom.

Freedom, in a poem, must mean freedom of meaning, the freedom to have a meaning of one's own. Such freedom is wholly illusory unless it is achieved against a prior plenitude of meaning, which is tradition, and so also against language. Language, in relation to poetry, can be conceived in two valid ways, as I have learned, slowly and reluctantly. Either one can believe in a magical theory of all language, as the Kabbalists, many poets, and Walter Benjamin did, or else one must yield to a thoroughgoing linguistic nihilism, which in its most refined form is the mode now called Deconstruction. But these two ways turn into one another at their outward limits. For Deconstruction, irony is not a trope but finally is, as Paul de Man says, "the systematic undoing . . . of understanding." On this view, language is not "an instrument in the service of a psychic energy." De Man's serene linguistic nihilism welcomes the alternative vision:

> The possibility now arises that the entire construction of drives, substitutions, repressions, and representations is the aberrant, metaphorical correlative of the absolute randomness of language, prior to any figuration or meaning.

Can we prevent this distinguished linguistic nihilism, and the linguistic narcissism of poets and occultists, from turning into one another? Is there a difference between an *absolute* randomness of language and the Kabbalistic magical absolute, in which language is totally over-determined? In Coleridge's version of the magical view, founded on the Johannine Logos, synecdoche or symbol also was no longer a trope, but was the endless restitution of performative rhetoric, or the systematic restoration of spiritual persuasion and understanding. This remains, though with many refinements, the logocentric view of such current theorists as Barfield and Ong.

Whether one accepts a theory of language that teaches the dearth of meaning, as in Derrida and de Man, or that teaches its plenitude, as in Barfield and Ong, does not seem to me to matter. All I ask is that the theory of language be extreme and uncompromising enough. Theory of poetry, as I pursue it, is reconcilable with either extreme view of poetic language, though not with any views in between. Either the new poet fights to win freedom from dearth, or from plenitude, but if the antagonist be moderate, then the agon will not take place, and no fresh sublimity will be won. Only the agon is of the essence. Why? Is it merely my misprision, to believe that good poems must be combative?

I confess to some surprise that my emphasis upon strong poets and poems should have given so much offence, particularly to British academic journalists, though truly they do live within a steadily weakening tradition, and to their American counterparts, who yet similarly do represent a waning Modernism. The surprise stems from reading historians as inevitable as Burckhardt, philosophers as influential as Schopenhauer, scholars as informative as Curtius, and most of all from reading Freud, who is as indescribable as he is now inescapable. These writers, who are to our age what Longinus was to the Hellenistic world, have defined our Sublime for us, and they have located it in the agonistic spirit. Emerson preceded all of them in performing the same definition, the same location for America. These literary prophets teach us that the Greeks and the Renaissance were fiercely competitive in all things intellectual and spiritual, and that if we would emulate them, we hardly can hope to be free of competitive strivings. But I think these sages teach a harsher lesson, which they sometimes tell us they have learned from the poets. What is weak is forgettable and will be forgotten. Only strength is memorable; only the capacity to wound gives a healing capacity the chance to endure, and so to be heard. Freedom of meaning is wrested by combat, of meaning against meaning. But this combat consists in *a reading encounter,* and in an interpretive moment within that encounter. Poetic warfare is conducted by a kind of strong reading that I have called misreading, and here again I enter into an area where I seem to have provoked anxieties.

Perhaps, in common parlance, we need two very different words for what we now call "reading." There is relaxed reading and alert reading, and the latter, I will suggest, is always an agon. Reading well is a struggle because fictions and poems can be defined, at their best, as works that are bound to be misread, that is to say, troped by the reader. I am *not* saying that literary works are necessarily good or bad in proportion to their difficulty. Paul Valéry observed that "one only reads well when one reads with some quite personal goal in mind. It may be to acquire some power. It can be out of hatred for the author." Reading well, for Valéry, is to make one's own figuration of power, to clear imaginative space for one's own personal goal. Reading well is therefore not necessarily a polite process, and may not meet the academy's social standards of civility. I have discovered, to my initial surprise, that the reading of poetry has been as much idealized as the writing of it. Any attempt to de-idealize the writing of poetry provokes anger, particularly among weak poets, but this anger is mild compared to the fury of journalists and of many academics when the mystique of a somehow detached yet still generous, somehow disinterested yet still energetic, reading-process is called into question. The innocence of reading is a pretty myth, but our time grows very belated, and such innocence is revealed as only another insipidity.

Doubtless a more adequate social psychology of reading will be developed, but this is not my concern, any more than I am much affected by the ways in which recent critical theories have attempted to adumbrate the reader's share. A theosophy of reading, if one were available, would delight me, but though Barfield has attempted to develop one in the mode of Rudolph Steiner, such an acute version of epistemological idealism seems to me remote from the reality of reading. Gnosis and Kabbalah, though heterodox, are at once traditional and yet also de-idealizing in their accounts of reading and writing, and I continue to go back to them in order to discover properly drastic models for creative reading and critical writing.

Gnostic exegesis of Scripture is always a salutary act of textual violence, transgressive through-and-through. I do not believe that Gnosticism is only an extreme version of the reading-process, despite its deliberate esotericism and evasiveness. Rather, Gnosticism as a mode of interpretation helps to make clear why all critical reading aspiring towards strength *must* be as transgressive as it is aggressive. It is in Kabbalah, or belated Jewish Gnosis, that this textual transgression is most apparent, thanks to the superb and invaluable labors of Gershom Scholem. Scholem's researches are a demonstration that our idealisms about texts are poor illusions.

When I observe that there are *no* texts, but only interpretations, I am not yielding to extreme subjectivism, nor am I necessarily expounding any particular theory of textuality. When I wrote, once, that a strong reading is the only text, the only lie against time that endures, one enraged reviewer called my assertion a critic's sin against the Holy Ghost. The holy ghost, in this case, turned out to be Matthew Arnold, greatest of School Inspectors. But Emerson made my observation long before me, in many contexts, and many others had made it before him. Here is one of them, Rabbi Isaac the Blind, thirteenth-century Provençal Kabbalist, as cited by Scholem:

> The form of the written Torah is that of the colors of white fire, and the form of the oral Torah has colored forms as of black fire. And all these engravings and the not yet unfolded Torah existed potentially, perceptible neither to a spiritual nor to a sensory eye, until the will [of God] inspired the idea of activating them by means of primordial wisdom and hidden knowledge. Thus at the beginning of all acts there was pre-existentially the not yet unfolded Torah. . . .

Rabbi Isaac goes on to insist that "the written Torah can take on corporeal form only through the power of the oral Torah." As Scholem comments, this means, "strictly speaking, there is no written Torah here on earth." Scholem is speaking of Scripture, of what we must call Text Itself, and he goes on to a formulation that I would say is true of all lesser texts, of all poems more belated than the Torah:

> Everything that we perceive in the fixed forms of the Torah, written in ink on parchment, consists, in the last analysis, of interpre-

> tations or definitions of what is hidden. *There is only an oral Torah:* that is the esoteric meaning of these words, and the written Torah is a purely mystical concept. . . . There is no written Torah, free from the oral element, that can be known or conceived of by creatures who are not prophets.

What Scholem wryly asserts does not dismay what I would call *the poet in the reader* (any reader, at least potentially) but it does dismay or provoke many professional readers, particularly in the academies. One of my most instructive memories will be always of a small meeting of distinguished professors, which had gathered to consider the qualifications of an individual whom they might ask to join their enterprise. Before meditating upon this person's merits, they spontaneously performed a little ritual of faith. One by one, in turn, they confessed their belief in the real presence of the literary text. It had an existence independent of their devotion to it. It had priority over them, would be there after they were gone, and above all it had a meaning or meanings quite apart from their interpretive activity. The literary text was *there.* Where? Why, in editions, definitive editions, upon which responsible commentaries might be written. Responsible commentaries. For "responsible," substitute what word you will, whatever anxious word might match the social pieties and professional civilities that inform the spirituality of such occasions.

I only *know* a text, any text, because I know a reading of it, someone else's reading, my own reading, a composite reading. I happen to possess a somewhat preternatural verbal memory, particularly for verse. But I do not know *Lycidas* when I recite it to myself, in the sense that I know *the Lycidas* by *the* Milton. *The* Milton, *the* Stevens, *the* Shelley, do not exist. In a recent issue of a scholarly magazine, one exegete of Shelley passionately and accurately declared his faith that Shelley was a far more gifted imagination than he could ever be. His humble but worthy destiny, he declared, was to help all of us arrive at *the* Shelley by a lifetime of patient textual, historical, and interpretive work. His outrage was plain in every sentence, and it moved me deeply, even though evidently I was the unnamed sinner who had compelled him to proclaim his passionate self-effacement.

Alas that words should be only words and not things or feelings, and alas again that it should be, as Stevens said, a world of words to the end of it. Words, even if we take them as magic, refer *only* to other words, to the end of it. Words will not interpret themselves, and common rules for interpreting words will never exist. Many critics flee to philosophy or to linguistics, but the result is that they learn to interpret poems as philosophy or as linguistics. Philosophy may flaunt its rigors but its agon with poetry is an ancient one, and never will end. Linguistic explanations doubtless achieve a happy intensity of technicality, but language is not in itself a privileged mode of explanation. Certainly the critic seeking *the* Shelley should be reminded that Shelley's poems *are* language, but the reminder will not be an indefinite nourishment to any reader. Philosophers of intertextuality and of rhetoricity usefully warn me that the meanings of an intertextual encounter are as undecidable and unreadable as any single text is, but I discover pragmatically that such philosophers at best teach me a kind of double-entry bookkeeping, which as a reader I have to discount. Every poem becomes as unreadable as every other, and every intertextual confrontation seems as much an abyssing as any other. I subtract the rhetoricity from both columns, from rhetoric as system of tropes, and from rhetoric as persuasion, and return to where I started. *Jedes Wort ist ein Vorurteil,* Nietzsche says, which I translate as: "Every word is a *clinamen.*" There is always and only bias, inclination, pre-judgment, swerve; only and always the verbal agon for freedom, and the agon is carried on not by truth-telling, but by words lying against time.

Freedom and lying are intimately associated in belated poetry, and the notion that contains them both might best be named "evasion." Evasion is a process of avoiding, a way of escaping, but also it is an excuse. Usage has tinged the word with a certain stigma, but in our poetry what is being evaded ultimately is fate, particularly the necessity of dying. The study of poetry is (or ought to be) the study of what Stevens called "the intricate evasions of as." Linguistically these evasions constitute trope, but I urge a study of poetry that depends upon a larger vision of trope than traditional or modern rhetoric affords us. The positions of freedom and the strategies of lying are more than images, more than figurations, more even than the operations that Freud named "defense." Searching for a term comprehensive enough to help in the reading of poems, I offered the notion of "revisionary ratios," and found myself working with six of these, a number not so arbitrary as it has seemed to some. Rather than enumerate and describe these ratios again, I want to consider something of the limits that traditional rhetoric has set upon our description of poems.

Rhetoric has been always unfitted to the study of poetry, though most critics continue to ignore this incompatibility. Rhetoric rose from the analysis of political and legal orations, which are absurd paradigms for lyrical poems. Helen Vendler pithily sums up the continued inadequacy of traditional rhetoric to the description of lyric:

> It remains true that the figures of rhetoric, while they may be thought to appear in a more concentrated form in lyric, seem equally at home in narrative and expository writing. Nothing in the figures of paradox, or irony, or metaphor, or imagery—or in the generic conventions of, say, the elegy—specifies a basis in verse.

John Hollander, who is our leading authority upon lyrical form, illuminates tropes by calling them "turns that occur between the meanings of intention and the significances of linguistic utterances." I want to expand Hollander's description so as to open up a hidden element in all criticism that deals with figuration. Any critic necessarily tropes or turns the concept of trope in giving a reading of a specific poem. Even our most sophisticated and rigorously theoretical critics are at work on a rhetoric of rhetoric when they believe themselves merely to be distinguishing between one trope and another. A trope is troped wherever there is a movement from sign to intentionality, whenever the transformation from signification to meaning is made by the test of what aids the continuity of critical discourse. The increasingly scandalous instance is in the supposed critical distinction between metonymy and metaphor, which has become a shibboleth for weak interpreters. Jakobsonian rhetoric is fashionable, but in my judgment is wholly inapplicable to lyric poetry. Against Jakobson, I follow Kenneth Burke in seeing that the fundamental dichotomy in trope is between irony and synecdoche or, as Burke says, between dialectic and representation. There is precious little dichotomy between metonymy and metaphor or, as Burke again says, between reduction and perspective. Metonymy and metaphor alike I would trope as heightened degrees of dialectical irony, with metaphor the more extended. But synecdoche is not a dialectical trope, since as microcosm it represents a macrocosm without necessarily playing against it.

In lyric poetry, there is a crucial gap between reduction or metonymy and the part-for-whole representation of synecdoche. Metonymy is a mode of repetition, working through displacement, but synecdoche is an initial mode of identification, as its close association with the ancient topoi of definition and division would indicate. The topoi associated with metonymy are adjuncts, characteristics and notation, all of them namings through supposed cause-and-effect. A metonymy *names,* but a synecdoche begins a process that leads to an *un-naming*. While metonymy hints at the psychology of compulsion and obsession, synecdoche hints at the vicissitudes that are disorders of psychic drives. Regressive behavior expresses itself metonymically, but sado-masochism is synecdochic, in a very dark sense. I verge upon saying that naming in poetry is a limitation of meaning, whereas un-naming restitutes meaning, and so adds to representation.

This way of connecting trope and psychic defense, which to me seems an inevitable aid in the reading of poetry, itself has encountered a good deal of psychic defense in my more unamiable critics. What is the justification for linking language and the ego, trope and defense, in relatively fixed patterns? Partly, the rationale would depend upon a diachronic, rather than a synchronic, view of rhetoric, that is, upon an analytic rhetoric that would observe the changing nature of both linguistic trope and psychic defense as literary history moved from the Ancient world to the Enlightenment, and then on to Milton as prophet of Post-Enlightenment poetry. But, in part, the explanation for reading trope as defense and defense as trope goes back to my earlier observations on criticism as the rhetoric *of* rhetoric, and so on each critic's individual troping of the concept of trope. If rhetoric has its diachronic aspect, then so does criticism as the rhetoric of rhetoric. A study of Post-Enlightenment criticism from its prophet, Dr. Johnson, on to our contemporaries would reveal that its rhetoric was reborn out of Associationist psychology, and that the crucial terms of that psychology themselves stemmed from the topoi of a rejected classical rhetoric, ostensibly rejected by the Enlightenment but actually troped rather than rejected.

This complex phenomenon needs to be studied in detail, and I am attempting such a study currently in a book on the Sublime and the concept of topos as image-of-voice in Post-Enlightenment poetry. Here I want only to extract a dilemma of the relation between style and idea in the perpetual, onward Modernizing march of all post-Miltonic poetry. From the poets of Sensibility down to our current post-Stevensian contemporaries, poetry has suffered what I have termed elsewhere an over-determination of language and consequently an under-determination of meaning. As the verbal mechanisms of crisis have come to dominate lyric poetry, in relatively fixed patterns, a striking effect has been that the strongest poets have tended to establish their mastery by the paradox of what I would call *an achieved dearth of meaning*. Responding to this achieved dearth, many of the strongest critics have tended to manifest *their* skill by attributing the dearth to their own synchronic view of language and so to the vicissitudes of *language itself* in producing meaning. A diachronic phenomenon, dependent upon Miltonic and Wordsworthian poetic *praxis,* is thus assigned to a synchronic cause. Deconstructionist criticism refuses to situate itself in its own historical dilemma, and so by a charming paradox it falls victim to a genealogy to which evidently it must remain blind. Partly, this paradox is due to the enormous and significant difference between Anglo-American poetic tradition, and the much weaker French and German poetic traditions. French poetry lacks not only early giants of the dimension of Chaucer, Spenser, and Shakespeare, but it also is devoid of any later figures whose strength could approximate Milton and Wordsworth, Whitman and Dickinson. There is also the oddity that the nearest French equivalent, Victor Hugo, remains absurdly unfashionable and neglected by his nation's most advanced critics. Yet the "achieved dearth of meaning" in French poetry is clearly exemplified more even by Hugo than by Mallarmé, just as in English it is accomplished more powerfully by Wordsworth and Whitman than it is by Eliot and Pound.

If this judgment (however unfashionable) is correct, then it would be sustained by a demonstration that the revisionary patterns of Modern poetry are set by Wordsworth and Whitman (or by Hugo, or in German by the later Goethe), and by the further demonstration that these fixed or all-but-fixed relations between trope and defense reappear in Baudelaire, Mallarmé, and Valéry, in Hölderlin and Rilke, in Yeats and Stevens and Hart Crane. These patterns, which I have mapped as a sequence of revisionary ratios, are not the invention of belated moderns but of inaugural moderns, the High Romantics, and of Milton, that mortal god, the Founder from whom Wordsworth and Emerson (as Whitman's precursor) derive.

Ratios, as a critical idea, go back to Hellenistic criticism, and to a crucial clash between two schools of interpretation, the Aristotelian-influenced school of Alexandria and the Stoic-influenced school of Pergamon. The school of Alexandria championed the mode of *analogy,* while the rival school of Pergamon espoused the mode of *anomaly.* The Greek *analogy* means "equality of ratios," while *anomaly* means a "disproportion of ratios." Whereas the analogists of Alexandria held that the literary text was a unity and had a fixed meaning, the anomalists of Pergamon in effect asserted that the literary text was an interplay of differences and had meanings that rose out of those differences. Our latest mimic wars of criticism thus repeat battles fought in the second century B.C. between the followers of Crates of Mallos, Librarian of Pergamon, and the disciples of Aristarchus of Samothrace, Librarian of Alexandria. Crates, as an Anomalist, was what nowadays Hillis Miller calls an "uncanny" critic or, as I would say, an "antithetical" critic, a student of the revisionary ratios that take place *between* texts. Richard McKeon notes that the method of Crates led to allegories of reading, rather than to Alexandrian or analogical New Criticism, and I am prepared to call my work an allegory of reading, though very different from the allegories of reading formulated by Derrida and de Man, legitimate rival descendants of Crates.

The breaking of form to produce meaning, as I conceive it, depends upon the operation of certain instances of language, revisionary ratios, and on certain topological displacements in language that intervene between ratios, displacements that I have been calling "crossings."

To account for these ratios, without defending here their name and their number, I have to return to my earlier themes of the aggression of reading and the transgression of writing, and to my choice of a psychic rather than a linguistic model in a quest for tropes that might illuminate acts of reading.

Anna Freud, in her classic study, *The Ego and the Mechanisms of Defense,* notes that

> . . . all the defensive measures of the ego against the id are carried out silently and invisibly. The most that we can ever do is to reconstruct them in retrospect: we can never really witness them in operation. This statement applies, for instance, to successful repression. The ego knows nothing of it; we are aware of it only subsequently, when it becomes apparent that something is missing.

As I apply Anna Freud, in a poem the ego is the poetic self and the id is the precursor, idealized and frequently composite, hence fantasized, but still traceable to a historical author or authors.

The defensive measures of the poetic self against the fantasized precursor can be witnessed in operation only by the study of a difference between ratios, but this difference depends upon our awareness not so much of presences as of absences, of *what is missing in the poem because it had to be excluded.* It is in this sense that I would grant a point made by John Bayley, that I am "fascinated by the sort of poetry that is *not really there,* and—even better—the kind that knows it never can be." But Bayley errs in thinking that this is only one tradition of the poetry of the last three centuries, because clearly it is the norm, or the condition of belated strong poetry. The authentic poem now achieves its dearth of meaning by strategies of exclusion, or what can be called litanies of evasion. I will quote a sympathetic British critic, Roger Poole, for a more useful account of this problematic element in our poetry:

> If a poem is really 'strong' it represents a menace. It menaces the way the reader thinks, loves, fears and is. Consequently, the reading of strong poetry can only take place under conditions of mutual self-defense. Just as the poet must not know what he knows, and must not state what he states, so the reader must not read what he reads. [The] question is not so much 'What does this poem mean?' as 'What has got left out of this poem to make of it the particularly expensive torso that it is?

To adumbrate Poole's observations a touch more fully, I would suggest that we all suffer from an impoverished notion of poetic allusion. No strong poem merely alludes to another, and what look like overt allusions and even echoes in strong poems are disguises for darker relationships. A strong authentic allusion to another strong poem can be only by and in what the later poem *does not say,* by what it represses. This is another aspect of a limitation of poetry that defines poetry: a poem can be *about* experience or emotion or whatever only by initially encountering another poem, which is to say a poem must handle experience and emotion as if they already were rival poems. Poetic knowledge is necessarily a knowledge by tropes, an experience of emotion as trope, and an expression of knowledge and emotion by a revisionary further troping. Since a poem is necessarily still further troped in any strong reading, there is a bewildering triple intertropicality at work that makes a mockery of most attempts at reading. I do not agree wholly with de Man that reading is impossible, but I acknowledge how very difficult it is to read a poem properly, which is what I have meant by my much-attacked critical trope of "misreading" or "misprision." With three layers of troping perpetually confronting us, the task of restituting meaning or of healing a wounded rhetoricity is a daunting one. Yet it can and must be attempted. The only alternative I can see is the triumph of Romantic irony in purified form by way of the allegory of reading formulated by Paul de Man. But this most advanced version of Deconstruction cheerfully accepts the risk warned against by de Man's truest precursor, Friedrich Schlegel: "The irony of irony is the fact that one becomes weary of it if one is offered it everywhere and all the time."

To evade such destructive weariness, I return to the poetic equivalent of Freud's concept of defense. The center of the poetic self, of the speaking subject that Demanian Deconstruction dissolves into irony, is narcissistic self-regard. Such poetic self-esteem is wounded by its realization of belatedness, and the wound or narcissistic scar provokes the poetic self into the aggressivity that Freud amazingly chose to call "defense." Even Freud, like all the rest of us, idealized the arts, it being Nietzsche's distinction that in this too he was the grand exception, though to some extent he shares this particular distinction with Kierkegaard. Because of such prevalent idealization, we all of us still resist the supposed stigma of identifying the strong poet's drive towards immortality with the triadic sequence of narcissism, wounded self-regard, and aggression. But change in poetry and criticism as in any human endeavor comes about only through aggression. Unless a strong poet strongly loves his own poetry, he cannot hope to get it written. When Robinson Jeffers writes that he hates his verses, every line, every word, then my response is divided between a sense that he lies, and a stronger sense that

perhaps he tells the truth, and *that* is the trouble. Alas that poetic self-love should not in itself be sufficient for strength, but it
is no good lamenting that it should be necessary for poetic
strength. Pindar, one of our earliest instances of lyric strength,
should have taught all of us that poetic narcissism is at the root of
any lyric Sublime. The first Olympic ode, still the truest paradigm for Western lyric, overtly celebrates Hieron of Syracuse, yet
the horse and rider more fully and implicitly celebrated are
Pegasus and Pindar. Lyric celebrates the poetic self, despite every
denial. Yet we refuse the lesson, even as Freud partly did. A
poet, as much as any man or woman among us, scarcely feels
complimented when described as narcissistic and aggressive. But
what *can* poetry give back, either as successful representation or
achieved pathos, and whether to poet or reader, except for a *restitution of narcissism?* And since paranoid thinking can be defined as
a complete shield against being influenced, what is it that saves
strong poets from paranoid thinking except for their early suscep-
tibility to poetic influence, an openness that *must* in time scar the
narcissism of the poet *qua* poet. For those who scoff still at the
idea of the anxiety of influence, I shall cite the second and belated
Pindar, Hölderlin, in a letter he wrote to his precursor, Schiller:

I have sufficient courage and judgment to free myself from other
masters and critics and to pursue my own path with the tranquil spirit necessary for such an endeavor, but in regard to
*you*, my dependence is insurmountable; and because I know the
profound effect a single word from you can have on me, I sometimes strive to put you out of my mind so as not to be overcome by
anxiety at my work. For I am convinced that such anxiety, such
worry is the death of art, and I understand perfectly well why it is
more difficult to give proper expression to nature when the artist
finds himself surrounded by masterpieces than when he is virtually
alone amidst the living world. He finds himself too closely involved with nature, too intimately linked with it, to consider the
need for rebelling against its authority or for submitting to it. But
this terrible alternation is almost inevitable when the young artist
is exposed to the mature genius of a master, which is more forceful

and comprehensible than nature, and thus more capable of enslaving him. It is not a case of one child playing with another child—the primitive equilibrium attained between the first artist and his world no longer holds. The child is now dealing with men with whom he will never in all probability be familiar enough to forget their superiority. And if he feels this superiority he must become either rebellious or servile. Or must he?

This passage, anguished in its sense of contamination, is cited by René Girard as another instance of the violence of thematicism that he names as a progression "from mimetic desire to the monstrous double." I would prefer to read it as an exercise in self-misprision, because in it a very strong poet evasively relies upon a rhetoric of pathos to portray himself as being weak. The revisionary ratio here employed against Schiller is what I call *kenosis* or repetition and discontinuity. Appearing to empty himself of his poetic godhood, Hölderlin actually undoes and isolates Schiller, who is made to ebb more drastically than the ephebe ebbs, and who falls hard where Hölderlin falls soft. This *kenosis* dares the profoundest evasion of naming as the death of art what is the life of Hölderlin's art, the ambivalent and agonistic clearing-away of Schiller's poetry in order to open up a poetic space for Hölderlin's own achievement. Freud, in his final phase, taught us what we may call "the priority of anxiety"—that is, the dominance of the pleasure principle by tendencies more primitive than it, and independent of it. Hölderlin teaches us the same, even as he denies his own teaching. Freud belatedly discovered that certain dreams in traumatic neuroses come out of "a time before the purpose of dreams was the fulfillment of wishes" and so are attempts "to master the stimulus retrospectively by developing the anxiety." Hölderlin, in his greatest odes, earlier discovered that poetic thoughts did not sublimate desires, but were endeavors to master a quasi-divine reality by developing the anxiety that came from the failure to realize poetic godhood. As a poet, Hölderlin knew what as a man he denies in his letter to Schiller, which is that the anxiety of influence is a figuration for Sublime poetry itself.

Defense therefore is the natural language of Hölderlin's poetic imagination and of every Post-Enlightenment imagination that can aspire convincingly to something like Hölderlin's Sublime strength. But in language itself defense is compelled to be manifested as trope. I have argued elsewhere for certain paradigmatic links between specific tropes and specific defenses, at least since Milton's day, and I will not repeat such argument here. But I have never elucidated the relation of trope to my revisionary ratios, and that will be my concern in the remainder of the theoretical portion of this essay, after which I will conclude by speculating upon the role of the ratios in the poetic breaking of poetic form. An excursus in practical criticism will follow, so as to apply my sequence of ratios to the interpretation of John Ashbery's recent long poem, *Self-Portrait in a Convex Mirror.*

It is certainly very difficult to chart anomalies, particularly *within* a poem yet in reference *to* the impingement of another poem. Revisionary ratios are thus at once intra-poetic *and* inter-poetic, which is a necessary doubling since the ratios are meant to map an internalizing of tradition. Tradition is internalized only when a total stance toward precursors is taken up by a new strong poet. Such a stance is a mode of deliberateness, but it can operate at many levels of consciousness, and with many shades between negation and avowal. As John Hollander observed, ratios are "at once text, poem, image and model." As text, a ratio names intertextual differences; as poem it characterizes a total relationship between two poets, earlier and later. As model, a ratio functions the way a paradigm works in the problem-solving of normal science. It is as image that a ratio is most crucial, for the revisionary ratios are, to cite Hollander again, "the varied positions of freedom" or "true position" for a poet.

Freud's patterns of psychic images are the defenses, a tropological system masking itself as a group of operations directed against change, but actually so contaminated by the drives it would deflect as to become a compulsive and unconscious process like the drives. But eventually Freud was to assert that "the theory of the drives is so to say our mythology. Drives are mythical entities, magnificent in their indefiniteness." To this audacity of the Founder I would add that defenses are no less mythological. Like tropes, defenses are turning-operations, and in language tropes and defenses crowd together in the entity rather obscurely called poetic images. Images are ratios between what is uttered and what, somehow, is intended, and as Kenneth Burke remarks, you cannot discuss images for very long without sliding into whole textures of relationships. Cannot *those* relationships be charted? If it is extravagant to create a new rhetoric, this extravagance, as Joseph Riddel says, "simply repeats the wandering or indirect movement of all trope." But trope, or the play of substitution, is purely a temporal process. Ratios of revision between earlier and later poets and poems are as much spatial as temporal, though the space be imaginative or visionary. Rhetorical criticism, even of the advanced deconstructive kind, treats a poem merely as a formal and linguistic structure. But strong poems manifest the will to utter permanent truths of desire, and to utter these *within* a tradition of utterance. The intention to prophesy is necessarily a dynamic of space as well as time, particularly when the prophecy insists upon finding its authority *within* a tradition of what has been prophesied. As soon as we speak of what is within a previous utterance, our discourse is involved in thematics, in topology or literary place. Themes are things placed into stance, stance is the attitude or position of the poet in the poem, and placing is a dynamic of desire seeking either its apotheosis or its entropic self-destruction.

A power of evasion may be the belated strong poet's most crucial gift, a psychic and linguistic cunning that energizes what most of us have over-idealized as the imagination. Self-preservation is the labor of the poem's litanies of evasion, of its dance-steps beyond the pleasure principle. Where a defensive struggle is carried on, there must be some self-crippling, some wounding of energies, even in the strongest poets. But the uncanny or Sublime energies of poetic evasion, operating through the graduated anomalies that are ratios of revision, constitute the value-creating power of the anxiety of influence. Ann Wordsworth summarizes this eloquently, when she speaks of "this ingenious ravelling, a process as determinant perhaps as dream-work" which is "the creative mind's capacity to *know* through the precursor, to *renew* through misprision, and to *expand* into the full range of human experience." Where my formulation and use of revisionary ratios have been most attacked is in their sequence, and in the recurrence of that sequence in so many poems of the last two hundred years. I have meant that we are to read *through* ratios and not *into* them, so that they cannot be regarded as reductive entities, but still their frequency causes disquiet. So it should, but hardly because revisionary ratios are my own paranoid code, as some journalists have suggested. And yet a few closing words on paranoid codes may be in place just here and now in this fictional time of Borges and Pynchon.

Commenting on *The Crying of Lot 49,* the book's best critic, Frank Kermode alas, observes that "a great deviation is called a sect if shared, paranoia if not." Kermode charmingly goes on to recall that "a man once undertook to demonstrate infallibly to me that *Wuthering Heights* was an interlinear gloss on Genesis. How could this be disproved? He had hit on a code, and legitimated all the signs." Kermode's point is that this is the danger that both Pynchon's Oedipa and the novel's reader confront. Warning us, Kermode asks us to remember that "deception is the discovery of the novel, not of its critics." If Kermode is correct in this, then I would call Pynchon, in just that respect, too much of a moralist and too little of a strong poet. If evasion is the discovery of the post-Miltonic poem, it is also the discovery of the poem's critics. Every belated poem that matters ends with either the narrative gesture, postponing the future, *by projecting it,* or else the prophetic gesture, hastening the future, *by introjecting it.* These defensive operations can be regarded as either the work of negation, intellectually freeing us from some of the consequences of repression, or the labor of paranoia, reducing reality to a code. I would hope to have done part of the work of negation for some readers and lovers of poetry besides myself. There is no reading worthy of being communicated to another unless it deviates to break form, twists the lines to form a shelter, and so makes a meaning through that shattering of belated vessels. That shattering is rhetorical, yes, but more than language is thus wounded or blinded. The poet of our moment and of our climate, our Whitman and our Stevens, says it best for me, and so I end with the eloquence of John Ashbery:

> The song makes no mention of directions.
> At most it twists the longitude lines overhead
> Like twigs to form a crude shelter. (The ship
> Hasn't arrived, it was only a dream. It's somewhere near
> Cape Horn, despite all the efforts of Boreas to puff out
> Those drooping sails.) The idea of great distance
> Is permitted, even implicit in the slow dripping
> Of a lute. How to get out?
> This giant will never let us out unless we blind him.

## II

I turn to a proof-text, Ashbery's long poem, *Self-Portrait in a Convex Mirror*. It would not have been thought a long poem by Browning, but five hundred and fifty-two lines is a long poem for our damaged attention-spans these days. Ashbery, like Stevens, is a profoundly Whitmanian poet, frequently despite appearances. Throughout Ashbery's career, he has centered upon full-scale poems, the great successes being *Fragment, The Skaters,* the prose *Three Poems, Fantasia on "The Nut-Brown Maid,"* and above all *Self-Portrait*. They are versions or revisions of *Song of Myself,* in some of the same subtle ways that Stevens wrote revisions of Whitman in *The Man with the Blue Guitar* and *Notes toward a Supreme Fiction*. Necessarily, Ashbery also revises Stevens, though more overtly in *Fragment* and *Fantasia* than in the very Whitmanian *Skaters* and *Three Poems*. Both Stevens and Whitman are ancestral presences in *Self-Portrait,* and so is Hart Crane, for the language of the poem engages, however covertly and evasively, the central or Emersonian tradition of our poetry.

Angus Fletcher, in his studies of Spenser, Milton, Coleridge, and Crane, has been developing a liminal poetics or new rhetoric of thresholds, and I follow Fletcher both in my notion of the topoi of "crossings" as images of voice, and in my account of the final revisionary ratio of *apophrades* or reversed belatedness, which is akin to the classical trope of *metalepsis* or transumption and to the Freudian "negation" (*Verneinung*) with its dialectical interplay of the defenses, projection and introjection. I will re-expound and freshly develop these Fletcherian ideas in the reading of Ashbery that follows.

Ashbery divides *Self-Portrait* into six verse-paragraphs, a happy division which I shall exploit, naming them by my apotropaic litany of evasions or revisionary ratios. Swerving easily away from Whitman and from Stevens, Ashbery begins his *clinamen* from tradition by a brilliant description of the painting that gives him his title:

> As Parmigianino did it, the right hand
> Bigger than the head, thrust at the viewer
> And swerving easily away, as though to protect
> What it advertises. A few leaded panes, old beams,
> Fur, pleated muslin, a coral ring run together
> In a movement supporting the face, which swims
> Toward and away like the hand
> Except that it is in repose. It is what is
> Sequestered.

This abrupt opening is itself evasive, the "As" being one of Stevens' "intricate evasions of as." The hand's defensive gesture is a reaction formation or rhetorical *illusio,* since what is meant is that the hand acts as though to advertise what it protects. Here a swerve is another mode of repose, so that defense does not so much protect as it sequesters, a word whose Late Latin antecedent had the meaning "to give up for safekeeping." Ashbery quotes Vasari's description of the halved wooden ball upon which Parmigianino painted what the poet calls the face's "receiving wave/of arrival." Unspoken is each wave's ebbing, but the absent image of departure informs the poem's countersong, which thus makes its initial entrance:

> The soul establishes itself.
> But how far can it swim out through the eyes
> And still return safely to its nest? The surface
> Of the mirror being convex, the distance increases
> Significantly; that is, enough to make the point
> That the soul is a captive, treated humanely, kept
> In suspension, unable to advance much farther
> Than your look as it intercepts the picture.

The poignance of the extreme dualism here will be almost constant throughout the poem. Such dualism is a surprise in Ashbery, yet the pathos is precisely what we expect from the self-portraitist of *Fragment* and *Three Poems*. Certainly the anguish of *Self-Portrait* has an intensity to it that marks Ashbery, yet generally not to this degree. I will suggest that *Self-Portrait*, though meditation rather than lyric, is a poem closely related to the *Ode on a Grecian Urn* and to Stevens' version of Keats' *Ode, The Poems of Our Climate*. Three reveries upon aesthetic distance and poetic coldness share a common sorrow, and manifest almost a common glory.

The soul is a captive, but art rather than the body appears to be the captor:

> The soul has to stay where it is,
> Even though restless, hearing raindrops at the pane,
> The sighing of autumn leaves thrashed by the wind,
> Longing to be free, outside, but it must stay
> Posing in this place. It must move
> As little as possible. This is what the portrait says.
> But there is in that gaze a combination
> Of tenderness, amusement and regret, so powerful
> In its restraint that one cannot look for long.

> The secret is too plain. The pity of it smarts,
> Makes hot tears spurt: that the soul is not a soul,
> Has no secret, is small, and it fits
> Its hollow perfectly: its room, our moment of attention.

We can remark that the actual painting looks rather like the actual Ashbery, and that this poet's characteristic expression could not be more accurately described than as "a combination/Of tenderness, amusement, and regret . . . powerful/In its restraint." The secret *is* irony, is the strong presence that is an abyss, the palpable absence that is the poet's soul. Times and places come together in the *attention* that makes the painter's and the poet's room into the one chamber. But this attention is a Paterian music, surpassing both painting and poetry:

> That is the tune but there are no words.
> The words are only speculation
> (From the Latin *speculum,* mirror):
> They seek and cannot find the meaning of the music.

Angus Fletcher, in his seminal study of "Threshold, Sequence and Personification in Coleridge," reminds us that while numerology suggests a timeless ontology, the *poetics* of number accept our time-bound duration. Poetry, as St. Augustine conceived it, is "the mirror or *speculum* of the world," a mirror that "temporalizes and historicizes number." Ashbery, as a rider of poetic motion, labors at the fiction of duration, but his evident ruefulness at becoming what Stevens' *Asides on the Oboe* called "the human globe" or "the man of glass" is strongly emphasized. The *clinamen* is away from Stevens' celebration of Emersonian centrality, or praise for "the man who has had the time to think enough," and towards a lament for the confinements of art and artist:

> We see only postures of the dream,
> Riders of the motion that swings the face
> Into view under evening skies, with no

False disarray as proof of authenticity.
But it is life englobed.
One would like to stick one's hand
Out of the globe, but its dimension,
What carries it, will not allow it.
No doubt it is this, not the reflex
To hide something, which makes the hand loom large
As it retreats slightly.

A representation conveyed only as a mode of limitation; this irony is the peculiar mark of the poem's initial movement of *clinamen,* its swerve away from its origins, which truly are not so much in Parmigianino as in Stevens, particularly in the Whitmanian Stevens of *Poem with Rhythms,* written just after *Asides on the Oboe,* a poem where "The hand between the candle and the wall/Grows large on the wall." The painter's hand as seen by Ashbery must stay within aesthetic limitation:

There is no way
To build it flat like a section of wall:
It must join the segment of a circle. . . .

Stevens, like the Whitman of *The Sleepers* whom he echoes earlier in *Poem with Rhythms,* breaks the limitation by an act of will, by the hyperbole of a Sublime power:

It must be that the hand
Has a will to grow larger on the wall,
To grow larger and heavier and stronger than
The wall; and that the mind
Turns to its own figurations and declares,
*"This image, this love, I compose myself*
*Of these. In these, I come forth outwardly.*
*In these, I wear a vital cleanliness,*
*Not as in air, bright-blue-resembling air,*
*But as in the powerful mirror of my wish and will."*

A mind that can turn to its own figurations and constitute an ego by love of those figurations, is a Whitmanian, transcendentalizing mind of summer. Such a mind is also that of Freudian Man, since Freud defines narcissism as being the self's love of the ego, a love that by such cathexis veritably *constitutes* the ego. The *speculum* or convex mirror of Ashbery precisely is not the powerful mirror of his wish and will, and in this inclination away from his fathers, the palpable Stevens and the ghostly Whitman, Ashbery establishes his true *clinamen*. But the cost is severe, and Ashbery accurately observes that his own "pure affirmation," like the painter's, "doesn't affirm anything." Or, to illuminate this properly ironic affirmation by using Fletcher's terms, Ashbery affirms only his own perpetual liminality, the threshold stance that he shares with Hart Crane and with the more delicate, fragile nuances of Whitman's more antithetical moments. Fletcher, writing on Coleridge, seems to be describing the first part of Ashbery's poem:

> While epic tradition supplies conventional models of the threshold, these conventions are always subject to deliberate poetic blurring. . . . poets have wished to subtilize, to dissolve, to fragment, to blur the hard material edge, because poetry hunts down the soul, with its obscure passions, feelings, other-than-cognitive symbolic forms. . . .

Ashbery hunts down the soul, following Parmigianino, and finds only two disparate entities, a hand "big enough/To wreck the sphere," and an ambiguous hollow, a room without recesses, only alcoves, a chamber that defeats change, "stable within/Instability," a globe like our earth, where "there are no words/For the surface, that is,/No words to say what it really is."

A threshold is a crossing, and at the close of this first verse-paragraph Ashbery deliberately fails to negotiate a first crossing, and so fails to get over a threshold of poetic election. The disjunction is from the artist's "pure/Affirmation that doesn't affirm anything" to "The balloon pops, the attention/Turns dully away." Since the attention is the memory that the soul's only room was "our moment of attention," the balloon's pop dislodges the earlier "ping-pong ball" of the painting's stable instability. A failed crossing of election leaves the poet helpless (by choice) as experience threatens to engulf his sense of his own pathos. Ashbery's second verse paragraph is his poem's *tessera*, its antithetical completion which fails all completion. The poet, necessarily unsure of his poethood's survival, is only the synecdoche for voices that overwhelm him:

> I think of the friends
> Who came to see me, of what yesterday
> Was like. A peculiar slant
> Of memory that intrudes on the dreaming model
> In the silence of the studio as he considers
> Lifting the pencil to the self-portrait.
> How many people came and stayed a certain time,
> Uttered light or dark speech that became part of you
> Like light behind windblown fog and sand,
> Filtered and influenced by it, until no part
> Remains that is surely you.

There is an affinity between this peculiar slant of memory's light, and Dickinson's oppressive certain slant of light that imaged death. Both are synecdoches of a kind that belongs to Coleridge's wounding sense of symbol or to Anna Freud's defense mechanism of turning against the self. Anna Freud said of a patient that "by turning her aggressive impulses inwards she inflicted upon herself all the suffering which she had formerly anticipated in the form of punishment by her mother." What I call the revisionary ratio of *tessera* is the poetic transformation of such turning against the self. Ashbery, *as poet,* is compelled to present himself as being only a mutilated part of a whole already mutilated. Why most strong poems in our tradition, from Wordsworth on, manifest this masochistic impulse of representation, *even as they strive to pull away from initial ironies,* is beyond my present capacity to surmise. Yet Ashbery's contribution to this necessity of representation clearly joins the Wordsworthian "enchantment of self with self":

> In the circle of your intentions certain spars
> Remain that perpetuate the enchantment of self with self:

Eyebeams, muslin, coral. It doesn't matter
Because these are things as they are today
Before one's shadow ever grew
Out of the field into thoughts of tomorrow.

Fletcher remarks that, in the context of poetic thresholds,
" 'sequence' means the process and the promise that something
will follow something else." Such process begins spatially, Fletcher adds, but ends "on a note of temporal description," perhaps
because sequence in a poem is a mode of survival, or fiction of duration. I have experienced my own defensive emotions concerning
the sequence of revisionary ratios that I find recurrent in so many
poems, quite aside from the defensive reactions I have aroused in
others. But the sequence is *there* in the sense that image and trope
tend to follow over-determined patterns of evasion. Thus, Ashbery's poem moves on to a third verse paragraph that is a *kenosis,*
an isolating defense in which poetic power presents itself as being
all but emptied out:

Tomorrow is easy, but today is uncharted,
Desolate, reluctant as any landscape
To yield what are laws of perspective
After all only to the painter's deep
Mistrust, a weak instrument though
Necessary. Of course some things
Are possible, it knows, but it doesn't know
Which ones. Some day we will try
To do as many things as are possible
And perhaps we shall succeed at a handful
Of them, but this will not have anything
To do with what is promised today, our
Landscape sweeping out from us to disappear
On the horizon.

This "today" seems not so much uncharted as non-existent.
Ashbery displaces "today" by "possible," "promises" or "dream"
throughout his third verse-paragraph. A sequence of "possible,"
"possible," "promised," "promises" and "possibilities" in lines

151–168 is replaced by seven occurrences of "dream" or "dreams" from lines 180–206, where the section ends. All these are metonymies for, reductions of "today," and perform the self-emptying action of *kenosis:* "out from us." Brooding on aesthetic forms, Ashbery attains to a poignant and characteristic sense of "something like living":

> They seemed strange because we couldn't actually see them.
> And we realize this only at a point where they lapse
> Like a wave breaking on a rock, giving up
> Its shape in a gesture which expresses that shape.

*Kenosis* is Ashbery's prevalent ratio, and his whole poetics is one of "giving up/Its shape in a gesture which expresses that shape." What but the force of the past, the strength of his own poetic tradition, could drive Ashbery on to his next threshold, the disjunctive gap or crossing of solipsism that he leaps between his poem's third and fourth verse paragraphs? The transition is from "a movement/Out of the dream into its codification" to the angelic or daemonic surprise of the face of Parmigianino/Ashbery. The Uncanny or Sublime enters both through repression of the memory of the face, and through a return of the repressed by way of what Freud termed Negation:

> As I start to forget it
> It presents its stereotype again
> But it is an unfamiliar stereotype, the face
> Riding at anchor, issued from hazards, soon
> To accost others, "rather angel than man" (Vasari).
> Perhaps an angel looks like everything
> We have forgotten, I mean forgotten
> Things that don't seem familiar when
> We meet them again, lost beyond telling,
> Which were ours once.

The great modern critic of Negation, foreshadowing the Deconstruction of Derrida and even more of de Man, is Walter Ben-

jamin. I do not believe that Ashbery cites Benjamin here, but it
is inevitable that any fresh Sublime should remind us of Benjamin, who joins Freud as the century's theorist of the Sublime.
Ashbery's tentative formula "Perhaps an angel looks like every-
thing/We have forgotten" is very close to Benjamin's meditation
upon his angel:

> The angel, however, resembles all from which I have had to
> part: persons and above all things. In the things I no longer have,
> he resides. He makes them transparent.

This is Benjamin's *aura* or light of the Sublime, truly visible
only in the shock of its disappearance, the flight of its repression.
Ashbery has lost, he goes on to say, "the whole of me" to the
strict otherness of the painter. Yet the loss becomes the Emer-
sonian-Stevensian *surprise,* the advent of power, in a passage that
plays against Stevensian images:

> We have surprised him
> At work, but no, he has surprised us
> As he works. The picture is almost finished,
> The surprise almost over, as when one looks out,
> Startled by a snowfall which even now is
> Ending in specks and sparkles of snow.
> It happened while you were inside, asleep,
> And there is no reason why you should have
> Been awake for it, except that the day
> Is ending and it will be hard for you
> To get to sleep tonight, at least until late.

Even the accent suggests very late Stevens, the perception of
"Transparent man in a translated world,/In which he feeds on a
new known." But instead of the Stevensian "clearness emerg-
ing/From cold," with a power surpassing sleep's power, Ashbery
opts for a lesser pathos, for an uneasiness, however Sublime,
rather than a transcendence. As always, Ashbery represses his own
strength, in his quest to maintain an evenness of tone, to avoid

climax-impressions. This results in a spooky Sublime, indeed more canny than uncanny, and the reader of Ashbery more than ever has to cultivate a patience for this limpid style, this mode of waiting without seeming to wait. "The surprise, the tension are in the concept/Rather than its realization." Yet even the concept is hidden, buried deep in the image of depth in this daemonic verse paragraph: "the face/Riding at anchor, issued from hazards." Throughout the poem, the painting is imaged as a ship, appearing to us "in a recurring wave/Of arrival," but still a "tiny, self-important ship/On the surface." Towards the close of the poem, in lines 478–89, a transumption of these earlier tropes will be accomplished with mysterious urgency, when "A ship/Flying unknown colors has entered the harbor." The portrait as ship suggests the peril of poetic art from Spenser to Stevens, but to Ashbery's reaader it seems another version of the oxymorons that concluded his magnificent earlier meditation, *Soonest Mended,* where the poet speaks of

> . . . learning to accept
> The charity of the hard moments as they are doled out,
> For this is action, this not being sure, this careless
> Preparing, sowing the seeds crooked in the furrow,
> Making ready to forget, and always coming back
> To the mooring of starting out, that day so long ago.

Parmigianino's self-portrait is another "mooring of starting out," and such an oxymoron (with its quasi-pun on "morning") is for Ashbery a characteristic sublimation of unfulfillable poetic desires. A greater sublimation comes in the poem's *askesis,* its fifth verse-paragraph, where Ashbery perspectivizes against both the painter and his own poetic self. The perspectives are bewildering, as the "outside" cities and landscapes are played off against the inner space of painting and of poem:

> Our landscape
> Is alive with filiations, shuttlings;
> Business is carried on by look, gesture,

Hearsay. It is another life to the city,
The backing of the looking glass of the
Unidentified but precisely sketched studio. It wants
To siphon off the life of the studio, deflate
Its mapped space to enactments, island it.

If the soul is not a soul, then the inside/outside, mind/nature
metaphor is rendered inadequate, aside from its built-in in-
adequacies of endless perspectivism. Ashbery boldly sets out to
rescue the metaphor he has helped to bury. A cold wind of aesthetic and vital change rises to destroy Ashbery's kind of urban
pastoral, and the painter, as the poet's surrogate, is urged to see
and hear again, albeit in a necessarily illusory present:

Your argument, Francesco,
Had begun to grow stale as no answer
Or answers were forthcoming. If it dissolves now
Into dust, that only means its time had come
Some time ago, but look now, and listen. . . .

But though Ashbery goes on to urge the normality and cor-
rectness of metaphor, such a rescue operation must fail, remind-
ing us perhaps that the prestige of metaphor and of sublimation
tends to rise and fall together in cultural history. A third and
most crucial threshold-crossing takes place as Ashbery moves
reluctantly away from metaphor and into the giant *metalepsis* or
ratio of *apophrades* that concludes and is the glory of his poem.
The long final sixth verse-paragraph (ll. 311–552) begins with a
surprised sense of achieved identification, introjecting both the
painting and the poet's death:

A breeze like the turning of a page
Brings back your face: the moment
Takes such a big bite out of the haze
Of pleasant intuition it comes after.

Before describing this crossing and the superb section it introduces, I digress again into Fletcher's theories of threshold,

sequence and personification, as they were my starting-point for thinking about transumption. Coleridge credited Spenser with being the great inventor in English poetry of the "land of Faery, that is, of mental space." Fletcher follows Coleridge in relating such mental space to daemonic agency, personification and topical allusion. What Fletcher's grandest innovation does is to alter our understanding of personification, by compounding it both with transumption and the pun. Complete projection or introjection is paranoia, which means, as Fletcher says, that "madness is complete personification." But most strong poets avoid this generative void, though all pause upon its threshold. John Hollander, following Fletcher, has traced the figurative power of poetic echo and its link to the Post-Romantic transformations of *metalepsis* or transumption, transformations which based themselves upon Milton's transumptive use of similes:

> . . . the peculiar quality of Miltonic simile, by which, as Dr. Johnson put it, he "crowds the imagination," is a mode of transumption—the *multitudinousness* of the Satanic legions in Book I is like that of autumn leaves, but unclaimed manifestly for the comparison are the other likenesses (both are fallen, dead) whose presence is shadowed only in the literalizing of the place name of Vallombrosa.

Hollander cites the mythographic commentary by George Sandys on Ovid's story of Echo, where Sandys quotes Ausonius and then adds that "the image of the voice so often rendred, is as that of the face reflected from one glasse to another; melting by degrees, and every reflection more weake and shady than the former." This, Hollander implies, is the predicament that Milton and his heirs escaped by making their images of voice transumptive. And this is precisely the predicament that Ashbery evades in *Self-Portrait,* and particularly in its sixth or transumptive section to which I now return.

The breeze whose simile is a page's turning, and that brings back the self-portrait, returns more than two hundred lines later in the closing passage of the poem:

                              . . . the ache
Of this waking dream can never drown out
The diagram still sketched on the wind,
Chosen, meant for me and materialized
In the disguising radiance of my room.

. . . . . . . . . . . . . . . . . . . . . . . . . . . . . . . . . . . . . . . . .
                    The hand holds no chalk
And each part of the whole falls off
And cannot know it knew, except
Here and there, in cold pockets
Of remembrance, whispers out of time.


   The wind transumes the breeze, returning the self-portrait to
an introjected earliness, an identification of poet and painter. The
pockets of remembrance, though cold as painting and poem are
cold, remain the winds whispering *out of* time, in a multiple play
upon "out of," which refers us back to Keats' cold pastoral that
teased us out of time, as did eternity. The echo of the *Grecian
Urn* reinforces the echo of the *Nightingale*'s "waking dream."
Death, as in Keats' odes, is what the figurations defend against,
quite directly. So, going back to the start of the sixth verse
paragraph, the page-turning similitude is necessarily followed directly by the introjection of death, in a Crossing of Identification
that links not only painter and poet, but also the tragic Alban
Berg and *Cymbeline*. Reflections upon the common mortality of
artists lead to earlier presages of aesthetic whispers out of time:


                    I go on consulting
This mirror that is no longer mine
For as much brisk vacancy as is to be
My portion this time. And the vase is always full
Because there is only just so much room
And it accommodates everything. This sample
One sees is not to be taken as
Merely that, but as everything as it
May be imagined outside time—

The vase, emblem both of Keats' *Ode* and Stevens' *The Poems of Our Climate,* is as full as the poet's own time is briskly vacant, the oxymoron strengthening Ashbery's own recovery of strength in the poem. A meditation upon Ashbery's familiar "permanent anomaly," a certain kind of erotic illumination, leads on to a new sense of earliness, a metaleptic reversal of the poem's ironic opening:

> All we know
> Is that we are a little early, that
> Today has that special, lapidary
> Todayness that the sunlight reproduces
> Faithfully in casting twig-shadows on blithe
> Sidewalks. No previous day would have been like this.
> I used to think they were all alike,
> That the present always looked the same to everybody
> But this confusion drains away as one
> Is always cresting into one's present.

What shadows this freshly achieved earliness is the doubt that still more art is needed: "Our time gets to be veiled, compromised/By the portrait's will to endure." Creation being out of our hands, our distance from even our own art seems to become greater. In this intensification of estrangement, Ashbery's meditation gradually rejects the paradise of art, but with enormous nostalgias coloring farewell. A sublime pun, fulfilling Fletcher's vision of threshold rhetoric, is the climax of this poignant dismissal, which reverberates as one of Ashbery's greatest passages, majestic in the aesthetic dignity of its mingled strength and sadness:

> Therefore I beseech you, withdraw that hand,
> Offer it no longer as shield or greeting,
> The shield of a greeting, Francesco:
> There is room for one bullet in the chamber. . . .

The chamber, room of poet's and painter's self-portraits, room as moment of attention for the soul not a soul, fitting perfectly the hollow of its tomb, is also the suicide (or Russian roulette?) of a self-regarding art. Ashbery's poem too is the shield of a greeting, its defensive and communicative functions inextricably mixed. Yet Ashbery's reading of his tradition of utterance, and my reading of Ashbery, are gestures of restitution. Achieved dearth of meaning is exposed as an oxymoron, where the "achieved" outweighs the "dearth." The antithetical critic, following after the poet of his moment and his climate, must oppose to the abysses of Deconstruction's ironies a supermimesis achieved by an art that will not abandon the self to language, the art of Ashbery's earlier *Fragment:*

> The words sung in the next room are unavoidable
> But their passionate intelligence will be studied in you.

# 2

## PAUL DE MAN

# Shelley Disfigured

> . . . while digging in the grounds for the new
> foundations, the broken fragments of a marble
> statue were unearthed. They were submitted to
> various antiquaries, who said that, so far as the
> damaged pieces would allow them to form an
> opinion, the statue seemed to be that of a muti-
> lated Roman satyr; or, if not, an allegorical fig-
> ure of Death. Only one or two old inhabitants
> guessed whose statue those fragments had com-
> posed.
>
> THOMAS HARDY,
> *"Barbara of the House of Grebe"*

## I

Like several of the English romantics' major works *The Triumph of Life,* Shelley's last poem, is, as is well known, a fragment that has been unearthed, edited, reconstructed and much discussed. All this archeological labor can be considered a response to the questions that articulate one of the text's main structures: ". . . 'And what is this? / Whose shape is that within the car? and why—' " (ll. 177–78)[1]; later repeated in a more subject-oriented, second-person mode: " 'Whence camest thou? and whither goest thou?/ How did thy course begin,' I said, 'and why?' " (ll. 296–97); finally repeated again, now in the first person: " 'Shew whence I came, and where I am, and why— . . .' " (l. 398). These questions can easily be referred back to the enigmatic text they punctuate and they are characteristic of the interpretive labor associated with romanticism. In the case of this movement, they acquire an edge of urgency which is often lacking when they are addressed to earlier periods, except when these periods are themselves mediated by the neo-hellenism, the neo-medievalism or the neo-baroque of the late eighteenth and the early nineteenth century. This is not surprising, since they are precisely the archeological questions that prompt us to deduce the present from the identification of the more or less immediately anterior past, as well as from the process that leads from then to now. Such an attitude coincides with the use of history as a way to new beginnings, as "digging in the grounds for the new foundations." Much is invested in these metaphors of architecture and of statuary on which seems to hinge our ability to inhabit the world. But if this curiosity about antecedents has produced admirable philological results and allowed, as in the case of *The Triumph of Life,* for the establishment of texts whose unreliability is at least controlled by more reliable means, the questions which triggered all this industry remain more than ever in suspense: What is the meaning of *The Triumph of Life,* of Shelley and of romanticism? What shape does it have, how did its course begin and why? Perhaps the difficulty of the answers is prefigured in the asking of the questions. The status of all these where's and what's and how's and why's is at stake, as well as the system that links these interrogative pronouns, on the one hand, to questions of definition and of temporal situation and, on the other hand, to questions of shape and of figure. Such questions allow one to conclude that *The Triumph of Life* is a fragment of something whole, or romanticism a fragment, or a moment, in a process that now includes us within its horizon. What relationship do we have to such a text that allows us to call it a fragment that we are then entitled to reconstruct, to identify and implicitly to complete? This supposes, among other things, that Shelley or romanticism are themselves entities which, like a statue, can be broken into pieces, mutilated or allegorized (to use Hardy's alternatives) after having been stiffened, frozen, erected or whatever one wants to call the particular rigidity of statues. Is the status of a text line the status of a statue? Yeats, one of Shelley's closest readers and disciples, wrote a fine poem about history and form called *The Statues,* which it would be rewarding to read in conjunction with *The Triumph of Life.* But there are more economic ways to approach this text and to question the possibility of establishing a relationship to Shelley and to romanticism in general. After all, the link between the present I and its antecedents is itself dramatized in the poem, most explicitly and at greatest length in the encounter between the narrator and the figure designated by the proper name Rousseau, who has himself much to say about his own predecessors.

## II

The unearthed fragments of this fragment, the discarded earlier versions, disclose that the relationship between Shelley and Rousseau, or between Rousseau and his ancestors, underwent considerable changes as the composition of the poem progressed. Consider, for instance, the passage in which the poet, guided at this moment by Rousseau, passes judgment upon his contemporaries and immediate predecessors, including the openly alluded to Wordsworth, with such vehemence that he condemns them all to oblivion.[2] He is reproached for this by Rousseau who intervenes to assert that he himself, as well as Voltaire, would have ascended to "the fane / Where truth and its inventors sit enshrined," if they had not been so faint-hearted as to lack faith in their own intellectual labor as well as, by implication, that of their ancestors. Those encrypted statues of Truth are identified as "Plato and his pupil" (presumably Aristotle) who "Reigned from the center to the circumference" and prepared the way for Bacon and modern science. Rousseau's and Voltaire's capitulation is not a sheer loss however, since Rousseau has gained insight that he is able to communicate in turn to the young Shelley. Donald Reiman, the editor of *The Triumph of Life,* glosses the passage as follows:

Rousseau . . . tries to impress on the Poet that it was exactly this attitude toward the past struggle of great men that led him and Voltaire to abandon their reforming zeal and succumb to life. Thus the poet's contemptuous allusion to Wordsworth turns against him as Rousseau endeavors to show the Poet how the mistakes of those who have preceded him, especially idealists like himself, can serve as a warning to him: Rousseau and Voltaire fell because they adopted the contemptuous attitude toward history that the poet now displays; the child *is* father of the man, and Shelley's generation, representing the full mastery of the age that dawned in the French Revolution, can learn from the mistakes of that age's earlier generations (those of Rousseau and Voltaire and of Wordsworth).

Although this is certainly not presented as an interpretation of the entire text, but only of this discarded passage, it remains typical of the readings generally given of *The Triumph of Life,* even when they are a great deal more complicated than this straightforward statement. It is a clear example of the recuperation of a failing energy by means of an increased awareness: Rousseau lacked power, but because he can consciously articulate the causes of his weakness in words, the energy is preserved and recovered in the following generation. And this reconversion extends back to its originators, since the elders, at first condemned, are now reinstated in the name of their negative but exemplary knowledge. The child *is* father of the man, just as Wordsworth lucidly said, both humbling and saving himself in the eyes of his followers. This simple motion can take on considerable dialectical intricacy without altering its fundamental scheme. The entire debate as to whether *The Triumph of Life* represents or heralds a movement of growth or of degradation is part of this same genetic and historical metaphor.[3] The unquestioned authority of this metaphor is much more important than the positive or negative valorization of the movement it generates.

The initial situation of Rousseau—allied with Voltaire and Wordsworth in a shared failure, as opposed to Plato, Aristotle and Bacon, and as opposed, by implication, to Shelley himself—changes in later versions. In the last available text, itself frozen into place by Shelley's accidental death, the hierarchy is quite different: Rousseau is now set apart quite sharply from the representatives of the Enlightenment (which include Voltaire next to Kant and Frederick the Great) who are condemned with some of the original severity, without Rousseau reproving him for it. No allusion to Wordsworth is included at this point, though Wordsworth is certainly present in other regions of the poem. Rousseau is now classified with Plato and Aristotle, but whereas these philosophers were held up as untarnished images of Truth in the earlier version, they are now fallen and, in the imagery of the poem, chained to the chariot of Life, together with "the great bards of old" (l. 247). The reasons for their fall, as well as the elements in their works and in their lives that both unite and distinguish them from Rousseau, are developed in passages that are not difficult to interpret from a thematic point of view. The resulting hierarchies have become more complex: we first have a class of entirely condemned historical personages, which includes representatives of the Enlightenment as well as the emperors and popes of Christianity (ll. 281 ff.); on a distinctly higher level, but nevertheless defeated, we find Rousseau, Plato, Aristotle and Homer. As possibly exonerated from this defeat, the poem mentions only Bacon, a remnant from the earlier passage who now has lost much of his function, as well as "the sacred few" (l. 128) who, unlike Adonais in the earlier poem, had no earthly destiny whatsoever, either because, by choice or destiny, they died too early or because, like Christ or Socrates, they are mere fictions in the writings of others. As for Shelley himself, his close proximity to Rousseau is now more strongly marked than in the earlier passage; the possibility of his escape from Rousseau's destiny has now become problematic and depends on one's reading of Rousseau's own story, which constitutes the main narrative sequence of the poem.[4]

Lengthy and complex as it is, Rousseau's self-narrated history provides no answer to his true identity, although he is himself shown in quest of such an answer. Questions of origin, of direction and of identity punctuate the text without ever receiving a clear answer. They always lead back to a new scene of questioning which merely repeats the quest and recedes in infinite regress: the narrator asks himself " 'And what is this? . . .' " (l. 177) and receives an enigmatic answer (" 'Life!' ") from an enigmatic shape; once identified as Rousseau, the shape can indeed reveal some other names in the pageant of history but is soon asked, by the poet, to identify itself in a deeper sense than by a mere name: " 'How did thy course begin . . . and why?' " Complying with this request, Rousseau narrates the history of his existence, also culminating in an encounter with a mysterious entity, " 'A shape all light . . .' " (l. 352) to whom, in his turn, he puts the question " 'whence I came, and where I am, and why—.' " As an answer, he is granted a vision of the same spectacle that prompted the poet-narrator's questioning in the first place; we have to imagine the same sequence of events repeating themselves for Shelley, for Rousseau and for whomever Rousseau chose to question in his turn as Shelley questioned him. The structure of the text is not one of question and answer, but of a question whose meaning, as question, is effaced from the moment it is asked. The answer to the question is another question, asking what and why one asked, and thus receding ever further from the original query. This movement of effacing and of forgetting becomes prominent in the text and dispels any illusion of dialectical progress or regress. The articulation in terms of the questions is displaced by a very differently structured process that pervades all levels of the narrative and that repeats itself in the main sequences as well as in what seem to be lateral episodes. It finally engulfs and dissolves what started out to be, like *Alastor, Epipsychidion* or even *Prometheus Unbound,* a quest (or, like *Adonais,* an elegy), to replace it by something quite different for which we have no name readily available among the familiar props of literary history.

Whenever this self-receding scene occurs, the syntax and the imagery of the poem tie themselves into a knot which arrests the process of understanding. The resistance of these passages is such that the reader soon forgets the dramatic situation and is left with only these unresolved riddles to haunt him: the text becomes the successive and cumulative experience of these tangles of meaning and of figuration. One of these tangles occurs near the end of Rousseau's narration of his encounter with the "shape all light" assumed to possess the key to his destiny:

> ". . . as one between desire and shame
> Suspended, I said . . .
> . . . . . . . . . . . . . . . . . . . . . . . . . . . . . . . . . . . .
> 'Shew whence I came, and where I am, and why—
> Pass not away upon the passing stream.'
>
> " 'Arise and quench thy thirst' was her reply.
> And as a shut lily, stricken by the wand
> Of dewy morning's vital alchemy,
>
> "I rose; and bending at her sweet command,
> Touched with faint lips the cup she raised,
> And suddenly my brain became as sand
>
> "Where the first wave had more than half erased
> The track of deer on desert Labrador,
> Whilst the fierce wolf from which they fled amazed
>
> "Leaves his stamp visibly upon the shore
> Until the second bursts—so on my sight
> Burst a new Vision never seen before.—"
>
> [ll. 398–410]

The scene dramatizes the failure to satisfy a desire for self-knowledge and can therefore indeed be considered as something of a key passage. Rousseau is not given a satisfactory answer, for the ensuing vision is a vision of continued delusion that includes him. He undergoes instead a metamorphosis in which his brain, the center of his consciousness, is transformed. The transformation is also said to be the erasure of an imprinted track, a passive, mechanical operation that is no longer within the brain's own control: both the production and the erasure of the track are not an act performed by the brain, but the brain being acted upon by something else. The resulting "sand" is not, as some commentators imply, an image of drought and sterility (this is no desert, but a shore washed by abundant waters).[5] "My brain became as sand" suggests the modification of a knowledge into the surface on which this knowledge ought to be recorded. Ought to be, for instead of being clearly imprinted it is "more than half erased" and covered over. The process is a replacement, a substitution, continuing the substitution of "brain" by "sand," of one kind of track, said to be like that of a deer, by another, said to be like that of a wolf "from which [the deer] fled amazed." They mark a stage in the metamorphosis of Rousseau into his present state or shape; when we first meet him, he is

> . . . what I thought was an old root which grew
> To strange distortion out of the hill side . . .

> And . . . the grass which methought hung so wide
> And white, was but his thin discoloured hair,
> And . . . the holes he vainly sought to hide

> Were or had been eyes.
> > [ll. 182–88][6]

The erasure or effacement is indeed the loss of a face, in French *figure*. Rousseau no longer, or hardly (as the tracks are not all gone, but more than half erased), has a face. Like the protagonist in the Hardy story, he is disfigured, *défiguré*, defaced. And also as in the Hardy story, to be disfigured means primarily the loss of the eyes, turned to "stony orbs" or to empty holes. This trajectory from erased self-knowledge to disfiguration is the trajectory of *The Triumph of Life*.

The connotations of the pair deer/wolf, marking a change in the inscriptions made upon Rousseau's mind, go some way in explaining the presence of Rousseau in the poem, a choice that has puzzled several interpreters.[7] The first and obvious contrast is between a gentle and idyllic peace pursued by violent aggression. Shelley, an assiduous reader of Rousseau at a time when he was being read more closely than he has been since, evokes an ambivalence of structure and of mood that is indeed specifically Rousseau's rather than anyone else's, including Wordsworth's. Rousseau's work is characterized in part by an introspective, self-reflexive mode which uses literary models of Augustinian and pietistic origin, illustrated, for instance, by such literary allusions as Petrarch and the *Astrée* and, in general, by the elements that prompted Schiller to discuss him under the heading of the contemporary idyll. But to this are juxtaposed elements that are closer to Machiavelli than to Petrarch, concerned with political power as well as with economic and legal realities. The first register is one of delicacy of feeling, whereas a curious brand of cunning and violence pervades the other. The uneasy mixture is both a commonplace and a crux of Rousseau interpretation. It appears in the larger as well as the finer dimensions of his writings, most obviously in such broad contrasts as separate the tone and import of a text such as *The Social Contract* from that of *Julie*. That the compatibility between inner states of consciousness and acts of power is a thematic concern of *The Triumph of Life* is clear from the political passages in the poem. In the wake of the in itself banal passage on Bonaparte, the conflict is openly stated:

> . . . much I grieved to think how power and will
> In opposition rule our mortal day—
>
> And why God made irreconcilable
> Good and the means of good; . . .
>
> [ll. 228–31]

Rousseau is unique among Shelley's predecessors not only in that this question of the discrepancy between the power of words as acts and their power to produce other words is inscribed within the thematics and the structure of his writings, but also in the particular form that it takes there. For the tension passes, in Rousseau, through a self which is itself experienced as a complex interplay between drives and the conscious reflection on these drives; Shelley's understanding of this configuration is apparent in this description of Rousseau as "between desire and shame / Suspended. . . ."

The opposition between will and power, the intellectual goal and the practical means, reappears when it is said, by and of Rousseau, that ". . . my words were seeds of misery—/ Even as the deeds of others . . ." (ll. 280–81). The divergence between words and deeds (by way of "seeds") seems to be suspended in Rousseau's work, albeit at the cost of, or rather because of, considerable suffering: "I / Am one of those who have created, even / If it be but a world of agony" (ll. 294–95). For what sets Rousseau apart from the representatives of the Enlightenment is the pathos of what is here called the "heart" ("I was overcome / By my own heart alone. . . ."). The contrast between the cold and sceptical Voltaire and the sensitive Rousseau is another commonplace of popular intellectual history. But Shelley's intuition of the "heart" in Rousseau is more than merely sentimental. Its impact becomes clearer in the contrast that sets Rousseau apart from "the great bards of old," Homer and Vergil, said to have ". . . inly quelled / The passions which they sung . . ." (ll. 274–75), whereas Rousseau has ". . . suffered what [he] wrote, or viler pain!" Unlike the epic narrators who wrote about events in which they did not take part, Rousseau speaks out of his own self-knowledge, not only in his *Confessions* (which Shelley did not like) but in all his works, regardless of whether they are fictions or political treatises. In the tradition of Augustine, Descartes and Malebranche, the self is for him not merely the seat of the affections but the primary center of cognition. Shelley is certainly not alone in thus characterizing and praising Rousseau, but the configuration between self, heart and action is given even wider significance when Rousseau compares himself to the Greek philosophers. Aristotle turns out to be, like Rousseau, a double structure held together by the connivance of words and deeds; if he is now enslaved to the eroding process of "life," it is because he does not exist singly, as pure mind, but cannot be separated from the "woes and wars" his pupil Alexander the Great inflicted upon the world. Words cannot be isolated from the deeds they perform; the tutor necessarily performs the deeds his pupil derives from his mastery. And just as "deeds" cause the undoing of Aristotle, it is the "heart" that brought down Plato who, like Rousseau, was a theoretician of statecraft and a legislator. Like Aristotle and like Rousseau (who is like a deer but also like a wolf) Plato is at least double; life "conquered [his] heart" as Rousseau was "overcome by [his] own heart alone." The reference to the apocryphal story of Aster makes clear that "heart" here means more than mere affectivity; Plato's heart was conquered by "love" and, in this context, love is like the intellectual eros that links Socrates to his pupils. Rousseau is placed within a configuration, brought about by "words," of knowledge, action and erotic desire. The elements are present in the symbolic scene from which we started out, since the pursuit of the deer by the wolf, in this context of Ovidian and Dantesque metamorphoses, is bound to suggest Apollo's pursuit of the nymphs as well as scenes of inscription and effacement.

The scene is one of violence and grief, and the distress reappears in the historical description of Rousseau with its repeated emphasis on suffering and agony, as well as in the dramatic action of defeat and enslavement. But this defeat is paradoxical: in a sense, Rousseau has overcome the discrepancy of action and intention that tears apart the historical world, and he has done so because his words have acquired the power of actions as well as of the will. Not only because they represent or reflect on actions but because they themselves, literally, are actions. Their power to act exists independently of their power to know: Aristotle's or Plato's mastery of mind did not give them any control over the deeds of the world, also and especially the deeds that ensued as a consequence of their words and with which they were directly involved. The power that arms their words also makes them lose their power over them. Rousseau gains shape, face or figure only to lose it as he acquires it. The enigma of this power, the burden of whatever understanding Shelley's poem permits, depends primarily on the reading of Rousseau's recapitulative narrative of his encounter with the "Shape all light" (ll. 308–433).

# III

Rousseau's history, as he looks back upon his existence from the "April prime" of his young years to the present, tells of a specific experience that is certainly not a simple one but that can be designated by a single verb: the experience is that of forgetting. The term appears literally (l. 318) and in various periphrases (such as "oblivious spell," l. 331), or in metaphors with a clear analogical vehicle such as "quell" (l. 329), "blot [from memory]" (l. 330), "trample" (l. 388), "tread out" (l. 390), "erase" (l. 406), etc. It combines with another, more familiar metaphorical strain that is present throughout the entire poem: images of rising and waning light and of the sun.

The structure of "forgetting," in this text, is not clarified by echoes of a platonic recollection and recognition (anamnesis) that enter the poem, partly by way of Shelley's own platonic and neo-platonic readings,[8] partly by way of Wordsworth's *Immortality Ode* whose manifest presence, in this part of the poem, has misled even the most attentive readers of *The Triumph of Life*. In the *Phaedo* (73) and, with qualifications too numerous to develop here, in Wordsworth's *Ode*, what one forgets is a former state which Yeats, who used the same set of emblems, compares to the Unity of Being evoked in Aristophanes' *Symposium* speech as the mainspring of erotic desire. Within a neo-platonic Christian tradition, this easily becomes a fitting symbol for the Incarnation, for a birth out of a transcendental realm into a finite world. But this is precisely what the experience of forgetting, in *The Triumph of Life*, is not. What one forgets here is not some previous condition, for the line of demarcation between the two conditions is so unclear, the distinction between the forgotten and the remembered so unlike the distinction between two well-defined areas, that we have no assurance whatever that the forgotten ever existed:

"Whether my life had been before that sleep
The Heaven which I imagine, or a Hell

Like this harsh world in which I wake to weep
I know not."

[ll. 332–35]

The polarities of waking and sleeping (or remembering and forgetting) are curiously scrambled, in this passage, with those of past and present, of the imagined and the real, of knowing and not knowing. For if, as is clear from the previous scene,[9] to be born into life is to fall asleep, thus associating life with sleep, then to "wake" from an earlier condition of non-sleeping into "this harsh world" of life can only be to become aware of one's persistent condition of slumber, to be more than ever asleep, a deeper sleep replacing a lighter one, a deeper forgetting being achieved by an act of memory which remembers one's forgetting. And since Heaven and Hell are not here two transcendental realms but the mere opposition between the imagined and the real, what we do not know is whether we are awake or asleep, dead or alive, forgetting or remembering. We cannot tell the difference between sameness and difference, and this inability to know takes on the form of a pseudo-knowledge which is called a forgetting. Not just because it is an unbearable condition of indetermination which has to be repressed, but because the condition itself, regardless of how it affects us, necessarily hovers between a state of knowing and not-knowing, like the symptom of a disease which recurs at the precise moment that one remembers its absence. What is forgotten is absent in the mode of a possible delusion, which is another way of saying that it does not fit within a symmetrical structure of presence and absence.

In conformity with the consistent system of sun imagery, this hovering motion is evoked throughout the poem by scenes of glimmering light. This very "glimmer" unites the poet-narrator to Rousseau, as the movement of the opening sunrise is repeated in Rousseau's encounter with the feminine shape, just as it unites the theme of forgetting with the motions of the light. The verb appears in the opening scene:

> . . . a strange trance over my fancy grew
> Which was not slumber, for the shade it spread
>
> Was so transparent that the scene came through
> As clear as when a veil of light is drawn
> O'er the evening hills they *glimmer;* . . .
>
> > [ll. 29–33, *emphasis added*] [10]

and then again, later on, now with Rousseau on stage:

> The presence of that Shape which on the stream
> Moved, as I moved along the wilderness,
>
> More dimly than a day-appearing dream,
> The ghost of a forgotten form of sleep,
> A light from Heaven whose half-extinguished beam
>
> Through the sick day in which we wake to weep
> *Glimmers,* forever sought, forever lost.—
> So did that shape its obscure tenour keep. . . .
>
> > [ll. 425–32, *emphasis added*]

It is impossible to say, in either passage, how the polarities of light and dark are matched with those of waking and sleep; the confusion is the same as in the previously quoted passage on forgetting and remembering. The light, in the second passage, is said to be like a dream, or like sleep ("the ghost of a forgotten form of sleep"), yet it shines, however distantly, upon a condition which is one of awakening ("the sad day in which we wake to weep"); in this light, to be awake is to be as if one were asleep. In the first passage, it is explicitly stated that since the poet perceives so clearly, he cannot be asleep, but the clarity is then said to be like that of a veil drawn over a darkening surface, a description which necessarily connotes covering and hiding, even if the veil is said to be "of light." Light covers light, trance covers slumber and creates conditions of optical confusion that resemble

nothing as much as the experience of trying to read *The Triumph
of Life,* as its meaning glimmers, hovers and wavers, but refuses
to yield the clarity it keeps announcing.

This play of veiling and unveiling is, of course, altogether
tantalizing. Forgetting is a highly erotic experience; it is like
glimmering light because it cannot be decided whether it reveals
or hides; it is like desire because, like the wolf pursuing the deer,
it does violence to what sustains it; it is like a trance or a dream
because it is asleep to the very extent that it is conscious and
awake, and dead to the extent that it is alive. The passage that
concerns us makes this knot, by which knowledge, oblivion and
desire hang suspended, into an articulated sequence of events that
demands interpretation.

The chain that leads Rousseau from the birth of his consciousness to his present state of impending death passes through a
well-marked succession of relays. Plato and Wordsworth provide
the initial linking of birth with forgetting, but this forgetting
has, in Shelley's poem, the glimmering ambivalence which makes
it impossible to consider it as an act of closure or of beginning
and which makes any further comparison with Wordsworth irrelevant. The metaphor for this process is that of "a gentle rivulet
. . . [which] filled the grove / With sound which all who hear
must needs forget / All pleasure and all pain . . ." (ll. 314–19).
Unlike Yeats', Shelley's river does not function as the "generated
soul," as the descent of the transcendental soul into earthly time
and space. As the passage develops, it enters into a system of relationships that are natural rather than esoteric. The property of the
river that the poem singles out is its sound; the oblivious spell
emanates from the repetitive rhythm of the water, which articulates a random noise into a definite pattern. Water, which has no
shape of itself, is moulded into shape by its contact with the
earth, just as in the scene of the water washing away the tracks, it
generates the very possibility of structure, pattern, form or shape
by way of the disappearance of shape into shapelessness. The repetition of the erasures rhythmically articulates what is in fact a
disarticulation, and the poem seems to be shaped by the undoing

of shapes. But since this pattern does not fully correspond to what it covers up, it leaves the trace which allows one to call this ambivalent shaping a forgetting. The birth of what an earlier Shelley poem such as *Mont Blanc* would still have called the mind occurs as the distortion which allows one to make the random regular by "forgetting" differences.

As soon as the water's noise becomes articulated sound it can enter into contact with the light. The birth of form as the interference of light and water passes, in the semi-synaesthesia of the passage, through the mediation of sound; it is however only a semi-synaesthesia, for the optical and auditory perceptions, though simultaneous, nevertheless remain treated in asymetrical opposition:

> A Shape all light, which with one hand did fling
> Dew on earth, as if it were the dawn
> Whose invisible rain forever seemed to sing
>
> A silver music on the mossy lawn
> *And still* before her on the dusky grass.
> Iris her many-coloured scarf had drawn.
>                 [ll. 352–57, *emphasis added*] [11]

The water of the original river here fulfills a double and not necessarily complementary action, as it combines with the light to form, on the one hand, Iris's scarf or rainbow and, on the other hand, the "silver music" of oblivion. A traditional symbol of the integration of the phenomenal with the transcendental world, the natural synthesis of water and light in the rainbow is, in Shelley, the familiar "dome of many-coloured glass" whose "stain" is the earthly trace and promise of an Eternity in which Adonais' soul is said to dwell "like a star." As such, it irradiates all the textures and forms of the natural world with the veil of the sun's *farbiger Abglanz,* just as it provides the analogical light and heat that will make it possible to refer to the poet's mind as "embers." The metaphorical chain which links the sun to water, to color, to heat, to nature, to mind and to consciousness, is certainly at work in the poem and can be summarized in this image of the rainbow. But this symbol is said to exist here in the tenuous mode of insistence, as something that *still* prevails (l. 356) despite the encroachment of something else, also emanating from water and sun and associated with them from the start, called music and forgetting. This something else, of which it could be said that it wrenches the final statement of *Adonais* into a different shape, appears in some degree of tension with the symbol of the rainbow.

The entire scene of the shape's apparition and subsequent waning (l. 412) is structured as a near-miraculous suspension between these two different forces whose interaction gives to the figure the hovering motion which may well be the mode of being of all figures. This glimmering figure takes on the form of the unreachable reflection of Narcissus, the manifestation of shape at the expense of its possession. The suspended fascination of the Narcissus stance is caught in the moment when the shape is said to move

> . . . with palms so tender
> Their tread broke not the mirror of its billow
> [ll. 361–62]

The scene is self-reflexive: the closure of the shape's contours is brought about by self-duplication. The light generates its own shape by means of a mirror, a surface that articulates it without setting up a clear separation that differentiates inside from outside as self is differentiated from other. The self that comes into being in the moment of reflection is, in spatial terms, optical symmetry as the ground of structure, optical repetition as the structural principle that engenders entities as shapes. "Shape all light" is referentially meaningless since light, the necessary condition for shape, is itself, like water, without shape, and acquires shape only when split in the illusion of a doubleness which is not that of self and other. The sun, in this text, is from the start the figure of this self-contained specularity. But the double of the sun can only be the eye conceived as the mirror of light. "Shape" and "mirror" are inseparable in this scene, just as the sun is inseparable from the shapes it generates and which are, in fact, the eye,[12] and just as the sun is inseparable from itself since it produces the illusion of the self as shape. The sun can be said "to stand," a figure which assumes the existence of an entire spatial organization, because it stands personified

> amid the blaze
> Of his own glory. . . .
> [ll. 349–50]

The sun "sees" its own light reflected, like Narcissus, in a well that is a mirror and also an eye:

> . . . the Sun's image radiantly intense
> Burned on the waters of the well that glowed
> Like gold. . . .
> [ll. 345–47]

Because the sun is itself a specular structure, the eye can be said to generate a world of natural forms. The otherness of a world that is in fact without order now becomes, for the eye, a maze made accessible to solar paths, as the eye turns from the blank radiance of the sun to its green and blue reflection in the world, and allows us to be in this world as in a landscape of roads and intents. The sun

> threaded all the forest maze
> With winding paths of emerald fire. . . .
> [ll. 347–48]

The boldest, but also the most traditional, image in this passage is that of the sunray as a thread that stitches the texture of the world, the necessary and complementary background for the eye of Narcissus. The water and pupil of the eye generate the rainbow of natural forms among which it dwells in sensory self-fulfillment. The figure of the sun, present from the beginning of the poem, repeats itself in the figure of the eye's self-erotic contact with its own surface, which is also the mirror of the natural world. The erotic element is marked from the start, in the polarity of a male sun and a feminine shape, eye or well, which is said to

bend her

Head under the dark boughs, till like a willow
Her fair hair swept the bosom of the stream
That whispered with delight to be their pillow.—

[ll. 363–66]

Shelley's imagery, often assumed to be incoherent and erratic, is instead extraordinarily systematic whenever light is being thematized. The passage condenses all that earlier and later poets (one can think of Valéry and Gide's Narcissus, as well as of the *Roman de la Rose* or of Spencer) ever did with light, water and mirrors. It also bears witness to the affinity of his imagination with that of Rousseau, who allowed the phantasm of language born rhapsodically out of an erotic well to tell its story before he took it all away. Shelley's treatment of the birth of light reveals all that is invested in the emblem of the rainbow. It represents the very possibility of cognition, even for processes of articulation so elementary that it would be impossible to conceive of any principle of organization, however primitive, that would not be entirely dependent on its power. To efface it would be to take away the sun which, if it were to happen to this text, for example, would leave little else. *And still,* this light is allowed to exist in *The Triumph of Life* only under the most tenuous of conditions.

The frailty of the stance is represented in the supernatural delicacy which gives the shape "palms so tender / Their tread broke not the mirror of {the river's} billow" and which allows it to "glide along the river." The entire scene is set up as a barely imaginable balance between this gliding motion, which remains on one side of the watery surface and thus allows the specular image to come into being, and the contrary motion which, like Narcissus at the end of the mythical story, breaks through the surface of the mirror and disrupts the suspended fall of its own existence. As the passage develops, the story must run its course. The contradictory motions of "gliding" and "treading" which suspended gravity between rising and falling finally capsize. The "threading" sunrays become the "treading" of feet upon a surface which, in this text, does not stiffen into solidity.[13] Shelley's poem insists on the hyperbolic lightness of the reflexive contact, since the reflecting surface is never allowed the smooth stasis that is necessary to the duplication of the image. The water is kept in constant motion: it is called a "billow" and the surface, although compared to a crystal, is roughened by the winds that give some degree of verisimilitude to the shape's gliding motion. By the end of the section, we have moved from "thread" to "tread" to "trample," in a movement of increased violence that erases the initial tenderness. There is no doubt that, when we again meet the shape (ll. 425 ff.) it is no longer gliding along the river but drowned, Ophelia-like, below the surface of the water. The violence is confirmed in the return of the rainbow, in the ensuing vision, as a rigid, stony arch said "fiercely [to extoll] the fortune" of the shape's defeat by what the poem calls "life."

This chain of metaphorical transformations can be understood, up to this point, without transposition into a vocabulary that would not be that of their own referents, not unlike the movement of the figure itself as it endeavors to glide incessantly along a surface which it tries to keep intact. Specifically, the figure of the rainbow is a figure of the unity of perception and cognition undisturbed by the possibly disruptive mediation of its own figuration. This is not surprising, since the underlying assumption of such a paraphrastic reading is itself one of specular understanding in which the text serves as a mirror of our own knowledge and our knowledge mirrors in its turn the text's signification. But we can only inadequately understand in this fashion why the shaped light of understanding is itself allowed to wane away, layer by layer, until it is entirely forgotten and re-

mains present only in the guise of an edifice that serves to cele-
brate and to perpetuate its oblivion. Nor can we understand the
power that weighs down the seductive grace of figuration until it
destroys itself. The figure of the sun, with all its chain of correla-
tives, should also be read in a non-phenomenal way, a necessity
which is itself phenomenally represented in the dramatic tension
of the text.

The transition from "gliding" to "trampling" passes, in the action that is being narrated, through the intermediate relay of
"measure." The term actively reintroduces music which, after
having been stressed in the previous scene (ll. 354–55), is at first
only present by analogy in this phase of the action (ll. 359–74).[14]
Measure is articulated sound, that is to say language. Language
rather than music, in the traditional sense of harmony and melody. As melody, the "song" of the water and, by extension, the
various sounds of nature, only provide a background that easily
blends with the seduction of the natural world:

> . . . all the place
>
> Was filled with many sounds woven into one
> Oblivious melody, confusing sense
> Amid the gliding waves and shadows dun. . . .
> [ll. 339–42]

As melody and harmony, song belongs to the same gliding motion that is interrupted only when the shape's feet

> to the ceaseless song
>
> Of leaves and winds and waves and birds and bees
> And falling drops moved in a measure new. . . .
> [ll. 375–77]

The "tread" of this dancer, which needs a ground to the extent
that it carries the weight of gravity, is no longer melodious, but
reduces music to the mere measure of repeated articulations. It
singles out from music the accentual or tonal punctuation which

is also present in spoken diction. The scene could be said to narrate the birth of music out of the spirit of language, since the determining property is an articulation distinctive of verbal sound prior to its signifying function. The thematization of language in *The Triumph of Life* occurs at this point, when "measure" separates from the phenomenal aspects of signification as a specular *representation,* and stresses instead the literal and material aspects of language. In the dramatic action of the narrative, measure disrupts the symmetry of cognition as representation (the figure of the rainbow, of the eye and of the sun). But since measure is any principle of linguistic organization, not only as rhyme and meter but as any syntactical or grammatical scansion, one can read "feet" not just as the poetic meter that is so conspicuously evident in the terza rima of the poem, but as any principle of signification. Yet it is precisely these "feet" which extinguish and bury the poetic and philosophical light.

It is tempting to interpret this event, the shape's "trampling" the fires of thought "into the dust of death" (ll. 388), certainly the most enigmatic moment in the poem, as the bifurcation between the semantic and the non-signifying, material properties of language. The various devices of articulation, from word to sentence formation (by means of grammar, syntax, accentuation, tone, etc.), which are made to convey meaning, and these same articulations left to themselves, independently of their signifying constraints, do not necessarily determine each other. The latent polarity implied in all classical theories of the sign allows for the relative independence of the signifier and for its free play in relation to its signifying function. If, for instance, compelling rhyme schemes such as "billow," "willow," "pillow" or transformations such as "thread" to "tread" or "seed" to "deed" occur at crucial moments in the text, then the question arises whether these particularly meaningful movements or events are not being generated by random and superficial properties of the signifier rather than by the constraints of meaning. The obliteration of thought by "measure" would then have to be interpreted as the loss of semantic depth and its replacement by what Mallarmé calls "le hasard infini des conjonctions" (*Igitur*).

But this is not the story, or not the entire story, told by *The Triumph of Life*. For the arbitrary element in the alignment between meaning and linguistic articulation does not by itself have the power to break down the specular structure which the text erects and then claims to dissolve. It does not account for the final phase of the Narcissus story, as the shape traverses the mirror and goes under, just as the stars are conquered by the sun at the beginning of the poem and the sun then conquered in its turn by the light of the Chariot of Life. The undoing of the representational and iconic function of figuration by the play of the signifier does not suffice to bring about the disfiguration which *The Triumph of Life* acts out or represents. For it is the alignment of a signification with any principle of linguistic articulation whatsoever, sensory or not, which constitutes the figure. The iconic, sensory or, if one wishes, the aesthetic moment is not constitutive of figuration. Figuration is the element in language that allows for the reiteration of meaning by substitution; the process is at least twofold and this plurality is naturally illustrated by optical icons of specularity. But the particular seduction of the figure is not necessarily that it creates an illusion of sensory pleasure, but that it creates an illusion of meaning. In Shelley's poem, the shape is a figure regardless of whether it appears as a figure of light (the rainbow) or of articulation in general (music as measure and language). The transition from pleasure to signification, from the aesthetic to the semiological dimension, is clearly marked in the passage, as one moves from the figure of the rainbow to that of the dance, from sight to measure. It marks the identification of the shape as the model of figuration in general. By taking this step beyond the traditional conceptions of figuration as modes of representation, as polarities of subject and object, of part and whole, of necessity and chance or of sun and eye, the way is prepared for the subsequent undoing and erasure of the figure. But the extension, which coincides with the passage from tropological models such as metaphor, synecdoche, metalepsis or prosopoeia (in which a phenomenal element, spatial or temporal, is necessarily involved) to tropes such as grammar and syntax (which function on the level of the letter without the intervention of an iconic factor) is not by itself capable of erasing the figure or, in the representational code of the text, of drowning the shape or trampling out thought. Another intervention, another aspect of language has to come into play.

The narrative sequence of Rousseau's encounter, as it unfolds from the apparition of the shape (l. 343) to its replacement (l. 434) by a "new vision," follows a motion framed by two events that are acts of power: the sun overcoming the light of the stars, the light of life overcoming the sun. The movement from a punctual action, determined in time by a violent act of power, to the gliding, suspended motion "of that shape which on the stream/ Moved, as I moved along the wilderness" (ll. 425–26) is the same motion inherent in the title of the poem. As has been pointed out by several commentators, "triumph" designates the actual victory as well as the *trionfo,* the pageant that celebrates the outcome of the battle. The reading of the scene should allow for a more general interpretation of this contradictory motion.

We now understand the shape to be the figure for the figurality of all signification. The specular structure of the scene as a visual plot of light and water is not the determining factor but merely an illustration (*hypotyposis*) of a plural structure that involves natural entities only as principles of articulation among others. It follows that the figure is not naturally given or produced but that it is posited by an arbitrary act of language. The appearance and the waning of the light-shape, in spite of the solar analogon, is not a natural event resulting from the mediated interaction of several powers, but a single, and therefore violent, act of power achieved by the positional power of language considered by and in itself: the sun masters the stars because it *posits* forms, just as "life" subsequently masters the sun because it posits, by inscription, the "track" of historical events. The positing power does not reside in Rousseau as subject; the mastery of the shape over Rousseau is never in question. He rises and bends at her command and his mind is passively trampled into dust without resistance. The positing power of language is both entirely arbitrary, in having a strength that cannot be reduced to necessity, and entirely inexorable in that there is no alternative to it. It stands beyond the polarities of chance and determination and can therefore not be part of a temporal sequence of events. The sequence has to be punctured by acts that cannot be made a part of it. It cannot begin, for example, by telling us of the waning of the stars under the growing impact of the sun, a natural motion which is the outcome of a mediation, but it must evoke the violent "springing forth" of a sun detached from all antecedents. Only retrospectively can this event be seen and misunderstood as a substitution and a beginning, as a dialectical relationship between day and night, or between two transcendental orders of being. The sun does not appear in conjunction with or in reaction to the night and the stars, but of its own unrelated power. *The Triumph of Life* differs entirely from such Promethean or titanic myths as Keats' *Hyperion* or even *Paradise Lost* which thrive on the agonistic pathos of dialectical battle. It is unimaginable that Shelley's non-epic, non-religious poem would begin by elegiacally or rebelliously evoking the tragic defeat of the former gods, the stars, at the hands of the sun. The text has no room for the tragedy of defeat or of victory among next-of-kin, or among gods and men. The previous occupants of the narrative space are expelled by decree, by the sheer power of utterance, and consequently at once forgotten. In the vocabulary of the poem, it occurs by *imposition* (l. 20), the emphatic mode of positing. This compresses the prosopopoeia of the personified sun, in the first lines of the poem, into a curiously absurd pseudo-description. The most continuous and gradual event in nature, the subtle gradations of the dawn, is collapsed into the brusk swiftness of a single moment:

> Swift as a spirit hastening to his task
> . . . the Sun sprang forth
> . . . and the mask
>
> Of darkness fell from the awakened Earth.
> [ll. 1–4][15]

The appearances, later in the poem, of the Chariot of Life are equally brusk and unmotivated. When they occur, they are not "descendants" of the sun, not the natural continuation of the original, positing gesture but positings in their own right. Unlike night following day, they always again have to be posited, which explains why they are repetitions and not beginnings.

How can a positional act, which relates to nothing that comes before or after, become inscribed in a sequential narrative? How does a speech act become a trope, a catachresis which then engenders in its turn the narrative sequence of an allegory? It can only be because we impose, in our turn, on the senseless power of positional language the authority of sense and of meaning. But this is radically inconsistent: language posits and language means (since it articulates) but language cannot posit meaning; it can only reiterate (or reflect) it in its reconfirmed falsehood. Nor does the knowledge of this impossibility make it less impossible. This impossible position is precisely the figure, the trope, metaphor as a violent—and not as a dark—light, a deadly Apollo.

The imposition of meaning occurs in *The Triumph of Life* in the form of the questions that served as point of departure for the reading. It is as a questioning entity, standing within the pathos of its own indetermination, that the human subject appears in the text, in the figures of the narrator who interrogates Rousseau and of Rousseau who interrogates the shape. But these figures do not coincide with the voice that narrates the poem in which they are represented; this voice does not question and does not share in their predicament. We can therefore not ask why it is that we, as subjects, choose to impose meaning, since we are ourselves defined by this very question. From the moment the subject thus asks, it has already foreclosed any alternative and has become the figural token of meaning, "Ein Zeichen sind wir/ Deutungslos . . ." (Hölderlin). To question is to forget. Considered performatively, figuration (as question) performs the erasure of the positing power of language. In *The Triumph of Life,* this happens when a positional speech act is represented as what it resembles least of all, a sunrise.

To forget, in this poem, is by no means a passive process. In the Rousseau episode, things happen because the subject Rousseau keeps forgetting. In his earliest stages, he forgets the incoherence of a world in which events occur by sheer dint of a blind force, in the same way that the sun, in the opening lines, occurs by sheer imposition. The episode describes the emergence of an articulated language of cognition by the erasure, the forgetting of the events this language in fact performed. It culminates in the appearance of the shape, which is both a figure of specular self-knowledge, the figure of thought, but also a figure of "thought's empire over thought," of the element in thought that destroys thought in its attempt to forget its duplicity. For the initial violence of position can only be half erased, since the erasure is accomplished by a device of language that never ceases to partake of the very violence against which it is directed. It seems to extend the instantaneousness of the act of positing over a series of transformations, but this duration is a fictitious state, in which "all seemed as if it had been not" (l. 385). The trampling gesture enacts the necessary recurrence of the initial violence: a figure of thought, the very light of cognition, obliterates thought. At its apparent beginning as well as at its apparent end, thought (i.e., figuration) forgets what it thinks and cannot do otherwise if it is to maintain itself. Each of the episodes forgets the knowledge achieved by the forgetting that precedes it, just as the instantaneous sunrise of the opening scene is at once covered over by a "strange trance" which allows the narrator to imagine the scene as something remembered even before it could take place.[16] Positing "glimmers" into a glimmering knowledge that acts out the aporias of signification and of performance.

The repetitive erasures by which language performs the erasure of its own positions can be called disfiguration. The disfiguration of Rousseau is enacted in the text, in the scene of the root and repeats itself in a more general mode in the disfiguration of the shape:

> . . . The fair shape waned in the coming light
> As veil by veil the silent splendor drops
> From Lucifer, amid the chrysolite
>
> Of sunrise ere it strike the mountain tops—
>
> [ll. 412–15]

Lucifer, or metaphor, the bearer of light which carries over the light of the senses and of cognition from events and entities to their meaning, irrevocably loses the contour of its own face or shape. We see it happen when the figure first appears as water-music, then as rainbow, then as measure, to finally sink away "below the watery floor" trampled to death by its own power. Unlike Lycidas, it is not resurrected in the guise of a star, but repeated on a level of literality which is not that of meaning but of actual events, called "Life" in Shelley's poem. But "Life" is as little the end of figuration as the sunrise was its beginning. For just as language is misrepresented as a natural event, life is just as falsely represented by the same light that emanates from the sun and that will have to engender its own rainbow and measure. Only that this light destroys its previous representation as the wolf destroys the deer. The process is endless, since the knowledge of the language's performative power is itself a figure in its own right and, as such, bound to repeat the disfiguration of metaphor as Shelley is bound to repeat the aberration of Rousseau in what appears to be a more violent mode. Which also implies, by the same token, that he is bound to forget him, just as, in all rigor, *The Social Contract* can be said to erase *Julie* from the canon of Rousseau's works, or *The Triumph of Life* can be said to reduce all of Shelley's previous work to nought.

# IV

The persistence of light-imagery, in the description of the Chariot of Life as well as in the inaugural sunrise, creates the illusion of a continuity and makes the knowledge of its interruption serve as a ruse to efface its actual occurrence. The poem is sheltered from the performance of disfiguration by the power of its negative knowledge. But this knowledge is powerless to prevent what now functions as the decisive textual articulation: its reduction to the status of a fragment brought about by the actual death and subsequent disfigurement of Shelley's body, burned after his boat capsized and he drowned off the coast of Lerici.

This defaced body is present in the margin of the last manuscript page and has become an inseparable part of the poem. At this point, figuration and cognition are actually interrupted by an event which shapes the text but which is not present in its represented or articulated meaning. It may seem a freak of chance to have a text thus molded by an actual occurrence, yet the reading of *The Triumph of Life* establishes that this mutilated textual model exposes the wound of a fracture that lies hidden in all texts. If anything, this text is more rather than less typical than texts that have not been thus truncated. The rhythmical interruptions that mark off the successive episodes of the narrative are not new moments of cognition but literal events textually reinscribed by a delusive act of figuration or of forgetting.

In Shelley's absence, the task of thus reinscribing the disfiguration now devolves entirely on the reader. The final test of reading, in *The Triumph of Life,* depends on how one reads the textuality of this event, how one disposes of Shelley's body. The challenge that is in fact present in all texts and that *The Triumph of Life* identifies, thematizes and thus tries to avoid in the most effective way possible, is here actually carried out as the sequence of symbolic interruptions is in its turn interrupted by an event that is no longer simply imaginary or symbolic. The apparent ease with which readers of *The Triumph of Life* have been able to dispose of this challenge demonstrates the inadequacy of our understanding of Shelley and, beyond him, of romanticism in general.

For what we have done with the dead Shelley, and with all the other dead bodies that appear in romantic literature—one thinks, among many others, of the "dead man" that " 'mid that beauteous scene / Of trees and hills and water, bolt upright / Rose, with his ghastly face . . ." in Wordsworth's *Prelude* (V, 448–50)—is simply to bury them, to bury them in their own texts made into epitaphs and monumental graves. They have been made into statues for the benefit of future archeologists "digging in the grounds for the new foundations" of their own monuments. They have been transformed into historical and aesthetic objects. There are various and subtle strategies, much too numerous to enumerate, to accomplish this.

Such monumentalization is by no means necessarily a naive or evasive gesture, and it certainly is not a gesture that anyone can pretend to avoid making. It does not have to be naive, since it does not have to be the repression of a self-threatening knowledge. Like *The Triumph of Life,* it can state the full power of this threat in all its negativity; the poem demonstrates that this rigor does not prevent Shelley from allegorizing his own negative assurance, thus awakening the suspicion that the negation is a *Verneinung,* an intended exorcism. And it is not avoidable, since the failure to exorcize the threat, even in the face of such evidence as the radical blockage that befalls this poem, becomes precisely the challenge to understanding that always again demands to be read. And to read is to understand, to question, to know, to forget, to erase, to deface, to repeat—that is to say, the endless prosopopoeia by which the dead are made to have a face and a voice which tells the allegory of their demise and allows us to apostrophize them in our turn. No degree of knowledge can ever stop this madness, for it is the madness of words. What *would* be naive is to believe that this strategy, which is not *our* strategy as subjects, since we are its product rather than its agent, can be a source of value and has to be celebrated or denounced accordingly.

Whenever this belief occurs—and it occurs all the time—it leads to a misreading that can and should be discarded, unlike the coercive "forgetting" that Shelley's poem analytically thematizes and that stands beyond good and evil. It would be of little use to enumerate and categorize the various forms and names which this belief takes on in our present critical and literary scene. It functions along monotonously predictable lines, by the historicization and the aesthetification of texts, as well as by their use, as in this essay, for the assertion of methodological claims made all the more pious by their denial of piety. Attempts to define, to understand or to circumscribe romanticism in relation to ourselves and in relation to other literary movements are all part of this naive belief. *The Triumph of Life* warns us that nothing, whether deed, word, thought or text, ever happens in relation, positive or negative, to anything that precedes, follows or exists elsewhere, but only as a random event whose power, like the power of death, is due to the randomness of its occurrence. It also warns us why and how these events then have to be reintegrated in a historical and aesthetic system of recuperation that repeats itself regardless of the exposure of its fallacy. This process differs entirely from the recuperative and nihilistic allegories of historicism. If it is true and unavoidable that any reading is a monumentalization of sorts, the way in which Rousseau is read and disfigured in *The Triumph of Life* puts Shelley among the few readers who "guessed whose statue those fragments had composed." Reading as disfiguration, to the very extent that it resists historicism, turns out to be historically more reliable than the products of historical archeology. To monumentalize this observation into a *method* of reading would be to regress from the rigor exhibited by Shelley which is exemplary precisely because it refuses to be generalized into a system.

## NOTES

1. All quotations from *The Triumph of Life* are from the critical edition established by Donald H. Reiman, *Shelley's 'The Triumph of Life,'* A *Critical Study* (University of Illinois Press, 1965). Together with G. M. Matthews' edition, " 'The triumph of Life': A New Text" in *Studia Neophilologica* XXXII (1960), pp. 271–309, this edition is authoritative. On the complex history of the text's composition and publication, see Reiman, pp. 119–28.

2. The passage appears as Appendix C in Reiman, p. 241:

Nor mid the many shapes around him [Napoleon] chained
Pale with the toil of lifting their proud clay

Or those gross dregs of it which yet remained
Out of the grave to which they tend, should I
Have sought to mark any who may have stained

Or have adorned the doubtful progeny
Of the new birth of this new tide of time
In which our fathers lived and we shall die

Whilst others tell our sons in prose or rhyme
The manhood of the child; unless my guide
Had said, "Behold Voltaire—We two would climb

"Where Plato and his pupil, side by side,
Reigned from the center to the circumference
Of thought; till Bacon, great as either, spied

"The spot on which they met and said, 'From hence
I soar into a loftier throne.'—But I—
O World, who from full urns dost still dispense,

"Blind as thy fortune, fame and infamy—
I who sought both, prize neither now; I find
What names have died within thy memory,

"Which ones still live; I know the place assigned
To such as sweep the threshold of the fane
Where truth and its inventors sit enshrined.—

"And if I sought those joys which now are pain,
If he is captive to the car of life,
'Twas that we feared our labour would be vain."

3. One can confront, for example, the following statements: "The bleak facts, however, are narrated with the verve of a poet who has tapped new sources of creative strength, and Shelley's dream-vision is set in the frame of a joyous morning in spring. The poem leaps into being, at once adducing a simile which is far from despairing. . . ." (Meyer H. Abrams, *Natural Supernaturalism,* 1971, p. 441) and ". . . I find the attempts of some critics [of *The Triumph*] to envision its potential climax as joyous and optimistic and its title as indicative of such a conclusion to be very mistaken" (Harold Bloom, *Shelley's Mythmaking,* 1959, p. 223).

4. There is considerable disagreement, among the critics of *The Triumph,* on the importance and the valorization of this passage, as there is much disagreement about the importance of Rousseau as a source of the poem—next to Dante, Spencer, Milton (*Comus*), Wordsworth, etc. Generally speaking, the interpreters who dismiss the importance of Rousseau also tend to interpret the figure of the "shape all light" as

unambiguously nefarious; see, for instance, H. Bloom, *op. cit.,* pp. 267–70 or J. Rieger, *The Mutiny Within: The Heresies of P. B. Shelley* (New York, 1967) and, on the obverse side of the question and among several others, Carlos Baker, *Shelley's Major Poetry* (Princeton, 1948), pp. 264–68 or, in a different vein, Kenneth Neill Cameron, *Shelley, The Golden Years* (Harvard, 1974). Cameron sees the scene of the shape's trampling Rousseau's thought into dust as "not destruction, but rebirth" (p. 467). Reiman, who stresses and documents the importance of Rousseau more than other readers, and whose conviction that the shape is Julie is so strong that he even finds her name inscribed in the manuscript, reads the figure as a figure of love and includes her in his claim that "Everywhere, in *The Triumph,* the dark side of human experience is balanced by positive alternatives" (p. 84). It is perhaps naive to decide on a clear valorization on this level of rhetorical complexity; one would have to determine for what function of language the shape is a figure before asking whether an alternative to its function is even conceivable.

5. Reiman (p. 67) correctly refers to a "sandy beach" but his commitment to a positive interpretation leads to irrelevant considerations on assumedly alternating movements of good and evil. The suggestion of a desert (rather than the "desert shore" of l. 164) is implicit in all commentators who quote l. 400 ("And suddenly my brain became as sand . . .") without the ensuing context of shore and waves.

6. Compare the landscape of aging in *Alastor:*

> And nought but gnarled roots of ancient pines
> Branchless and blasted, clenched with grasping roots
> The unwilling soil. A gradual change was here,
> Yet ghastly. For, as fast years flow away,
> The smooth brow gathers, and the hair grows thin
> And white, and where irradiate dewy eyes
> Had shone, gleam stony orbs. . . .

> [ll. 530–36]

7. Shelley's consistently very high opinion of Rousseau is supported by the references to Rousseau in his writings and correspondence. For a brief summary of this question, see for example K. N. Cameron, *op. cit.,* p. 648. The Rousseau text Shelley most admired is *Julie.*

8. On Shelley's platonism, see James A. Notopoulos, *The Platonism of Shelley* (Durham, N.C., 1949) which abundantly documents Shelley's ex-

tensive involvement with the platonic tradition but fails to throw light on the most difficult passages of *The Triumph of Life*. The ambivalent treatment of Plato in *The Triumph* is read by Notopoulos as a denunciation of homosexuality.

9. "In the April prime / . . . . . / I found myself asleep / Under a mountain. . . ." The condition of being alive is also referred to as "that hour of rest" (l. 320) and Shelley refers to "a sleeping mother . . ." (l. 321) and "no other sleep" that will quell the ills of existence.

10. One may wish to read, against common usage, the verb to glimmer with full transitive force: the veil of light *glimmers* the hills. . . .

11. The same construction recurs later on, this time with reversed emphasis, measure insisting against the melodies of the "sweet tune":

> And still her feet, no less than the sweet tune
> To which they moved, seemed as they moved, to blot
> The thoughts of him who gazed on them. . . .
>
> [ll. 382–84]

12. See also, in the *Hymn of Apollo:*

> I am the eye with which the Universe
> Beholds itself and knows itself divine. . . .
>
> [ll. 31–32]

The sunrise of *The Triumph* and that of the *Hymn* (1820) differ to the precise extent that the identification sun/eye is no longer absolute in the later poem.

13. As in an otherwise similar scene in Mallarmé's *Hérodiade,* where the emphasis falls on the hardness of the mirror as frozen water:

> O miroir!
> Eau froide par l'ennui dans ton cadre gelée. . . .

14. When the shape's hair sweeping the river is said to be "As the enamoured is upborne in dream / O'er the lily-paven lakes mid silver mist / To wondrous music . . ." (ll. 367–69).

15. "Swift as a spirit . . ." is reminiscent of the *Spirit of Plato (From the Greek)*: "I am the image of swift Plato's spirit,/Ascending heaven; Athens doth inherit / His corpse below," which implies the identifica-

tion of the sun with a non-natural, in this case spiritual, element. The dichotomy between a natural, historical world and the world of the spirit, though still at work in the poem and allowing for readings such as Bloom's or Rieger's, is here superseded by a different dimension of language. The thematic assertion of this no longer platonic conception of language occurs in the similarity between Rousseau's and Plato's hierarchical situation in history. This is hardly a condemnation of Plato (or of Rousseau) but a more evolved understanding of the figural powers of language.

16. ll. 33–39.

# 3

## JACQUES DERRIDA

---

# Living On

## Translated by James Hulbert

But who's talking about living?

In other words on living?

This time, "in other words" does not put the same thing into other words, does not clarify an ambiguous expression, does not function like an "i.e." It amasses the powers of indecision and adds to the foregoing utterance its capacity for skidding. Under the pretext of commenting upon a terribly indeterminate, shifting statement, a statement difficult to pin down [*arrêter*], it gives a reading or version of it that is all the less satisfactory, controllable, unequivocal, for being more "powerful" than what it comments upon or translates. The supposed "commentary" of the "i.e." or "in other words" has furnished only a textual supplement that calls in turn for an overdetermining "in other words," and so on and so forth.

In other words on living? This time it sounds to you more surely like a quotation. This is its second occurrence in what you

---

BORDER LINES. *10 November 1977.* Dedicate "Living On" to my friend Jacques Ehrmann. Recall that it was in response to his invitation, and to see him, that I first came to Yale. He had the good fortune to sign J. E. when he wrote his initials. This permitted him to inscribe my copy of his book *"Textes" suivi de "La mort de la littérature,"* published anonymously, as follows: "To J. D. in friendly remembrance of this '10 November' on which J. E. called you." J. E. [the letters that

75

have every reason to suppose is a common context, although you have no absolute guarantee of it. If it is a sort of quotation, a sort of "mention," as the theoreticians of "speech acts" feel justified in saying, we must understand the entire performance "in other words on living?" as having quotation marks around it. But once quotation marks demand to appear, they don't know where to stop. Especially here, where they are not content merely to *surround* the performance "in other words on living?": they divide it, rework its body and its insides, until it is distended, diverted, out of joint, then reset member by member, word by word, realigned in the most diverse configurations (like a garment spread out on a clothesline with clothespins). For example, several pairs of quotation marks may enclose one or two words: "living on" ["*survivre*"], "on" living ["*sur*" *vivre*], "on" "living," on "living," producing each time a different semantic and syntactic effect; I still have not exhausted the list, nor have I brought the hyphen into play. Translating (almost, in other words) the Latin *dē*, the French *de*, or the English "of," "on" immediately comes to contaminate what it translates with meanings that it imports in turn, those other meanings that rework "living on" or "surviving" (*super, hyper,* "over," *über,* and even "above" and "beyond"). It would be superficial to attribute this contamination to contingency, contiguity, or contagion. At least, chance makes *sense* here, and that's what interests me.

Be alert to these invisible quotation marks, even within a word: *survivre,* living on. Following the triumphal procession of an "on," they trail more than one language behind them.

Forever unable to saturate a context, what reading will ever

---

spell *je,* "I"] are also the last letters of these "texts," their final paraph [*paraphe,* also "initials"], in his untranslatable signature. *24-31 December 1977.* Here, economy, the law of the *oikos* (house, room, tomb, crypt), the law of reserves, reserving, savings, saving: inversion, reversion, revolution of values [*valeurs,* also "securities," "meanings"]—or of the course of the sun—in the law of the *oikos* (*Heimlichkeit/Unheimlichkeit*). That makes three languages I'm writing in, and this is to appear, sup-

master the "on" of living on? For we have not exhausted its ambiguity: each of the meanings we have listed above can be divided further (e.g., living on can mean a reprieve or an afterlife, "life after life" or life after death, more life or more than life, and better; the state of suspension in which it's over—*and* over again, and you'll never have done with that suspension itself) and the triumph *of* life can also triumph *over* life and reverse the procession of the genitive. I shall demonstrate shortly that this is not wordplay, not on your life. What tack shall we take [*depuis quel bord;* lit., "from what side," "edge," "border," "shore" . . .] to translate the ambiguity of an in-other-words? I know, I am already in some sort of untranslatability. But I'll wager that that will not stop the procession of one language into another, the massive movement of this procession, this *cortège,* over the border of another language, into the language of the other.

(In fact, the hymen or the alliance *in the language of the other,* this strange vow by which we are committed in a language that is not our mother tongue, is what I wish to speak of here. I wish to commit myself with this vow, following the coupled pretexts of *The Triumph of Life* and *L'arrêt de mort.* But thus far the commitment is my own; it is still necessary that you be committed, already, to translating it.)

And to go write-on-living? If that were possible, would the writer have to be dead already, or be living on? Is this an alternative?

Will it be possible for us to ask whoever asked the initial question, "But who's talking about living?", what inflection governs his or her question? By definition, the statement [*énoncé*] "But

---

posedly, in a fourth. A question to the translators, a translator's note that I sign in advance: What is translation? Here, economy. To write in a *telegraphic* style, for the sake of economy. But also, *from afar,* in order to get down to what *é-loignement, Ent-fernung,* "dis-tance," *mean* in writing and in the voice. Telegraphics and telephonics, that's the theme. My desire to take charge of the Translator's Note myself. Let them also read this band as a telegram or a film for developing (a film "to be

who's talking about living?", like every other statement, does not require the presence or assistance of any party, male or female. The statement survives them a priori, lives on after them. Hence no context is saturable any more. No one inflection enjoys any absolute privilege, no meaning can be fixed or decided upon. No border is guaranteed, inside or out. Try it. For example:

1. "But *who*'s talking about living?": the question stresses the identity of the speaker, without ruling out the possibility (a further complication) that it refers to the subject of the question "But who's talking about living?", and so forth.

2. "But who's *talking about living?*": in other words, who can really speak about living? Who is in a position to? Who is already on the other side [*bord*], little enough alive, or alive enough, to dare to speak about living, not about one life, nor even about life, but about living, the immediate, present, even impersonal process of an act of living that nevertheless guarantees even the spoken word that it conveys and that it thus defies to *speak on living:* it is impossible to use living speech to speak of living—unless it is possible *only* with living speech, which would make the aporia even more paralyzing. Is this the point at which a triumphant procession unfinishes? " 'Then, what is Life?' I said. . . ." The structure of this line, very close to the end (the end of the poem *and* Shelley's end), the "I said" and the self-quotation are perhaps not so foreign to the canonical question of the supposed "unfinished" quality of a *"Triumph."*

3. "But who's talking about '*living*'?": an implicit quotation of "living," a "mention" of the word or the concept, which is not the same thing and doubles the possibilities. In other words: who is saying what about "living," the word or the thing, the sig-

---

processed," in English?): a procession underneath the other one, and going past it *in silence,* as if it did not see it, as if it had nothing to do with it, a double band, a "double bind," and a blindly jealous double . . . what Hillis Miller would call a "double blind" ("double blind-alley" in "The Mirror's Secret"). Double proceedings, double *cortège,* double triumph. *The Triumph of Life, L'arrêt de mort* (how will they have translated this title? Better to leave it in "French," assuming that it

nifier or the concept, if we suppose that in this case these oppositions are pertinent in the least, and that "living," precisely, does
not go beyond their bounds?

4. In French, the language, "my" language, which I am
speaking here but which you are already translating, a context
governed by the everyday nature of oral exchange would, *in most
cases,* put the principal accent on the following intended meaning, which I translate in an approximate way like this: Is it really
a question of living? In other words, who said that we *had* to
live? But who's talking about living? Must we live, really? Can
"living," "live," be taken as an imperative, an order, a necessity?
Where do you get this axiomatic, valuational certainty that we
(or *you*) must live? Who says that living is worth all the trouble?
That it's better to live than to die? That, since we've started, we
have to keep on living? In other words living on? (The sentence
in the second line has put in for a transfer and brought about its
displacement.) In other words, then, what is life (" 'Then, what
is Life?' I said. . . ."), a *quoted* question that, for want of a sat-
urating context, we can always understand as having two meanings, at least:

   a.  the meaning of *meaning* or of *value* (Does life have meaning,
sense? Does it have the slightest value? Is it worth living? Who's
talking about living?—and so forth)
   b.  the meaning of *being* (What is the essence of life? What is
Life? What is the living-ness [*l'être-vivant*] of life?—and so forth).

These two meanings (at least two) inhabit *The Triumph of Life* and
rework its supposedly "unfinished" edge. *The Triumph* talks about

---

belongs to a determinable language; but then in what language will this
text appear?), each "triumph" (there are two triumphs) forming the
double band or "double bind" of double proceedings. This would be a
good place for a translator's note, for example, about *everything* that has
been said elsewhere on the subject of the "double bind," the double
band, the double procession, and so forth (a quotation *in extenso,* among
others, of *Glas,* which itself . . . and so forth): this, as a measure of the

living. But what does it say about it? A great deal, far too many
things, but this much at least, in its writing-on-living: it *is,* itself, the poem, and it gives itself a name, *The Triumph of Life.* In
a sense still to be determined, it lives-on. But—I must say it in
the syntax of my language to defy the translators to decide, at
each moment—*in/after whose name, or the name of what,* does it live
on? Does it live on in/after Shelley's name? This deserves a translators' note explaining both *survivre au nom de* and what happens
in French when *triomphe de la vie* [triumph of life] is transformed
into *triompher de la vie* [to triumph over life]. This is not playing
with language, as one might easily suspect. I maintain, not without delaying the proof a bit longer, that this is a question of what
takes place *in* the poem and of what remains of it, beyond any opposition between finished and unfinished, whether we mean the
end of the last poem or that of the man who drowned "off Lerici"
on 8 July 1822, "writing *The Triumph of Life*" (as is said in one
account of *Shelley's Life,* with a chronological table in five divisions, "Dates," "Events," "Residence," "Finance," "Chief
Works").

"Who's talking about living?" I am treating this sentence as a
quotation; there can be no doubt about it now. And you may
even have the feeling that all I've been doing is commenting on
this opening sentence that came, with no quotation marks, from
who knows where. But wasn't this attack already a quotation? I
was apparently the one who decided to write that, without asking
for anyone's authorization, not taking it out of any well-defined
corpus, not indicating any copyright. But I immediately began to
reconstitute all sorts of corpora or contexts from which I might

---

impossible. How can one text, assuming its unity, give or present
another to be read, without touching it, without saying anything about
it, practically without referring to it? How can two "triumphs" read
each other, each one *and* the other, without even knowing each other, at
a distance? At a distance and without knowing each other, like the two
"women" in *L'arrêt de mort.* The "mad hypothesis," the manic hubris of
a reading toward which the other procession (what happens [*se passe*] be-

have taken it. One of the most general or broadest of the categories that might limit such a corpus would be something like
the language called French, or a family of languages more or less
susceptible of translation of or into French. This reconstitution is
far from finished. I set down here as an axiom and as that which
is to be proved, that the reconstitution cannot be finished. This is
my starting point: no meaning can be determined out of context,
but no context permits saturation. What I am referring to here is
not richness of substance, semantic fertility, but rather structure:
the structure of the remnant or of iteration. But I have given this
structure many other names, and what matters here is the secondary aspect of nomination. Nomination is important, but it is
constantly caught up in a process that it does not control.

Since I began, and since you read the question "Who's talking
about living?" (wherever it came from), the word *bord* [edge,
brink, verge, border, boundary, bound, limit, shore] has imposed
itself more than once.

If we are to approach [*aborder*] a text, for example, it must have
a *bord*, an edge. Take this text. What is its upper edge? Its title
("Living On")? But when do you start reading it? What if you
started reading it after the first sentence (another upper edge),
which functions as its first reading head but which itself in turn
folds its outer edges back over onto inner edges whose mobility—
multilayered, quotational, displaced from meaning to meaning—
prohibits you from making out a shoreline? There is a regular *submerging* of the shore.

When a text quotes and requotes, with or without quotation
marks, when it is written on the brink, you start, or indeed have

---

tween the two women, one of whom he imagines—if only to rule out
the notion—to have drowned herself) is directed, *obviously* has nothing
to do with Shelley's drowning, or even with the event thus recorded in
one chronology: "*Date:* 1816, December *Events:* Harriet found drowned.
Shelley marries Mary." Or with "glu de l'étang lait de ma mort noýe"
["snare" (more literally "[bird]lime") "of the pond, milk of my drowned
death"; extensive resonances from "gl-," "l'étang," "lait" . . .] (in

already started, to lose your footing. You lose sight of any line of demarcation between a text and what is outside it.

(This is where my scenario breaks off, unfinished—it would have related, *on the one hand,* all the "triumphs of death" of the Italian *quattrocento,* the ironical or antithetical quotation of a genre by *The Triumph of Life,* the supposed unfinished quality at the apparent lower edge of a poem by Shelley at the moment when, in greatest proximity to the signature, at the apparent lower edge of the poem, the signatory is drowned, loses his footing, loses sight of the shore, and, *on the other hand,* all the drownings in Blanchot's stories, the drownings that I cited in "Pas" as well as the others, all the representations [*mises en scène*] of a shoreline that disappears or is overrun at the edge of *Thomas l'obscur,* a book that is remarkable—and re-marked—from its opening sentences on:

Thomas sat down and looked at the sea. He remained motionless for a time, as if he had come there to follow the movements of the other swimmers and, although the fog prevented him from seeing very far, he stayed there, obstinately, his eyes fixed on the bodies floating with difficulty. Then, when a more powerful wave reached him, he went down onto the sloping sand and slipped among the currents, which quickly immersed him.

> [*Thomas the Obscure,* new version,
> translated by Robert Lamberton
> (New York: David Lewis, 1973)]

or

---

*Glas*), which I would like to have translated here. Beyond all this grand phantasmic organization and these real or fictitious events, I wish to pose the question of the *bord,* the edge, the border, and the *bord de mer,* the shore. [These "Border Lines," in French, are entitled "Journal de bord"—usually translated "shipboard journal," but here also "journal on *bord.*"] (*The Triumph of Life* was written in the sea, at its edge, between land and sea, but that doesn't matter.) The question of the bor-

I sought, this time, to approach [*aborder*] him. I mean that I tried
to make him understand that even though I was there I could go
no further, and that I in turn had used up my resources. In truth, I
had long had the impression that I was at the end of my rope.
"But you aren't," he remarked.

[These are the "first" words of Blanchot's *Celui qui ne m'accompagnait pas.*] You may ask what I mean by that: do Blanchot's
stories, his *récits,* treat, in their own way, *The Triumph of Life,*
and even the supposed unfinished quality that separates it from
its ending, and even what separates it from its supposed signatory
and his drowning? For now, I shall not answer this question, but
ask one of my own: What is to say that the supposed signatory of
a piece of writing must answer for it, and answer at every turn
the questions of this person or that, telling them "exactly" what
the "story" is?)

   If we are to approach a text, it must have an edge. The question of the text, as it has been elaborated and transformed in the
last dozen or so years, has not merely "touched" "shore," *le bord*
(scandalously tampering, changing, as in Mallarmé's declaration,
*"On a touché au vers"*), all those boundaries that form the running
border of what used to be called a text, of what we once thought
this word could identify, i.e., the supposed end and beginning of
a work, the unity of a corpus, the title, the margins, the signa-
tures, the referential realm outside the frame, and so forth. What
has happened, if it has happened, is a sort of overrun [*déborde-
ment*] that spoils all these boundaries and divisions and forces us
to extend the accredited concept, the dominant notion of a

---

derline precedes, as it were, the determination of all the dividing lines
that I have just mentioned: between a fantasy and a "reality," an event
and a non-event, a fiction and a reality, one corpus and another, and so
forth. Here, from week to week in this pocket-calendar or these minutes
[*procès-verbal*], I shall perhaps endeavor to create an effect of *superimposing,* of superimprinting one text on the other. Now, each of the two
"triumphs" writes (on [*sur*]) textural superimprinting. What about this

"text," of what I still call a "text," for strategic reasons, in part—a "text" that is henceforth no longer a finished corpus of writing, some content enclosed in a book or its margins, but a differential network, a fabric of traces referring endlessly to something other than itself, to other differential traces. Thus the text overruns all the limits assigned to it so far (not submerging or drowning them in an undifferentiated homogeneity, but rather making them more complex, dividing and multiplying strokes and lines)—all the limits, everything that was to be set up in opposition to writing (speech, life, the world, the real, history, and what not, every field of reference—to body or mind, conscious or unconscious, politics, economics, and so forth). Whatever the (demonstrated) necessity of such an overrun, such a *dé-bordement,* it still will have come as a shock, producing endless efforts to dam up, resist, rebuild the old partitions, to blame what could no longer be thought without confusion, to blame difference *as* wrongful confusion! All this has taken place in non-reading, with no work on what was thus being demonstrated, with no realization that it was never our wish to extend the reassuring notion of the text to a whole extra-textual realm and to transform the world into a library by doing away with all boundaries, all framework, all sharp edges (all *arêtes:* this is the word that I am speaking of tonight), but that we sought rather to work out the theoretical and practical system of these margins, these borders, once more, from the ground up. I shall not go into detail. Documentation of all this is readily available to anyone committed to breaking down the various structures of resistance,

---

"on," this *"sur,"* and its surface? An effect of superimposing: one procession is superimposed on the other, accompanying it without accompanying it (Blanchot, *Celui qui ne m'accompagnait pas*). This operation would never be considered legitimate on the part of a teacher, who must give his references and tell what he's talking about, giving it its recognizable title. You can't give a course on Shelley without ever mentioning him, pretending to deal with Blanchot, and more than a few others.

his own resistance as such or as primarily the ramparts that bolster a system (be it theoretical, cultural, institutional, political, or whatever). What are the borderlines of a text? How do they come about? I shall not approach the question frontally, in the most general way. I prefer, within the limits that we have here, a more indirect, narrower channel, one that is more concrete as well: at the edge of the narrative, of the text *as* a narrative. The word is *récit,* a story, a narrative, and not *narration,* narration. The reworking of a textual problematic has affected this aspect of the text as narrative (the narrative of an event, the event of narrative, the narrative as the structure of an event) by placing it in the foreground.

(I note parenthetically that *The Triumph of Life,* which it is not my intention to discuss here, belongs in many ways to the category of the *récit,* in the disappearance or overrun that takes place the moment we wish to close its case after citing it, calling it forth, commanding it to appear.

1. *There is* the *ré-cit* of double affirmation, as analyzed in "Pas" [in *Gramma,* No. 3/4 (1976)], the "yes, yes" that must be cited, must recite itself to bring about the alliance [*alliance,* also "wedding band"] of affirmation with itself, to bring about its ring. It remains to be seen whether the double affirmation is *triumphant,* whether the triumph is affirmative or a paradoxical phase in the work of mourning.

2. *There is* the double narrative, the narrative of the vision enclosed in the general narrative carried on by the same narrator. The line that separates the enclosed narrative from the other—

---

And your transitions have to be readable, that is, in accordance with criteria of readability very firmly established, and long since. At the beginning of *L'arrêt de mort,* the superimposing of the two "images," the image of Christ and, "behind the figure of Christ," Veronica, "the features of a woman's face—extremely beautiful, even magnificent"—this superimposing is readable "on the wall of [a doctor's] office" and on a "photograph." Inscription and reimprinting, reimpression, of light in

......................................

And then a Vision on my brain was rolled.

———————

......................................

—marks the upper edge of a space that will never be closed. What is the *topos* of the "I" who quotes himself in a narrative [of a dream, a vision, or a hallucination] within a narrative, including, in addition to all his ghosts, his *hallucinations of ghosts,* still other visions within visions (e.g., "a new Vision never seen before")? What is his *topos* when he quotes, in the present, a past question formulated in another sort of present [". . . 'Then, what is Life?' I said. . . ."] and which he narrates as something that presented itself in a vision, and so on?

3. *There is* also the ironic, antithetical, underlying re-citation of the "triumphs of death" that adds another level of coding to the poem. What are we doing when, to practice a "genre," we quote a genre, represent it, stage it, expose its *generic law,* analyze it practically? Are we still practicing the genre? Does the "work" still belong to the genre it re-cites? But inversely, how could we make a genre work without referring to it [quasi-] quotationally, indicating at some point, "See, this is a work of such-and-such a genre"? Such an indication does not belong to the genre and makes the statement of belonging an ironical exercise. It interrupts the very belonging of which it is a necessary condition. I must abandon this question for the moment; it's capable of

---

both texts. *La folie du jour.* The course of the sun, day, year, anniversary, double revolution, the palindrome and the anagrammatic version or reversion of *écrit, récit,* and *série.* The series (*écrit, récit, série,* etc.). Note to the translators: How are you going to translate that, *récit* for example? Not as *nouvelle,* "novella," nor as "short story." Perhaps it will be better to leave the "French" word *récit.* It is already hard enough to understand, in Blanchot's text, in French. An essential question for the

disrupting more than one system of poetics, more than one literary pact.)

What is a narrative—this thing that we call a narrative? Does
it take place? Where and when? What might the taking-place or
the event of a narrative be?

I hasten to say that it is not my intention here, nor do I claim,
nor do I have the means, to answer these questions. At most, in
repeating them, I would like to begin a minute displacement, the
most discreet of transformations: I suggest, for example, that we
replace what might be called *the question of narrative* ("What is a
narrative?") with *the demand for narrative*. When I say *demande* I
mean something closer to the English "demand" than to a mere
request: inquisitorial insistence, an order, a petition. To know
(before we know) what narrative is, the narrativity of narrative,
we should perhaps first recount, return to the scene of one origin
of narrative, to the narrative of one origin of narrative (will that
still be a narrative?), to that scene that mobilizes various forces,
or if you prefer various agencies or "subjects," some of which
*demand* the narrative of the other, seek to extort it from him, like
a secret-less secret, something that they call the truth about what
has taken place: "Tell us exactly what happened." The narrative
must have begun with this demand, but will we still call the *mise
en scène* [representation, staging] of this demand a narrative? And
will we even still call it *mise en "scène,"* since that origin concerns
the eyes [*touche aux yeux*] (as we shall see), the origin of visibility,
the origin of origin, the birth of what, as we say in French, "sees
the light of day" [*voit le jour,* is born] when the present leads to
presence, presentation, or representation? "Oh, I see the daylight

---

translator. The *sur,* "on," "super-," and so forth, that is my theme
above, also designates the figure of a passage by *trans*-lation, the *trans-*
of an *Übersetzung*. Version [*version;* also "translation into one's own
language"], transference, and translation. *Übertragung*. The simultaneous transgression and reappropriation of a language [*langue*], its law,
its economy? How will you translate *langue?* Let us suppose then that
here, at the foot of the other text, I address a translatable message, in

[*je vois le jour*], oh God," says a voice in *La folie du jour,* a "narrative" ["*récit*"] (?) by Maurice Blanchot. (This title, *La folie du jour,* appears only in what would be called, according to a certain convention, the "second version," in book form this time [Fata Morgana, 1973; in English, "The Madness of the Day," tr. Lydia Davis, *TriQuarterly,* No. 40 (Fall 1977), pp. 168–177, quoted throughout], of a *"récit"* first published in a literary magazine [*Empédocle,* 2, 1949] under the title "Un récit?" Is it the *same* text, except for the title? Or are these two versions of the same *écrit* [piece of writing], the same *"récit"?* Usually, from one version to the next, the title remains the same. What is a version? What is a title? What borderline questions are posed here? I am here seeking merely to establish the necessity of this whole problematic of judicial framing and of the jurisdiction of frames. This problematic, I feel, has not been explored, at least not adequately, by the institution of literary studies in the university. And there are essential reasons for that: this is an institution built on that very system of framing. In the case of *La folie du jour,* the matter is even more complicated, as we shall see little by little, and this complication involves a certain *"sur"* ["on," "super-" etc.], or what I have called elsewhere, in *La Dissémination,* a certain "overcasting" [*surjet*]. For now, let us point out that the question mark [in "Un récit?"] appears as an integral part of the title only on the cover of the review *Empédocle,* under the general heading "Sommaire" ["contents"]. Under the same heading, on the inside of the review, on a sort of flyleaf [*page de garde*] before the text itself, the question mark disappears. This disappearance

the style of a telegram, to the translators of every country. Who is to say in what language, *exactly* what language, if we assume that the translation has been prepared, the above text will appear? It is not untranslatable, but, without being opaque, it presents at every turn, I know, something to stop [*arrêter*] the translation: it forces the translator to transform the language into which he is translating or the "receiver medium," to deform the initial contract, itself in constant deformation,

is confirmed on the first page of the *récit,* where the title is repeated: "Un récit." Whether this variation, which Andrzej
Warminski pointed out to me, is deliberate or not, it managed to
construct its own narrative of variation, in its relative specificity,
only by means of such protective structures [*structures de garde*]
and institutions as the registering of copyright, the Library of
Congress or the Bibliothèque Nationale, or something like a
flyleaf.) Thus a voice says, "Oh, I see the daylight, oh God!" in
*La folie du jour,* a *"récit"* (?) by Maurice Blanchot, a story whose
title runs wild and drives the reader mad, (*s'*)*affole* in every sense
of the word and in every direction: *la folie du jour,* the madness of
today, of the day today, which leads to the madness that comes
from the day, is born of it, as well as the madness of the day
itself, itself mad (another genitive): the madness of the *jour* in the
sense of *diës,* day, and in the sense of light, brightness. The title
seems to refer at times to the "I went mad," "only my innermost
being was mad," of the "narrator" (an impossible narrator,
though, incapable of responding to the demand for narrative,
mad for light: ". . . and if seeing would infect me with madness, I madly wanted that madness"), at times to the madness of
a "character" following the narrator on the street ("a strange sort
of lunatic"), at times, in another genitive, to "the madness of the
day" itself, in a phrase that is a homonym of the title and is taken
from or grafted onto the body of the story. ("Finally I became
convinced that I was face to face with the madness of the day.
That was the truth: the light was going mad, the brightness had
lost all reason. . . .") In a dissemination as glorious as it is

---

in the language of the other. I anticipated this difficulty of translation,
if only up to a certain point, but I did not calculate it or deliberately
increase it. I just did nothing to avoid it. On the contrary, I shall try
here, in this short steno-telegraphic band, for the greatest translatability
possible. Such will be the proposed contract. For the problems that I
wished to formalize above all have an irreducible relationship to the
enigma, or in other words the *récit,* of translation. I have sought to

fleeting, the *sēma jour,* the "same" *jour,* the other, is both *ajouré* and *ajourné* ["perforated" and "adjourned, postponed"; derived from the two senses of *jour*]—in itself, so to speak, in the precarious instability of its title. The madness of the day, of this moment, is momentary. The abyss that carries it away is expressed (for example) when a voice says, "Oh, I see the daylight [*jour*], oh God." It is not the narrator's voice but a feminine one [i.e., referred to by the pronoun *elle*] that discreetly sets free (by means of a sort of game that tires the narrator, he says) all the powers of a language by making it apparently untranslatable: "Suddenly, she [*elle*] would cry out, 'Oh, I see the daylight, oh God,' etc. I would protest that this game was tiring me out enormously, but she was insatiable for my glory." The game did not consist solely or surely (look at the paragraph) in wordplay. But language is involved from the first. The feminine voice that says "I see the daylight"—insatiable for the "glory" of the "I" of the story, for his triumph—this voice is spoken, is translated by language: "I am born" (*voir le jour also* means "to be born" in French), but also "I see" (things) and, what's more, "I see" light, glory, the element of visibility, the visibility of that which is visible, the phenomenality of the phenomenon; thus I see vision, both eyesight and what it can see, the stage [*scène*] and the possibility of representation [*scène*], the scene of visibility, a *primal scene,* I might say, quoting the title of a very short text [i.e., "Une scène primitive"], a "broken window" by Blanchot, a text whose powerful enigma I do not wish to touch on here. Visibility should—not be visible. According to an old, omnipotent logic that has reigned since Plato, that which enables us to see should remain

---

present these problems [*les mettre en scène*], but the stage on which they appear, as will be seen, is one where the unrepresentable is in full force. Thus I have sought to present them *practically,* and in a sense *performatively,* in accordance with a notion of the performative that I feel must be dissociated, by an act of deconstruction, from the notion of presence with which it is generally linked. The maximal translatability of this band: impoverishment by univocality. Economy and formalization, but

invisible: black, blinding. *La folie du jour* is a story of madness [*historie de la folie*], of that madness that consists in seeing the light, vision or visibility, from an experience of blindness. If from "life" we appeal to "light," from *vie* to *vision,* we can speak here of *sur-vie,* of living on in a life-after-life or a life-after-death, as *sur-vision,* "seeing on" in a vision-beyond-vision. To see sight or vision or visibility, to see beyond what is visible, is not merely "to have a vision" in the usual sense of the word, but to see-beyond-sight, to see-sight-beyond-sight. As in Ponge's "Le soleil placé en abîme," the story of glory engulfs or clouds over a sort of paternal figure, placing it in an abyss-structure, in vision-beyond-vision. The story obscures the sun ("the sun their father," says *The Triumph of Life*) with a blinding light. (Thus perhaps the mother lives on, and on, as a ghost—phantom or revenant—an absolute figurant, a walk-on who walks on and on, in accordance with the "obsequent logic" to which I referred in *Glas.* I am my father who is dead and my mother who is alive, anounces Nietzsche at the midpoint of his life, in *Ecce Homo,* after passing through blindness.) To see vision, to see on beyond sight: this abyss-like madness of an utterly primal scene, the scene of scenes, stages, representation, is simulated and dissimulated in the narrative in the reassuring form (for those who want to be reassured) of spectacles [*spectacles*] within bounds, determinate "visions" or "scenes" that serve in a way to allegorize the abyss and contain the madness. The word "vision" itself is ambiguous enough to make this economy possible.

The feminine voice that says, "Oh, I see the daylight, oh God," is, as we have said, insatiable for the "glory" of the speaker who

---

in the opposite sense to that of what takes place in the upper band: there, too, are economy and formalization, but by semantic accumulation and overloading, until the point when the logic of the undecidable *arrêt de mort* brings and opens polysemia (and its economy) in the direction of dissemination. Why have I chosen to stress the translation-effect here? 1. Effects of transference, of superimposing, of textual superimprinting between the two "triumphs" or the two *"arrêts" and* within

says "I" in *La folie du jour*. This speaker has supposedly triumphed over blindness. I do not know whether it is possible to consider the "glories" of *The Triumph of Life* and those of *La folie du jour* as translating one another, and if so, which translating which, and in what ways. If we are not restricted to literal recurrences of the word "glory," then that translation can go every which way. Its detours become both endless and inevitable. Let us say that I interrupt them here. I stop [*Je m'arrête*]. Thus I shall not quote "Outdoors, I saw something briefly [*j'eus une courte vision;* also "I had a brief vision"]" from *La folie du jour,* at the hinge of the text, to give it the resonance of an echo translating "And then a Vision on my brain was rolled," which is at once the linking point and the opening of the narrative in *The Triumph of Life.* After the "brief vision," before the traumatic accident in which "I nearly lost my sight, because someone crushed glass in my eyes," the accident that left him at first with his eyes bandaged (to be translated, I suppose, by "eyes banded" or by "banded eyes" as in lines 100 and 103 of *The Triumph of Life*), the beginning of the end is there for us to read. The beginning of the end describes in an abyss-structure [i.e., in an inserted miniature representing the whole] the structure of the "narrative," the *"récit"* (?) entitled *La folie du jour.* This "narrative" *seems* indeed to *begin* with a certain sentence that will subsequently be quoted towards the end as part of the narrative, unless the first sentence quotes in advance the one that comes at the end and that relates the first words of a narrative. I shall return to this structure, which deprives the text of any beginning and of any decidable

---

each of them. Both are written in a certain (arrested [*arrêté*]) relationship of translation. 2. The *hymen* (alliance, wedding-band, reaffirmation, "Yes, yes," "Come, come" and so forth) is related, in *L'arrêt de mort,* thematically related, to what commits us "in the language of the other." 3. Above all, by making manifest the limits of the prevalent concept of translation (I do not say of translatability in general), we touch on multiple problems said to be of "method," of reading and

edge or border, of any heading or letterhead [en-tête]. (Entête is the word with which Chouraqui translates the beginning of Genesis:

> ENTÊTE [in-head] Elohim created heaven and earth.
> The earth was in shambles,
> darkness upon the face of the abyss,
> the breath of Elohim moving upon the face of the waters.
>
> Elohim says:
> > "There will be light."
> > And there is light.
>
> Elohim sees the                 light: Oh, the good.
> Elohim separates the            light from the darkness.
> Elohim cries to the             light: "Day."
> To the darkness, he cries: "Night."
>
> And it is evening and it is morning:
> day, unique.

After the "brief vision," before the injury from which "I nearly lost my sight," he tells himself that this brief vision, in mid-story, marks the beginning of the end:

> This brief scene roused me to the point of delirium. I don't suppose I could fully explain it to myself and yet I was sure of it, that I had seized the moment when the day, having come face to face with a real event, would now hasten to its end. Here it comes, I said to myself, the end is coming; something is happening, the end is beginning. I was overcome with joy.

---

teaching. The line that I seek to recognize within translatability, between two translations, one governed by the classical model of transportable univocality or of formalizable polysemia, and the other, which goes over into dissemination—this line also passes between the critical and the deconstructive. A politico-institutional problem of the University: it, like all teaching in its traditional form, and perhaps all teaching whatever, has as its ideal, with exhaustive translatability, the effacement

(There are writings entitled, for example, *Entête* [Genesis], the Gospels, Revelation [Apocalypse], and so forth. I would like to speak of them here, to attempt to read them, to move to them from, for example, *The Triumph of Life, La folie du jour, L'arrêt de mort* . . . and the story, the narrative, of "Living On" as differance, with an *a,* between archeology and eschatology, as differance *in* apocalypse. That will be a while in coming.)

---

What is judiciously called the question-of-narrative covers, with a certain modesty, a demand for narrative, a violent putting-to-the-question, an instrument of torture working to wring the narrative out of one as if it were a terrible secret, in ways that can go from the most archaic police methods to refinements for making (and even letting) one talk that are unsurpassed in neutrality and politeness, that are most respectfully medical, psychiatric, and even psychoanalytic. For reasons that should be obvious by now, I shall not say that Blanchot offers a *representation,* a *mise en scène,* of this demand for narrative, in *La folie du jour:* it would be better to say that it is there to be read, "to the point of de*lire*ium," as it throws the reader off the track. For the same reasons, I do not know whether the text can be classified as being of the genre (Genette: the *mode* [mode; mood of a verb]) *"récit,"* a word that Blanchot has repeatedly insisted upon and contested, reclaimed and rejected, set down and (then) erased, and so forth. In addition to these general reasons there is a singular characteristic, involving precisely the (internal and external) *boundaries* or *edges* of

---

of language [*la langue*]. The deconstruction of a pedagogical institution and all that it implies. What this institution cannot bear, is for anyone to tamper with [*toucher à;* also "touch," "change," "concern himself with"] language, meaning *both* the *national* language *and,* paradoxically, an ideal of translatability that neutralizes this national language. Nationalism and universalism. What this institution cannot bear is a transformation that leaves intact neither of these two complementary poles.

this text. The boundary from which we believe we approach *La folie du jour*, its "first word" ("I"), opens with a paragraph that *affirms* a sort of triumph of life at the edge of death. The triumph must be excessive (in accordance with the "boundlessness" of hubris) and very close to what it triumphs over. This paragraph begins a narrative, it seems, but does not yet recount anything. The narrator introduces himself in that simplest of performances, an "I am," or more precisely an "I am neither . . . nor . . . ," which immediately removes the performance from presence. The end of this paragraph notes especially the double excess of every triumph of life: i.e., the excessive double affirmation, *of* triumphant life, of death which triumphs *over* life.

> I am neither learned nor ignorant. I have known joys. That is saying too little: I am alive, and this life gives me the greatest pleasure. And what about death? When I die (perhaps any minute now), I will feel immense pleasure. I am not talking about the foretaste of death, which is stale and often disagreeable. Suffering dulls the senses. But this is the remarkable truth, which I am certain of: I feel boundless pleasure in living, and I will take boundless satisfaction in dying.

A number of signs make it possible to recognize a man in the first-person speaker. But in the *double* affirmation seen (remarked upon) in the syntax of triumph as *triomphe-de*, triumph *of* and triumph *over*, the narrator comes close to seeing a trait that is particularly feminine, a trait of feminine beauty, even.

---

It can bear more readily the most apparently revolutionary ideological sorts of "content," if only that content does not touch the borders of language [*la langue*] and of all the juridico-political contracts that it guarantees. It is this "intolerable" something that concerns me here. It is related in an essential way to that which, as it is written above, brings out the limits of the concept of translation on which the university is built, particularly when it makes the teaching of language, even

Men want to escape death, strange animals that they are. And some of them cry out "Die, die" because they want to escape life. "What a life. I'll kill myself. I'll give in." That is pitiful and strange; it is a mistake.

Yet I have met people who have never told life to be quiet or told death to go away—almost always women, beautiful creatures.

Later, on the next-to-last page, we learn that this opening paragraph (the upper edge of *La folie* . . .) corresponds in its content and form, if not in its occurrence, to the beginning of the account [*récit*] that the narrator tries to take up [*aborder*] in response to the demands of his interrogators. This creates an exceedingly strange space: what appeared to be the beginning and the upper edge of a discourse *will have been* merely part of a narrative that forms a part of the discourse in that it *recounts* how an attempt was made—in vain!—to force a narrative out of the narrator. The starting edge will have been the quotation (at first not recognizable as such) of a narrative fragment that in turn will merely be quoting its quotation. For all these quotations, quotations of requotations with no original performance, there is no speech act not already the iteration of another, no circle and no quotation marks to reassure us about the identity, oppostion, or distinction of speech events. The part is always greater than the whole, the edge *of* the set [*ensemble*] is a fold [*pli*] *in* the set (" 'Happy those for whom the fold/ Of . . .' "), but as *La folie du jour* unfolds, explains itself [*s'explique*] without ever giving up its "fold" to another discourse not already its own, it is better if I quote. If I quote, for example, these last two pages:

---

literatures, and even "comparative literature," its principal theme. If *questions of method* (here, a translators' note: I have published a text that is untranslatable, starting with its title, "Pas," and in "La double séance," referring to "dissemination in the refolding [*repli*] of the *hymen*": "Pas de méthode" ["no method," but also "a methodical step"] for it: no path comes back in its circle to a first step, none proceeds from the simple to the complex, none leads from a beginning to an end. ('A

I had been asked, "Tell us exactly what happened." A story [*Un récit*]? I began: I am neither learned nor ignorant. I have known joys. That is saying too little. I told them the whole story [*histoire*], and they listened with interest, it seems to me, at least in the beginning. But the end was a surprise to all of us. "That was the beginning," they said. "Now get down to the facts." How so? The story [*récit*] was finished!

I was forced to realize that I was not capable of forming a story out of these events. I had lost the thread of the narrative [*l'histoire*]: that happens in a good many illnesses. But this explanation only made them more insistent. Then I noticed for the first time that there were two of them and that this departure from the traditional method, even though it was explained by the fact that one of them was an eye doctor, the other a specialist in mental illness, kept making our conversation seem like an authoritarian interrogation that was being supervised and guided by a strict set of rules. Of course neither of them was the police chief. But because there were two of them, there were three, and this third was firmly convinced, I am sure, that a writer, a man who speaks and argues with distinction, is always capable of recounting facts that he remembers.

A story [*récit*]? No. No stories [ *pas de récit*], never again.


By definition, there is no end to a discourse that would seek to describe the invaginated structure of *La folie du jour*. Invagination is the inward refolding of *la gaine* [sheath, girdle], the inverted reapplication of the outer edge to the inside of a form where the outside then opens a pocket. Such an invagination is possible from the first trace on. This is why there is no "first" trace. We have just seen, on the basis of this example refined to

---

book neither begins nor ends: at most it pretends to.' . . . 'Every method is a fiction.') *Point de méthode* ["absolutely no method," but also "a point of method"]: that doesn't rule out a certain course to be followed" [*La dissémination*, p. 303]. The translators will not be able to translate this *pas* and this *point*. Will they have to indicate that this reminder is to be related to what is called the "unfinished" quality of Shelley's *Triumph* and the impossibility of fixing [*arrêter*] the opening

the point of madness, how "the whole story [to which] they listened" is the one (the same but another at the same time) that,
like *La folie du jour,* begins "I am neither learned nor ignorant.
. . . ." But this "whole story," which corresponds to the totality
of the "book," is also only a part of the book, the narrative that is
demanded, attempted, impossible, and so forth. Its end, which
comes before the end, does not respond to the request of the
authorities, the authorities who demand an *author,* an *I* capable of
organizing a narrative sequence, of remembering and telling the
truth: "exactly what happened," "recounting facts that he remembers," in other words saying "I" (I am the same as the one to
whom these things happened, and so on, and thereby assuring
the unity or identity of narratee or reader, and so on). Such is the
demand for the story, for narrative, the demand that society, the
law that governs literary and artistic works, medicine, the police,
and so forth, claim to constitute. This demand for truth is itself
recounted and swept along in the endless process of invagination.
Because I cannot pursue this analysis here, I merely situate the
place, the locus, in which *double invagination* comes about, the
place where the invagination of the upper edge on its outer face
(the supposed beginnging of *La folie du jour*), which is folded
back "inside" to form a pocket and an inner edge, comes to extend
beyond (or encroach on) the invagination of the lower edge, on its
inner face (the supposed end of *La folie du jour*), which is folded
back "inside" to form a pocket and an outer edge. Indeed the
"middle" sequence ("I had been asked, 'Tell us exactly what happened.' A story? I began: I am neither learned nor ignorant. I
have known joys. That is saying too little. I told them the whole

---

and closing boundaries of *L'arrêt de mort,* all problems treated, in another mode, in the procession above? Will they relate this untranslatable *pas* to the double "knot" of double invagination, a central motif of
that text, or, along with its entire semantic family, to all the occurrences of "path," "past," "pass" in Shelley's *Triumph?* )—if the question
of teaching (not only the teaching of literature and the humanities) runs
throughout this book, if my participation is possible only with supple-

story and they listened with interest, it seems to me, at least in
the beginning. But the end was a surprise to all of us. 'That was
the beginning,' they said. 'Now get down to the facts.' How so?
The story was finished!"), this antepenultimate paragraph, recalls, subsumes, quotes without quotation marks the first sentences of *La folie du jour* (I am neither learned nor . . . .),
including in itself the entire book, including itself, but only after
anticipating, by quoting it in advance, the question that will
form the lower edge or the final boundary of *La folie du jour*—or
*almost* final, to accentuate the dissymmetry of effects. The question "A story?", posed as a question in response to the demand
(Do they demand a story, a *récit,* of me?) in the antepenultimate
paragraph, will be taken up again in the final sequence ("A story?
No. No stories, never again."), but again, just as in the previous
instance, this repetition does not follow (chronologically or logically) what nevertheless seems to come before it in the first line,
in the immediate linearity of reading. We cannot even speak here
of a future perfect tense, if this still presumes a regular modification of the present into its instances of a present in the past, a
present in the present, and a present in the future. In this requotation of the story [*ré-citation du récit*], intensified or reinforced
here by the requotation of the *word "récit,"* it is impossible to say
which one quotes the other, and above all which one forms the
border of the other. Each includes the other, comprehends the
other, which is to say that neither comprehends the other. Each
"story" (and each occurrence of the word "story," each "story" in
the story) is part of the other, makes the other a part (of itself),
each "story" is at once larger and smaller than itself, includes it-

---

mentary interpretation by the translators (active, interested, inscribed in
a politico-institutional field of drives, and so forth), if we are not to pass
over all these stakes and interests (what happens in this respect in the
universities of the Western world, in the United States, at Yale, from
department to department? How is one to step in? What is the key here
for decoding? What am I doing here? What are they making me do?
How are the boundaries of all these fields, titles, corpora, and so forth,

self without including (or comprehending) itself, identifies itself with itself even as it remains utterly different from its homonym. Of course, at intervals ranging from two to forty paragraphs, this structure of *crisscross double invagination* ("I am neither learned nor [. . . .] A story? I began: I am neither learned nor [. . . .] The story was finished! [. . .] A story? No. No stories, never again.") never ceases to refold or superpose or *overemploy* itself in the meantime, and the description of this would be interminable. I must content myself for the moment with underscoring the supplementary aspect of this structure: the chiasma of this *double invagination* is always possible, because of what I have called elsewhere the iterability of the mark. Now, if we have just seen a strikingly complex example of this in the case of a *récit,* a story, using the word *"récit,"* reciting and requoting both its possibility and its impossibility, double invagination can come about in any text, whether it is narrative in form or not, whether it is of the genre or *mode "récit"* or not, whether it speaks of it or not. Nevertheless—and this is the aspect that interested me in the beginning—double invagination, wherever it comes about, has in itself the *structure of a narrative* [*récit*] *in deconstruction.* Here the narrative is irreducible. Even before it "concerns" a text in narrative form, double invagination constitutes the story of stories, the narrative of narrative, the *narrative of deconstruction in deconstruction:* the apparently outer edge of an enclosure [*clôture*], far from being simple, simply external and circular, in accordance with the philosophical representation of philosophy, makes no sign beyond itself, toward what is utterly *other,* without becoming double or dual, without making itself be "represented," refolded,

---

laid out? Here I can only locate the necessity of all these questions), then we must pause to consider [*on devra s'arrêter sur*] translation. It brings the *arrêt* of everything, decides, suspends, and sets in motion . . . even in "my" language, within the presumed unity of what is called the corpus of a language. *9–16 January 1978.* What will remain unreadable for me, in any case, of this text, not to mention Shelley, of course, and everything that haunts his language [*langue*] and his writ-

superposed, *re-marked* within the enclosure, at least in what the structure produces as an effect of interiority. But it is precisely this structure-effect that is being deconstructed here.

If "No. No stories, never again" belongs to *La folie du jour* as it is inscribed at its edge, at the edge of a text that recounts the demand for an impossible story, a text that was first called "Un récit," and so on, the story effaces itself from the story by making itself more noticeable, by re-marking itself, with a "double exposure," a superimprinting. And the history of the story or the story of history is the story of effacement *as* superimprinting of all the logic of the "double bind" or of double invagination that is reaffirmed in that story. It is not absolutely necessary that this superimprinting by effacement also stress the word *récit,* the name of the *mode* or genre, but it makes for a remarkable supplement . . . especially if the designation [*la "mention"*] *"récit"* is part of the title without being part of it, between the title and the rest. This is what happens with the first titles of *La folie du jour* and "in" the text that bears these titles, but it is also what happens between the two versions of *L'arrêt de mort.* The first one (1948) carries, beneath the title, if not as a subtitle, the designation *"récit."* This disappears in the second version (1971), which also effaces the last two pages, an enigmatic epilogue that threatened to gather together, under the authority of a meta-story, the two "stories," independent and indeed disparate, that precede it. Here we cannot go deeply into this event, this double effacement, which is a story in itself: the two versions form (without forming) a single corpus registered at the Bibliothèque Nationale in the name of Maurice Blanchot. I allude to this institution to indicate

---

ing. What will remain unreadable for me of this text, once it is translated, of course, still bearing my signature. But even in "my" language, to which it does not belong in a simple way. One never writes either in one's own language or in a foreign language. Derive all the consequences of this: they involve each element, each term of the preceding sentence. Hence the triumph (necessarily double and equivocal, because it is also a phase of mourning). Hence the triumph as the triumph of

with one reference all the problems that I cannot go into here, problems of the mark that superimposes by effacement (judicial, political problems and the like, involving the convention or the fiction that guarantees an author his due [*les "droits d'auteur,"* royalties; lit., an author's rights], the unity of an author's corpus, the presumption of the "real" author in his proper name as set down in the registry office, which distinguishes him from the narrator, and so on: I reserve all these questions under the title *"du droit à la littérature"* ["from law to literature"/"of the right to literature"]). This double effacement, I say, is a story in itself, a story of "story," a "story" of the story [*un "récit" du récit*]. It is enough, in *La folie du jour,* to disrupt or unhinge the demand for narrative [*la demande du récit*], to strike the instigators with impotence but also to sustain them as instigators on the basis of that impotence. As to the double version, it is no contingent accident: it is fated, even within what in copyright law is considered to be one and the same version. Like the meaning "genre" or *"mode,"* or that of "corpus" or the unity of a "work," the meaning of version, and of the unity of a version, is overrun, exceeded, by this structure of invagination: not merely cancelled or invalidated but exposed in the precariousness of its effect, the fragility of the conventional artifices that provisionally guarantee it, all the historical fictions that certify its *carte d'identité.* Thus, on the basis of what happens to the *récit,* to *"récit"* from one version of *L'arrêt de mort* to another or even within what is considered a single "version" of *La folie du jour*—on the basis of what happens to the subtitle "récit" or the title "Un récit (?)" from one version of the two *récits* (?) to the other, we understand better

---

translation. *Übersetzung* and "translation" overcome, equivocally, in the course of an equivocal combat, the loss of an object. A text lives only if it lives *on* [*sur-vit*], and it lives *on* only if it is *at once* translatable *and* untranslatable (always "at once . . . and . . .": *hama,* at the "same" time). Totally translatable, it disappears as a text, as writing, as a body of language [*langue*]. Totally untranslatable, even within what is believed to be one language, it dies immediately. Thus triumphant trans-

how the unity of one version can be *encroached* upon by an essential *unfinishedness* that cannot be reduced to an incompleteness or an inadequacy. I register, I record this remark on the shore of what is called the unfinishedness of *The Triumph of Life,* at the moment when Shelley is drowned. I do so without claiming to understand what people mean in this case by "unfinished," or to decide anything. I do so only to recall the immense procedures that should come before a statement about whether a work is finished or unfinished. Where are we to situate the event of Shelley's drowning? And who will decide the answer to this question? Who will form a narrative of these borderline events [*événements de bord*]? At whose demand?

## THE TRIUMPH OF LIFE

Once we have accentuated the question of narrative as demand for narrative, once the response to this demand indeterminably invaginates every border, then this will affect all the questions with which I began: the question of narrative (What is a *récit?*), that of *la Chose* (What is a thing and that thing that is called a narrative or that is called to from a narrative? What is the demand for [*de,* also "of"] *la Chose?* And so on . . .), that of the place and of taking place, of the topography of the event, which will lead us to a certain "Come" [*"Viens"*] and a certain *"pas"* ["step," "not"] which opens the door to the impossible possibility of what comes about [*arrive*] in its taking place.

Within the boundaries of this session, I shall propose a fragment, itself unfinished, detached from a more systematic reading

---

lation is neither the life nor the death of the text, only or already its living *on,* its life after life, its life after death. The same thing will be said of what I call writing, mark, trace, and so on. It neither lives nor dies; it lives *on.* And it "starts" only with living on (testament, iterability, remaining [*restance*], crypt, detachment that lifts the strictures of the "living" *rectio* or direction of an "author" not drowned at the edge of his text). The relative synonymy or intertranslatability that I seek to pro-

of Shelley, a reading oriented by the problems of *narrative* [*récit*] as *reaffirmation* (yes, yes) of life, in which the *yes,* which says nothing, describes nothing but itself, the performance of its own event of affirmation, repeats itself, *quotes, cites* itself, says *yes-to* itself as (to an-) other in accordance with the ring, requotes and recites a commitment that would not take place outside this repetition of a performance without presence. This strange ring says *yes* to life only in the overdetermining ambiguity of the triumph *de* ["of," "over"] life, *sur* ["over," "on," etc.] life, the triumph marked in the "on" of "living on" [*le sur d'un survivre*].

All this syntax, almost untranslatable, is sealed in the French expression *l'arrêt de mort.*

In order that my fragmentary discourse may remain somewhat intelligible, concrete, coherent, I shall refer to the example of the former *"récit"* that has this title, *L'arrêt de mort.* In this text you will recognize the "narrative voice" that Blanchot, in *L'entretien infini,* distinguishes from the "narratorial voice." The narrative voice, he says, is "a neutral voice that utters [*dit*] the work from the placeless place where the work is silent." The placeless place where the work is silent: a silent voice, then, withdrawn into its "voicelessness" [*"aphonie"*]. This "voicelessness" distinguishes it from the "narratorial voice," the voice that literary criticism or poetics or narratology strives to locate in the system of the narrative, of the novel, or of the narration. The narratorial voice is the voice of a subject recounting something, remembering an event or a historical sequence, knowing who he is, where he is, and what he is talking about. It responds to some "police," a force of order or law ("What 'exactly' are you talking about?": the

---

duce above between *arrêt de mort* and triumph of life. It also means that these two *titles* can always, in addition to or beyond any other possible reference, designate the very thing to which they give a title, that is, the text below, the writing of the "poem" or *"récit"* that *bears* the title. The triumph of life or *l'arrêt de mort* would be *the* text, this text, its element, its condition, its effect. This assumes a certain functioning of titles, and that we analyze its laws, its relationship to the law and to the

truth of equivalence). In this sense, all organized narration is "a matter for the police," even before its genre (mystery novel, cop story) has been determined. The narrative voice, on the other hand, would *surpass* police investigation, if that were possible. In *La folie du jour,* we can say that the authoritarian demand puts pressure on a narrative voice to turn into a narratorial voice and to bring about [*donner lieu à*] a narrative that would be *identifiable,* collected, connected, in its subject and in its object. Now, the narrative voice ("I" or "he," "a third person that is neither a third person nor the simple cover of impersonality") has no fixed [*arrêté*] place. It takes place placelessly, being both *atopical,* mad, extravagant, and *hypertopical,* both placeless and over-placed. Blanchot speaks of that which "designates 'its' place *both* as the place at which it [*il,* the neuter *it* of the narrative voice] would always be missing and that therefore would remain empty, *and* as surplus space, always one place too many: hypertopia" ("L'absence de livre," in *L'entretien infini* [Paris: Gallimard, 1969], p. 564n). The neuter *il,* "it," of the narrative voice, is not an "I," not an ego, even if it is represented in the narrative by "I," "he," or "she." We might wonder—and this is one of the questions that will run through my reading of this fragment—why the neuter of the *il* that is not an "I," not an ego, is represented in French, according to Blanchot, by a pronoun that privileges the affinity or apparently fortuitous and external resemblance between the masculine *il* ["he"] and the neuter *il* ["it"]. Atopia, hypertopia, place-*less* place [*lieu* sans *lieu*], this narrative voice calls out to this "-less" [*sans,* without] syntax, which in Blanchot's text so often comes to neutralize (without positing, without negating) a word,

---

judicial conventions of "literature." This schema is not its own *telos,* not self-mirroring or mere *mise en abyme;* at least the "double bind" that structures these titles, as I seek to demonstrate it, keeps this reflecting representation from folding back upon itself or reproducing itself within itself in perfect self-correspondence [*adéquate à elle-même*], from dominating or including itself, tautologically, from translating itself into its own totality. Writing and triumph. Nietzsche: *"Writing in order to*

a concept, a term (*x*-less *x*): "-less" or "without" without privation or negativity or lack ("without" without *without, less*-less
"-less"), the necessity of which I have attempted to analyze in "Le
'sans' de la coupure pure" and "Pas." This "-less" syntax enters
at least twice (and that's no accident) into the (definitionless)
definition of the narrative voice. We have already read "placeless
place," and now we come to "at a distanceless distance," in a
passage that makes the ghost return [*fait revenir le revenant*],
"ghostly," "phantom-like" *revenance* (the element of haunting that
inundates, if you will, *The Triumph of Life*, its "ghosts," "phantoms," "ghostly shadows," and the like):

> The narrative voice that is on the inside only insofar as it is on the
> outside, at a distance, cannot become incarnate: although it can
> certainly borrow the voice of a judiciously chosen character or even
> create the hybrid function of a mediator (this voice that is the ruin
> of all mediation), it is still always different from that which utters
> it; it is that indifferent indifference that alters the personal voice.
> Let's use our imaginations [*par fantaisie*] and call it ghostly,
> phantom-like. [. . . .]
>    [. . . .] The narrative voice is the bearer of that which is
> neutral [*porte le neutre*].

The neutral and not neutrality, the neutral beyond dialectical
contradiction and all opposition: such would be the possibility of
a "narrative," a "*récit*," that would no longer be simply a form, a
genre, or a literary *mode,* and that goes, that is borne, beyond
the system of philosophical oppositions. The neutral cannot be
governed by any of the terms involved in an opposition within

---

*triumph*. Writing should always mark a triumph" (*Opinions et sentences
mêlées*, aphorism 152; I quote from a French translation now in use but
quite inadequate, precisely in its triumph. Nietzsche writes: "*Schreiben
und Siegen-wollen.*—Schreiben sollte immer einen Sieg anzeigen . . ."").
See what he says then of the triumph (*Überwindung*) over oneself, i.e., he
claims, without using force (*Gewalt*) on others. He opposes the triumph
that he prescribes for literature, to that of "dyspeptics who write only at

philosophical language and natural language. And yet it is not outside of language: it is, for example, narrative voice. Despite the negative form that it takes on in grammar (*ne-uter*, neither-nor) and that betrays it, it surpasses negativity. It is linked rather to the double affirmation (yes, yes, come, come) that re-quotes [*ré-cite*] itself and becomes involved in the *récit*.

One text reads another. How can a reading be settled on [*arrêter*]? For example, we can say that *The Triumph of Life* reads *L'arrêt de mort,* among other things. And, among other things, vice versa. Each "text" is a machine with multiple reading heads for other texts. To read *L'arrêt de mort,* starting with the title in its endless mobility, I can always be guided by another text—for example, in this case, by a certain passage from *Le pas au-delà* [Paris: Gallimard, 1973], which, more than twenty years later, also seems to provide a "commentary" for the title *L'arrêt de mort:*

◆*Taking three steps, stopping, falling, and immediately securing oneself in this fragile fall.*

◆*Survivre,* living *on:* not *living* or (not living) *maintaining oneself,* lifeless, in a state of pure supplement, a movement of supplementing life, but rather stopping [*arrêter*] the dying, a stopping [*arrêt*] that does not stop [*arrête*] it, that on the contrary makes it go on, makes it *last* [*durer*]. '*Speak on the* arrête [coined word; cf. arête: ridge, cutting edge, backbone, fish bone, arris]—*the line of instability—of the spoken word.' As if it were present at the exhaustion of dying: as if night, having started too early, at the earliest moment of day, doubted that it would ever come to night.*

the very moment when they are unable to digest something, or from the moment that the morsel [*morceau*] sticks in their teeth. . . ." The problem of the *mors* [literally "(bridle-)bit"] (how can *mors* be translated?), set forth in *Glas* and "Fors." Obviously (and this is the place to note [*marquer*] it, in this short telegraphic band addressed to the translators and that I am burying here underneath the other one), I can try for a certain intertranslatability (*triumphant* and *arrested*) of *The Triumph of*

◆It is almost certain that at certain moments we realize it: to keep speaking—this afterlife, life-after-life of the spoken word, speaking on—is a way of making ourselves aware that for a long time we have not been speaking any more.


◆Praise of the faraway *near*.


◆Come, come [*viens, viens, venez*], you to whom injunction, prayer, urging, expectation [*attente*] could never be appropriate [*convenir*].

In the first of these sequences, you will have noticed the shift to italics. This indicates quite uniformly the transition from a more assertive, theoretical, impersonal mode to a more fictional, narrative one. (The interweaving of these modes complicates this opposition even more, but let's not get into that here.) For example, *durer,* "last," already italicized, glides into [*amorce continûment*] the serial interlacement. This enduring, lasting, going on, stresses or insists *on* the "on" of a living on that bears the entire enigma of this supplementary logic. Survival and *revenance,* living on and returning from the dead: living on goes beyond both living and dying, supplementing each with a sudden surge and a certain reprieve, deciding [*arrêtant*] life *and* death, ending them in a decisive *arrêt,* the *arrêt* that puts an end to something and the *arrêt* that condemns with a sentence [*sentence*], a statement, a spoken word or a word that goes on speaking. Now, the

---

*Life* and *L'arrêt de mort,* here, only on the basis of work undertaken elsewhere, the code of which cannot fail to enter into the translation. *Glas,* "Pas," "Fors," to limit myself to this sequence of hardly translatable titles, lead elsewhere, but I stress them more because in them the relationship to the work of mourning is more thematic, as is work on the Freudian concept of the work of mourning. Now, we know that according to Freud "triumph" corresponds to a phase, manic in type, in the

homonymy of *"arrête,"* if we can call these words homonyms, the verb and the noun (*"arrêt qui ne l'arrête pas,"* "a stopping that does not stop it"; *"parle sur l'arrête,"* "speak on the *arrête,* the ridge, the arris, the 'arrist' "), is made complete by means of some tampering with spelling. This is rare in Blanchot's writing, but all the more significant. And we are further justified in paying attention to this by the fact that it is repeated elsewhere, thirty pages earlier, when the noun *arête* (cutting edge, ridge, etc.) receives an extra *r* [in the context of a discussion of the words "I do not know"]: " 'Do not—I know' indicates the double power for attack that the two terms, in isolation, retain: the decisiveness of the knowing, the cutting edge of the negative, the *arrête* that in each case impatiently ends everything." *Arrête,* with two *r*'s, is thus indeed that which orders the *arrêt* (stopping/decision), but the ar(r)ête, as a noun, is also that sharp dividing line, that angle of instability on which it is impossible to settle, to *s'arrêter.* Thus this dividing line functions also *within* the word and traces in it a line of vacillation. This line runs within *L'arrêt de mort,* within what the *arrêt de mort* says, the expression "arrêt de mort," the title *L'arrêt de mort*—all of which are to be distinguished.

How then is the title of the book to be read? First, *is* it readable? Its open polysemia plays with the language to the point of stopping [*arrêter*] any translation of it. In his introduction to [the translation by Lydia Davis of] a fragment of *L'arrêt de mort* (*Georgia Review,* Summer 1976), Geoffrey Hartman asks rightly: "Is *'arrêt de mort,'* then, 'death sentence' or 'suspension of death'?" (Which I shall play at translating into my language as follows: Does *The Triumph of Life* triumph over life [*triomphe de la vie*] or

---

process of mourning. All the difficulties recognized by Freud in "Trauer und Melancholie": mania and melancholia have the same "content," and the states of "joy," "jubilation," and "triumph" (*Freude, Jubel, Triumph*) that characterize mania require the same "economic" conditions as melancholia, and so on. A movement from *Überwindung* to *Triumphieren.* Mania brings about phases of triumphant jubilation analogous to those that appear paradoxically in depression and in melancholic inhibition

express the triumph of life [*triomphe de la vie*]?) "Death Sentence," the title chosen for the fragment of the "novella" (*récit* is also untranslatable) presented under this title (this designation as a "novella") to the American reader, does translate one meaning of the expression *arrêt de mort*. In French an *arrêt* comes at the end of a trial, when the case has been argued and must be judged. The judgment that constitutes the *arrêt* closes the matter and renders a legal decision. It is a sentence. An *arrêt de mort* is a sentence that condemns someone to death. It is indeed a question of *une chose,* a thing, as case, *cause, causa,* and of a decision about *la chose.* As it happens, *la Chose* is here (as in Blanchot's text) Death, and the decision (verdict, sentence) of death concerns death as cause and as end. Death does not come *naturally,* just as *la Chose* does not. Death has an obscure relationship to decision, or more precisely to some sentence, some language that constitutes an *act* ("acts and deeds," "acts of a congress") and leaves a trace. *L'arrêt de mort* makes death a decision. *I* bestow, *I* give [*donne*] death. He, *il,* gives death: the *Il* (who says "I," who occupies the place of the narratorial voice, the place of the narrator in the *récit*) gives death, after *declaring,* announcing, *signifying,* and then *suspending* it. And *he* (I) does indeed *give* death, both as a gift and as a murder. In French *donner la mort* means first of all "to kill."

Here, first of all, [in Lydia Davis' translation, now complete, published as *Death Sentence* (Barrytown, New York: Station Hill, 1978) and quoted throughout, with permission and with occasional modifications for the sake of continuity] is the moment in which death is signified, announced, like a condemnation that

---

when the object seems to return. But in manic triumph, what the ego "has overcome and what it triumphs over" (*was es überwunden hat und worüber es triumphiert*) is concealed from it. How is this dissimulation possible? Freud's dissatisfaction in this text, and in *Beyond the Pleasure Principle,* whose entire problematic should be introduced here. Speculations on the improbable death drive. Always one step more [*un pas de plus*], and no thesis [*et pas de thèse*]. Freud is still—bereft of an answer,

calls forth death and calls J. to death—assent, consent, that is also a sentence (J. is *condemned* in every sense of the word, given up and given over):

> After I spoke to the doctor, I told her, "He gives you another month."
>
> "Well, I'll tell that to the queen mother, who doesn't believe I'm really ill."
>
> I don't know whether she wanted to live or die. During the last few months, the disease she had been fighting for ten years had been making her life more limited every day, and now she cursed both the disease and life itself with all the violence she could rouse. Some time before, she had thought seriously of killing herself. One evening I advised her to do it. That same evening, after listening to me, unable to talk because of her shortness of breath, but sitting up at her table like a healthy person, she wrote down several sentences [*lignes*] that she wished to keep secret. I got these sentences from her, in the end, and I still have them. [. . . .]
>
> No mention of me. I could see how bitter she had felt when she heard me agree to her suicide. When I think it over carefully, as I did afterwards, I realize that this consent was hardly excusable, was even dishonest, since it vaguely rose from the thought that the disease would never get the better of her, she fought so. Normally, she should have been dead long ago, but not only was she not dead, she had continued to live, love, laugh, run around the city, like someone whom illness could not touch. Her doctor had told me that from 1936 on he had considered her dead.   [translation modified]

---

unable to kiss it good-bye [*faire son deuil de la réponse*]. Here, in "Trauer und Melancholie," the most difficult phase seems to concern the difference between normal *Überwindung* and "triumph." Of course, the mania must have "overcome" (*überwunden*) the loss of the object or the mourning for this loss or the object itself. Hence the libidinal explosion of the manic, who, "famished," rushes to new cathexes, new objects. (During her "life after life" [*"sur-vie"*] or "resurrection," J., like the nar-

Condemned (by the disease, the doctor, the "narrator"), J. should have been dead already. She thus lives *on,* more alive than ever, though. The disease has not got the better of her, *n'a pas eu* raison *d'elle,* another expression that is hard to translate: *avoir raison de* is here to overcome, to *triumph over.* Over life, to be precise, which does not give in to that *ratio* and of which it is difficult to give a reasoned account.

In truth it is also J. who makes the decision that condemns her to death: J., who will have to, will have had to die, should have died (but will we ever know whether she died, whether death came for her?), makes the decision, takes it upon herself to decide and enjoins the narrator from deciding. She orders him to kill her, to "give her death." She decides her death [*arrête sa mort*], takes up the decree of death herself. This is the penultimate page of the first part (which also forms an independent whole) of an erstwhile *"récit"* strangely cut up into two wholes and suspended around this undecidable *arrêt de mort.* The verb *arrêter,* made reflexive as *s'arrêter,* stopping (itself) [*s'arrêtant*], twice marks a boundary that brings things to an end only to let them start or start over or start on again [*repartir*]. (The pulse "stopped [*s'arrêta*], then began to beat again[ . . . ]." [. . . .] "What is extraordinary begins at the moment I stop [*je m'arrête*].") Here, she demands death, which he gives her; she gives it to herself [i.e., takes her own life] with the hand of the narrator. As we read this, we should remember that J. *was dead* before, since she had *returned* to life at the narrator's bidding, in response to his call. Having died once, she had already lived on. This double death is a triumph of life *and* of death. Here is the passage:

---

rator, is surprisingly gay, and "she ate much more than I did.") But if "normal" mourning does in fact "overcome" the loss of the object, how can we explain the fact that after it has run its course (*nach ihrem Ablaufe*) it gives no indication of anything that would provide the necessary economic conditions for a "phase of triumph"? After a long digression—namely by way of "ambivalence" as one of the three necessary conditions for melancholia—Freud evokes the "regression of the libido

I never saw her more alive, nor more lucid. Maybe she was in the last instant of her agony [*agonie*], but even though she was incredibly beset by suffering, exhaustion and death, she seemed so alive to me that once again I was convinced that if she didn't want it, and if I didn't want it, nothing would ever get the better of her. While attack followed attack—but there was no more trace of coma nor any fatal symptoms—when the others were out of the room, her hand which was twitching on mine suddenly controlled itself and clasped mine with the greatest impatience and with all the affection and all the tenderness it could. At the same time she smiled at me in a natural way, even with amusement. Immediately afterwards she said to me in a low and rapid voice, "Quick, a shot." (She had not asked for one during the night.) I took a large syringe, in it I mixed two doses of morphine and two of a sedative, four doses altogether of narcotics. The liquid was fairly slow in penetrating, but since she saw what I was doing she remained very calm. She did not move at any moment. Two or three minutes later, her pulse became irregular, it beat violently, stopped, then began to beat again, heavily, only to stop again, this happened many times, finally it became extremely rapid and light, and "scattered like sand."

I have no better way of describing it [*Je n'ai aucun moyen d'en écrire davantage*]. I could say that during those moments J. continued to look at me with the same affectionate and willing [*consentant*] look and that this look is still there, but unfortunately I'm not sure of that. As for the rest, I don't want to say anything. The difficulties with the doctor became a matter of indifference to me. I myself see nothing important in the fact that this young woman was dead, and returned to life at my bidding, but I see an astounding miracle in her fortitude, in her energy, which was great

---

towards narcissism" as the only effective factor. But he suddenly suspends, calls a halt, postpones, in a gesture for the sake of economy that concerns precisely economy. We must halt (*haltmachen*), he says in conclusion, until we know the "economic nature" of physical pain and of the mental pain that is "analogous" to it. Earlier, as he *often* does, he uses the judicial expression *Verdikt* (verdict, sentence, *arrêt*) to designate the operation of Reality with respect to the lost object. Each time that

enough to make death powerless as long as she wanted. One thing must be understood: I have said nothing extraordinary or even surprising. What is extraordinary begins at the moment I stop. But I am no longer able to speak of it.

This last sentence marks, if you will, the lower or final border of the "first" of the two *"récits"* entitled *L'arrêt de mort.* This outer edge or border can also be considered an inner fold. This fold is marked by indecision in more ways than one: not only because the "stopping" is an instance of a beginning or a new beginning but also because the temporality of "this young woman was dead" sinks into an indefinite past, and because "unfortunately" we are "not sure" of the sentence, of her "willing" "consent" to the death sentence. The reason for the interruption finally oscillates among three types of movement, at least ("I have no way [. . .]"; "I could, but [. . .]. As for the rest, I don't want to say anything"; "But I am no longer able to speak of it").

Thus he stops, *il s'arrête,* when it comes to the "rest."

As defined (indefinitely) in the passage from *Le pas au-delà,* the *arrêt de mort* is not only the decision that determines [*arrêtant*] what cannot be decided: it also arrests death by suspending it, interrupting it, deferring it with a "start" [*sursaut*], the startling starting over, and starting on, of living on. But then what suspends or holds back death is the very thing that gives it all its power of undecidability—another false name, rather than a pseudonym, for differance. And this is the pulse of the "word" *arrêt,* the arrhythmic pulsation of its syntax in the expression *arrêt de mort. Arrêter,* in the sense of suspending, is suspending

we recall the lost object and the libido once linked to it returns, Reality gives its verdict, i.e., "that the object no longer exists." Then, if the ego does not want to be condemned to the same fate and if it values the narcissistic satisfactions that remain for it, it decides to break off its "tie" (*Bindung*) to the destroyed object. *23–30 January 1978.* In short, will it be possible to reduce the theme of double affirmation to the meaning of triumph, in the Freudian sense? The risk is that we may

the *arrêt,* in the sense of decision. *Arrêter,* in the sense of deciding, arrests the *arrêt,* in the sense of suspension. They are ahead
of or lag behind one another. One marks delay; the other, haste.
There are not merely two senses or two syntaxes of *arrêt* but,
beyond a playful variability, the *antagony* [*antagonie; cf. agonie,*
"death throes," and *antagonisme*] from one *arrêt* to the other. The
antagony lasts from one to the other, one relieving the other in an
*Aufhebung* that never lets up, *arrêt* arresting *arrêt,* both senses,
both ways. The *arrêt* arrests *itself* [*s'arrête*]. The indecision of the
*arrêt intervenes* not *between* two senses of the word *arrêt* but *within*
each sense, so to speak. For the suspensive *arrêt* is *already* undecided *because it suspends,* and the decisive *arrêt* undecided because what it decides, death, *la Chose,* the neuter, is the undecidable itself, installed by decision in its undecidability. Like
death, the *arrêt* remains (rests, *s'arrête,* arrests itself) undecidable.
Crisis: everything seems to begin in a period of crisis (1938,
Munich, then "the end of 1940"), then with a "strange attack
[*crise*]" when someone goes into *"râles"* ["breathing hoarsely" (tr.
Davis); also "death-rattle"] after opening a closet where the
"proof" of the story was, perhaps, to be found, and so forth.
Crisis is the urgency [*instance,* also "instance," "lawsuit," "tribunal"] of impossible decision, *krinein,* the "judgment" that it is
impossible to reach, to *arrêter,* in the *arrêt de mort.* Since *arrêt* arrests *arrêt,* since the suspensive *arrêt* arrests the decisive *arrêt* and
vice versa, the *arrêt de mort* arrests the *arrêt de mort.* Such is the
arrhythmic pulsation of the title before it scatters like sand. The
*arrêt* arrests *itself,* but in stopping [*s'arrêtant*] (as *arrêt*), it imparts
movement, sets things in motion [*donne le mouvement*]. It makes

---

find the negativity of mourning, of economic resentment, and of melancholia as well, in the "yes, yes." Can it be avoided? But for Freud himself what he calls "triumph" is not clear, and all the re-reading that I attempted at Yale of the athetic nature of *Beyond the PP* could be brought
to bear here. What I have said elsewhere ("Ja ou le faux-bond") about
the *deuil du deuil* [i.e., "relinquishing mourning itself"], and of half-
mourning. The *arrêt de mort* as *verdict:* it is obvious, and the translators

them come and go, go and come again. It *gives* life; it *gives* death.
And it gives them to itself, with a *consent* that "unfortunately" is
not "sure," fortunately not sure. The *arrêt* arrests itself. It stands
(but gets no foothold), stays (with no mainstay) on this unstable
line, this ridge [*arête*] that relates it to itself (the *arrêt* arresting *it-*
*self*) without being able to constitute it in self-reflection and
reappropriation of self. It remains [*reste*] on the *arête* of itself
without remaining to itself, in itself, for itself. It *a-rests* (for) itself. No consciousness, no perception, no watchfulness can gather
up this remnance, this *restance;* no attentiveness can make it
present, no "I," no ego; hence its essential relationship to ghosts,
fantasies, daydreams, to *Phantasieren* (Freud) or the "waking
dream" (*The Triumph of Life*). This epochal [etym. *epokhē,*
"pause"; in phenomenology, "bracketing"] suspension that retains the title and assures the compulsive pulsation of *L'arrêt de*
*mort,* is also an "ingenious" decision, one of those that are made
[*s'arrêtent*] only in a language, one language, and escape signature
by any "I" or ego. But in the same way, linked to what is untranslatable in a language, this decision becomes *unreadable.* I
maintain that this title is unreadable. If reading means making
accessible a meaning that can be transmitted as such, in its own
unequivocal, translatable identity, then this title is unreadable.
But this unreadability does not arrest reading, does not leave it
paralyzed in the face of an opaque surface: rather, it starts reading
and writing and translation moving again. The unreadable is not
the opposite of the readable but rather the ridge [*arête*] that also·
gives it momentum, movement, sets it in motion. "The impossibility of reading should not be taken too lightly" (Paul de Man).

---

must take this into account, that in "everyday" language, in "normal"
conversation, the expression *arrêt de mort* is unambiguous. It means
"death sentence." The syntax is clear: the *arrêt* is a verdict, a decision
that has been *arrêtée,* decided, determined, and that itself decides and
determines, and its relationship to the object of the preposition (*de mort*)
is, of course, the same as in *condamnation à mort.* But "literary" convention, the suspension of "normal" contexts, the context of everyday con-

If we say that the unreadable gives, presents, permits, yields something to be read [*l'illisible donne à lire*], this is not a compromise formula. Unreadability is no less radical and irreducible for all that—absolute, yes, you read me.

We had just read, in *L'arrêt de mort,* just before the end of the "first" *"récit,"* just before the "central" ridge of the corpus, the decisive *arrêt de mort,* in which death is given and no longer deferred. True, this takes place in the course of an event that is hard to situate and about which we cannot be sure that it took place or that it was the effect of a consenting sentence. Here, now, is the account of the other *arrêt de mort,* the suspensive *arrêt,* which gives respite, which gives an unexpected "start" to the dying J., or rather the dead J.: for this suspension is a resurrection. I extract this passage from the "first" "part" (neither part not whole, nor *pars totalis,* nor strictly speaking even first; no word is right any more, not even the quotation marks) of *L'arrêt de mort,* from the "first" of the two *"récits."* I slice things up somewhat barbarously and illegitimately, as we always do, counting on an implicit contract, the impossible contract: that you read "everything" and that at every moment you know the "whole" "corpus" by heart, with a living heart that beats unceasingly [*sans arrêt*], without even a pulsation. . . .

Shortly before, J. had asked her doctor for death, as one asks for a favor, and for life:

> During that scene, J. said to him, "If you don't kill me, then you're a murderer." Later I came across a similar phrase, attributed to Kafka. Her sister, who would have been incapable of inventing

---

versational usage or of writing legitimatized by law—starting with legislating writing or the body of laws that sets the norm for legal language itself—the functioning of the title, the transformation of its relationship to the context and of its referentiality (I locate here the necessity of a very complex analysis: What does a title entitle, designate, delimit? Does it designate something other than what it entitles, i.e., the thing "entitled," the text or book? Or something other than itself?

> something like that, reported it to me in that form and the doctor
> just about confirmed it. (He remembered her as saying, "If you
> don't kill me, you'll kill me.")

The doctor, like the narrator, can receive this sentence only as a
demand for what is impossible: a contradictory double demand, a
double petition to which the only possible response is to desist
from granting it. This sentence [*sentence*] ("If you don't kill me,
then you're a murderer") states, or rather produces, institutes, a
law whose very structure puts you in a position of fatal transgression. And yet, by the same token, you obey it even in the
transgression that it defines. Hence the infinite violence of what
can strictly be called a "double bind," double obligation, double
demand. The disjunction allows of no respite, no hope for recon-
ciliation; it is unceasing, *sans arrêt*. The narrator is subjected to
the violence of this untractable law, like the demand for an impossible narrative. The same law, that of the *arrêt de mort,* relates
this "double bind" and the double invagination described above.
The narrator is here opposed to the doctor (as he is opposed to the
doctors in *La folie du jour*), but he is also on the same side with
respect to J.'s order. He "signifies," relates, decides [*arrête*],
"gives" death, he is the "author" of death, but in all this he is
only obeying a demand: a demand at once impossible to satisfy
and satisfied the moment it is formulated, because it envisages its
own transgression. This is how death is given, how one "gives"
death to another or to oneself: oneself or a*nother,* it comes out the
*same.* Murder is inevitable, and it is doubtless this uncompromising law of *arrêt* that the doctor's memory seeks to attenuate by

---

But who or what is it? And where? And how does it relate to self-quotation? And so on and so forth.): all this forbids (prevents, inhibits, stops
[*arrête*]) a translation of the title *L'arrêt de mort* by its "homonym" in everyday language or by "death sentence." This translation, like any
other, leaves something out, an untranslated remnant. It arrests movement. Illegitimately: for "literature" and in general "parasitism," the
suspension of the "normal" context of everyday conversation or of "civil-

transforming the sentence "If you don't kill me, then you're a murderer" into "If you don't kill me, you'll kill me." The *arrêt de mort* contains within itself this "double bind" that makes every death a crime, an event foreign to nature, related to law, *causa, la Chose,* and a law that can be posited only in its own transgression. In "On tue un enfant (fragmentaire)," Blanchot writes: "There is death and murder—words that I defy anyone to distinguish seriously and that must nevertheless be separated—for this death and this murder, it is an impersonal, inactive, irresponsible 'One' [*'On'*] who must answer." (This fragment, in *Le Nouveau Commerce* [1976], uses the vocabulary of the *arrêt* to designate the strange law that extends beyond the limits of [Hegelian] dialectic but still leaves a mark on it: "[. . .] The result, perhaps absurd, was that what shook dialectic, the unexperienceable experience of death, arrested it immediately: an *arrêt* of which the subsequent progression [*procès*] retained a sort of memory, as of an aporia that must always be reckoned with." This progression is here first the one that goes from Hegel's "first philosophy" to speculative idealism.)

Thus there is a double *arrêt de mort:* "If you don't kill me, then you're a murderer." J. demands this morphine, this double-acting pharmaceutical, this death that "I" will give her. But in the interval "I" will have arrested (suspended) death—left or given an interval, a pause—the eventless event of this *arrêt de mort.* Before he is summoned, *from afar,* by a *tele*phoned "Come," before he is told, "Come, please come, J. is dying" (*J. se meurt:* this construction with the reflexive pronoun is familiar enough in French, but aside from a perceptible connotation from Bossuet's use of the

---

ian" usage of the language, in short everything that makes it possible to move from "death sentence" to "suspension of death" in the French expression *arrêt de mort,* can always come about (*de facto* and *de jure*) in "everyday" usage of the language, in language and in discourse. The dream of translation without remnants, a metalanguage that would guarantee orderly flow between "entry language" and "exit language" [e.g., of a translating computer], between semantic radicals properly

expression in a famous funeral oration for a princess, this way of saying "she is dying" derives through repetition a literal element of reflexivity—*elle* SE *meurt,* she dies for herself, of herself, unto herself: her death sentence is decidedly her own)—before this "Come," or at least before he quotes it, "I" mentions an exchange between the nurse, Dangerue (a proper name that recalls us to our projected systematic reading of all the names or initials of proper names in Blanchot's stories), and J., who "asked her, 'Have you ever seen death?' 'I have seen dead people, Miss.' 'No, death!' The nurse shook her head. 'Well, soon you will see it.' "

It is thus not a question of *one* death, one dead woman, a person who is dead or living on, between life and death—not one dead woman, one death, that is decided or undecided in this *arrêt de mort,* but *death, la mort (personne de mort:* no dead person, the person of death)—*la Chose*—*itself* as *other.* And "I," who has just been summoned ("Come"), arrives like death, as death comes about, *as* death, almost dead [i.e., "dead on his feet"]. When someone says in French *"Je suis mort,"* he is playing with the word *mort, between* the noun ["death"] and the (masculine) adjective ["dead"], which can change everything (in what you would call a "sea-change"). The attribute *mort* leaves the "I" alive, otherwise, but the noun also puts him beyond the reach of the event that might happen to him, that might come about accidentally.

He is summoned—"Come"—by telephone. It was necessary to recount the exchange with the nurse before his arrival in order to suggest that the narrator and death are identical ("Soon you will see it"). Now, the telephone had hardly been hung up, the nurse will tell him later, when "her pulse [. . .] scattered like sand": a

---

bordered (*arrêtés*). Who will distinguish rigorously between these languages, here? Confusion of languages, of tongues. Shelley's activity as a translator: in the strictly linguistic sense, in which it was important, and in the "textual" sense, which cannot be separated from the other. Particularly in the case of *The Triumph* (Dante, Milton, Rousseau, and so on, and all those whom Bloom calls the "precursors" in the triumphant course or procession, as well as "in the chariot-vision"). But he

sign of death, a death sentence, in an instant as elusive as the last grain of sand in the time of hourglasses, death also as the result of the dissemination of the rhythm of life with no finishing stroke [*coup d'arrêt*], unbordered and unbounded arrhythmy on a beach that is a continuation of the sea. The unexpected expression (her pulse "scattered like sand") will be repeated, quoted "in quotation marks" at the moment of the second death, on the last page, after the resurrection. This is the passage that I read earlier. J. appears dead, she died at the end of the telephone call, while the narrator was being told to "Come." She is dying, *elle "se meurt"* while the "Come" runs along the line and instantly reaches (comes to) the narrator. He is told to "Come," *and* she's dead. He arrives at the apartment, finds the door open, and J.'s death is announced to him with "vulgarity." This word recurs twice to describe the doctor, the one whose relationship to the identity of death is most secure and who is always more or less, as in *La folie du jour,* a medical expert, a representative of authority or social conventions, whose language he speaks ("It's a blessed release for the poor creatures"). (Vulgarity and foolishness are two values or non-values that, along with indiscretion, which is inseparable from them, are most reprehensible in Blanchot's view—or in the narrator's in any case. But since every value leads over into its opposite, this entails certain problems.) "I" arrives in the dead woman's room. The *room* is the privileged place of *la Chose* in all these stories, domestic but utterly foreign (*unheimlich*), left in the coldest anonymity, sealed off, usually a hotel room, in any case devoid of any other description, reduced to the most indispensable constants of Western habitation: a bed on the *edge* of which

---

translates *himself*. The temptation, here, of an exhaustive reading, both of *The Triumph* and of everything else, beginning with all of Shelley's *glas* [death-knells], "On Death," "Death," "Autumn: A Dirge," the fragment "The Death Knell Is Ringing," again "A Dirge," *Adonais,* etc., etc. The same temptation with Blanchot: beginning with *L'arrêt de mort,* a starting point chosen by chance *and* of necessity, to recognize a "logic" that would enable us to read *everything,* in *L'arrêt de mort* and

one sits, at times an armchair that one tries to reach, a door, a lock, and, in *L'arrêt de mort,* keys ("Yale" keys: *"du genre Yale"*); outside, corridors and stairways.

He ("I") arrives in this death-chamber, the dead woman's room.

I shall now read at great length, in the most neutral voice I can manage, and without stopping to make comments at every point, far from it. I stress only the instant of summons: J.'s first name makes her return to life, makes her be born, even, and makes her triumph over life, starting with a silent "Come" that resonates with all the "Come" 's that I have tried to recite in "Pas." Then there will be the appearance of *la Chose* which does not appear, even though it is there, forbidding that it be spoken of, which, a little later, will be called the *event.* The reaffirmation, the *récit,* of life marks its discreet triumph in a "gaiety" (the words "gay" and "gaiety" recur five or six times) the memory of which is terrifying, would "be enough to kill a man." Gaiety, reaffirmation, triumph *over* (triumph of the "on," "over," *sur, hyper* . . .): over life and of life, life after life and after death, at the same time between life and death in the crypt, more than life, when it's over (*and* over again), reprieve and hypervitality, a supplement of life that is *better* than life *and better* than death, a triumph of life and of death; a living-on that is better than truth and that would be (if such living-on could ever be) *la Chose par excellence: sur-vérité,* truth beyond truth, truth beyond life and death. Here is the passage:

> [. . .] and it dawned on me [*cette lumière me traversa*] that at a cer-
> tain moment in the night she must have felt defeated, too weak to

---

elsewhere, down to the smallest element, the grain of sand, the letter, the space. . . . A wager: I feel at once its possibility and its impossibility, each equally essential. The same wager as that of translation, without remnant [*sans reste*], *du reste* ["moreover"/"of the remnant"]. Everything that, in the text above, goes back to the dissemination of sand (beach, seaside, hour-glass). The temptation to translate (turn over, transfer) Blanchot's hour-glass into Shelley's ". . . and whose hour/

live until morning, when I would see her, and that she had asked the doctor's help in order to last a little longer, one minute longer, the one minute which she had so often demanded silently and in vain. This is what that poor fool mistook for anger, and doubtless he had given in to her by coming, but he was already too late: at a time when she could no longer do anything, he could do even less, and his only help had been to cooperate with that sweet and tranquil death he spoke of with such sickening familiarity. My grief began at that moment.

It dawns on the narrator that at one moment in the night, in that battle between life and death, which is also a battle between day and night, she was almost "defeated." Then she *triumphed*—like the day [*jour*]—by lasting until morning. The "triumph of life" as a "triumph of light": it is with the throes of death [*l'agonie*], the battle between life and death as between light and night, that both *The Triumph of Life* and *L'arrêt de mort* are concerned. But this antagonism follows the syntax of a revolution. One spills over [*verse*] into the other, the ring makes one come back and come down to the other in a version or translation in which each word is committed and caught up in the language of the other, and inverted to become the opposite of itself. Thus the minute of living on is retained as a minute of truth beyond truth: almost nothing, a suspended moment, a "start" [*sursaut*], the time it takes to take someone's pulse and to turn over the hourglass.

He has entered the room "full of strangers."

I would have liked to understand why, after having resisted so stubbornly for so many interminable years, she had not found the

---

Was drained to its last sand in weal or woe,/ So that the trunk survived both fruit & flower." ". . . And suddenly my brain became as sand. . . ." Then comes the play of animal tracks [*traces*], "erased" or "visibly stamp[ed]," and the "burst" of the "new Vision.") Correspondence [also "Change here . . ."]. For Patmos. Vision. Apocalypse. Revelation. The translators will have to return again to the apocalyptic text of *Glas*. They should explain the necessary immodesty of these self-

strength to hold out for such a short time longer. Naively, I
thought that interval had been a few minutes, and a few minutes
was nothing. But for her those few minutes had been more than a
lifetime, more than that eternity of life which they talk about, and
hers had been lost then. What Louise said to me when she telephoned—"She is dying"—was true, was the kind of truth you perceive in a flash, she was dying, she was almost dead, the wait had
not begun at that moment; at that moment it had come to an end;
or rather the last wait had gone on nearly the duration of the telephone call: at the beginning she was alive and lucid, watching all
of Louise's movements; then still alive, but already sightless and
without a sign of acceptance when Louise said, "She is dying"; and
the receiver had hardly been hung up when her pulse, the nurse
said, scattered like sand.   [translation modified]

"More than a lifetime, more than that eternity of life . . .":
this "more," this more-than-life [*sur-vie*], marks, at least in the
passage I have just quoted, a temporal extension of life, in the
form of a reprieve. Before dying, in these "few minutes," she
lived "more than a lifetime [*plus qu'une vie*]." This excess, which in
life triumphs over life and in time is worth more than the eternity of life, is already completely different from life or the eternity of life, but it *presents* itself, if that expression were still possible, before the *arrêt de mort,* before the death of J., "in," "life."
After J.'s death, after Louise, who "must have read in my face
that something was about to happen that she knew she did not
have the right to see, nor anyone else in the world," has taken ev-
eryone away, the narrator remains alone with the dead woman.
He is seated "on the edge of the bed." He describes her with her

---

references and self-quotations. I am writing here about self-quotation,
its necessity and its mirages. And then, all writing is triumphant.
Writing is triumph (*Schreiben und Siegen-wollen*), manic life-after-life in-
surance. That is what makes it unbearable. Essentially indiscreet and
exhibitionistic. Even if we read no "that's me there" in it. And the
increase in discretion is only a surplus-value of triumph, a supplement
of triumph—enough to make you sick. This is what I am saying. I say

"stillness of a recumbent effigy and not of a living being." Mortuary sculpture, death masks and impressions, wills, embalming, and the crypt, everything that preserves [*garde*] the dead, at the same time living and dead, beyond life and beyond death—this persistent motif must be followed in the "two" "*récits*" that compose *L'arrêt de mort.* "She who had been absolutely alive was already no more than a statue." Her hands still bear the contracted trace of "the immense battle which [she] had fought." Then comes the call and the resurrection, the triumph of life, the moment when "this young woman [who] was dead [ . . . ] returned to life at my [call]." He calls (to) J. by her fist name, but this first name is never spoken in the account [*récit*] that he gives of its utterance. This utterance [*profération*] is forbidden to the *récit*. The name must not be spoken publicly, aloud. The initial keeps [*garde*] the secret like a grave—jealously. J.'s resurrection will be announced afterwards as a piece of good "news." We shall take into account, later, the fact that the other woman, in the other *récit,* is called Nathalie.

> I leaned over her, I called to her loudly by her first name; and immediately—I can say there wasn't a second's interval—a sort of breath came out of her compressed mouth, a sigh which little by little became a light, weak cry; almost at the same time—I'm sure of this—her arms moved, tried to rise. At that moment, her eyelids were still completely shut. But a second afterwards, perhaps two, they opened abruptly and they opened to reveal something terrible which I will not talk about, the most terrible look which a living being can receive, and I think that if I had shuddered at that instant, and if I had been afraid, everything would

---

it against Nietzsche, perhaps: triumph over oneself is also pursuit of power (*Gewalt*). Hence, and I come back to this, the apocalyptic text of *Glas.* What I write here is related to reading, writing, teaching as apocalypse, to apocalypse as a revelation, to apocalypse in its eschatological and catastrophic sense, to the *Apokalupsis Ioannou,* the Revelation of St. John the Divine. The translators will quote *Glas,* including this passage that begins on page 220—"After developing the X-ray negative

have been lost, but my tenderness was so great that I didn't even think about the strangeness of what was happening, which certainly seemed to me altogether natural because of that infinite movement which drew me towards her, and I took her in my arms, while her arms clasped me, and not only was she completely alive from that moment on, but perfectly natural, gay and almost completely recovered.   [translation modified]


Between the call—the only time her name is spoken, this name that is not even disclosed—and a resurrection that is marked only by a breath, there was no time ("there wasn't a second's interval"). The first "breath," the first "sigh" (we use *le dernier soupir,* "one's last breath," literally "the last sigh," to mean death), the first "cry" of the woman who has just been born, did not *follow* a call, which was nothing but a first name, spoken out loud. Ressurection, birth, or triumph of life thus will not have been the effect of a cause, but rather an absolute event, a cause even, the cause, the *causa, la Chose,* the first name itself: since now no interval or interruption separates the call from the first breath, we do not even know any more who spoke that name for whom. She heard it before the other had finished speaking it. She is called as (is) the other, and it is like the name that is given for the first time, at birth. The time of this response that weds (*responsa*) the call, accompanies it rather than follows it, performs it as a naming rather than succeeds it, even makes it possible by giving itself unconditionally—this time is contemporary with the end of *L'arrêt de mort*: ". . . and to that thought I say eternally, 'Come,' and eternally it is there." The "and" ("and immedi-

---

of testamentary chrisms and graveclothes (why anointing and binding in both testaments?), after attacking, analyzing, toning their relics in a sort of developing bath, why not seek in them the remains of John [*Jean*]? Gospel and Revelation violently cut up, fragmented, redistributed, with spaces, shifts in accents, lines skipped and moved around, as if they came to us over a faulty teletype, a switchboard at an overloaded telephone exchange: 'The light shineth in the darkness and the darkness

ately," "and eternally") weds in a timeless time the one called
and the caller, the imperative "come" and the coming of the one
who comes. In this sense, we can no longer describe the call
(demand, order, desire . . .) and the response in the usual terms
and according to the usual distinctions of an analysis of locu-
tionary acts. The "come"-effect of the "first name" transcends all
these categories (strictly speaking, it can thus be called "transcendental": *qui transcendit omne genus*), and this event, at once ordinary and extraordinary, is also what *L'arrêt de mort* "recounts."
But it recounts it while performing it in secret. The cryptic insistence of this secret is marked not only by the initial of a first
name that is neither noun nor verb nor pronoun (the initial, at
most, of the pronoun *Je,* J.): this insistence is constantly re-
marked, remarkable, noticeable, especially, as in the case of every
crypt, in its relationship to the law, in an interdiction. Thus the
narrator says repeatedly that he cannot say. He is forbidden to
say. So—he says. And if the *arrêt de mort* is related to judicial
decision, law, it is also an *arrêt* that arrests—with a sentence, a
verdict—speech and the right to speak. ("As for the rest, I don't
want to say anything. [ . . . . ] I have said nothing extraordinary or even surprising. What is extraordinary begins at the
moment I stop [*je m'arrête*]. But I am no longer able to speak of
it.") The same interdiction encrypts the resurrection at the moment when he sees the terrible *Chose,* which we know he does not
see as something, something other than an act of seeing, a look,
eyes, when J.'s eyelids "opened to reveal something terrible
which I will not talk about, the most terrible look [ . . . ]."
Before, you remember, Louise had seen in the narrator's face

---

. . . glory . . . who is worthy to take the book and to open the seals
thereof . . .' "—and concludes on page 222: "As the name indicates,
the apocalyptic, in other words capital unveiling, lays bare, in truth,
self-hunger. In *Pompes funèbres* you remember, on the same page: 'Jean
was taken away from me. . . . Jean needed a compensation. . . . I was
hungry for Jean' [tr. Frechtman, *Funeral Rites*]. That is called a colossal
compensation. The absolute fantasy as having oneself absolutely [*s'avoir*

"that something was about to happen that she knew she did not have the right to see, nor anyone else in the world [ . . . ]." The *arrêt de mort* is thus the interdictory decision that arrests *L'arrêt de mort* (the "*récit*" with this title) on the verge of the event that it does not have the right to recount, but that also puts it into operation, puts it to work, makes it recount, decides, induces it to recount, starting from this interdictory suspension, makes it set out again toward the impossible narrative, to recount that (which) it will not recount. The text comments on the title (a *parergon* or *cartouche* between the work and what is outside it, as the locus *du droit à la littérature*), a title that is thus part of it without belonging to it; but the title also states the impossibility of the text or erstwhile *récit* that it will have entitled, the impossibility of the *intitulé* [title, heading, that which is entitled]. *L'arrêt de mort*: of the *intitulé*. Or of the *en-tête*. The condition for its possibility and impossibility. An entire conjugation, in all the tenses, of law and duty [*devoir*] (I must, I had to, I should not have, I must not, I shall have to refrain from, it will turn out that I should not have [in French, all expressible by conjugated forms of the verb *devoir*]), all the steps taken by the inderdictory *pas*, in every tense [*temps*] and every mood [*mode*]. The *double bind* and the *double invagination* of this interdiction make it possible for us to read [*donnent à lire*] the unreadability of this impossible event (the after-life of resurrection), of this "news." Thus:

> [. . .] as she asked me how long I had been there, it seemed to me she was remembering something, or that she was close to remembering it, and that at the same time she felt an apprehension

---

*absolu;* cf. *savoir absolu,* "absolute knowledge"] in one's most mournful glory: to swallow oneself up so as to be next-to-oneself; to turn oneself into a mouthful [*bouchée;* John 13:26: "sop," "piece of bread"]; be(come) (in a word *bander* [bind, bend, blindfold, get a hard-on, etc.]) one's own bit [*mors*]. . . ." The apocalyptic theme of *Glas,* of course, is due not only to the fact that the Greek word (*apokalupsis*), another phenomenon of translation, was one recourse of the Septuagint to translate the verb

that was linked to me, or my coming too late, or the fact that I had seen and taken by surprise something I shouldn't have seen. All that came through her voice. I don't know how I answered. Right away she relaxed and became absolutely human and real again.

Strange as it may seem, I don't think I gave one distinct thought, during that whole day, to the event which had allowed J. to talk to me and laugh with me again. It is simply that in those moments I loved her totally, and nothing else mattered. I only had enough self-control to go find the others and tell them J. had recovered. I don't know how they took the news [*nouvelle*] [. . .].

The narrator reports that he reported—a *nouvelle,* a *récit,* in short, a "novella" and a piece of good news—like an evangelist who has returned (from the dead) to report J.'s resurrection. The Christ parallel (an *arrêt* that puts someone to death, an *arrêt de mort* in accordance with the resurrection that says, "I am the truth and the life," the triumph of life . . .) is supported by more than one witness (martyr, you might say) or piece of evidence in the narration. An effect of "superimposing" of images inscribes itself *en abyme,* beginning with the visit to the doctor, the one who first condemns J. to death. He is a believer:

The first day, he greeted me with this statement: "I am fortunate enough to have faith, I am a believer. What about you?" On the wall of his office there was an excellent photograph of the Turin Sudario, a photograph in which he saw two images superimposed on one another: one of Christ and one of Veronica; and as a matter of fact I distinctly saw, behind the figure of Christ, the features of a woman's face—extremely beautiful, even magnificent in its

---

*gilah,* which means "to reveal" in Hebrew (to reveal in particular the genitals, the ear, and the eyes; in "Freud et la scène de l'écriture" I refer to Ezekiel [on this, see what Bloom says about the Chariot of Yahweh and *The Triumph*] and to a certain sequence: "Then did I eat [the scroll of the law]; and it was in my mouth as honey for sweetness." A similar passage in Revelation: ". . . I took the little book . . . and ate it up; and it was in my mouth sweet as honey: and as soon as I had eaten it,

strangely proud expression. One last thing about this doctor: he was not without his good qualities; he was, it seems to me, a good deal more reliable in his diagnoses than most.

What this "superimposing," multiplied *en abyme,* comes down to, is not a constitution of the Gospel as a paradigm or a model for reference, as if *L'arrêt de mort* powerfully quoted, or cryptically put back into operation, back to work, a great, exemplary narration. Nor is it the other way around: for one might also be tempted to read *L'arrêt de mort* as the analytic regression towards a sort of original *récit,* nuclear event-ness, an invariable sequence of which the Gospels would be only an example, a variation, a case. The relationship, it seems to me, is of a different sort: it is one of seriality without paradigm. If there is a *récit,* it is to the extent that no paradigm can determine or arrest it. Serial repetition involves paradigm-"effects" but reinserts them in the series; and this reinsertion is already, still, put into operation in *L'arrêt de mort,* which, in itself "alone" (if that's the right word), constitutes a series of *récits* (at least two), *récits* at once analogous (hence the series) and utterly different, offering no guarantee of analogy. It is by the way remarkable, since we alluded to Veronica's veil, that this episode of the Passion does not appear in any of the canonical Gospels, as Pierre Madaule points out in his *Une tache sérieuse?: récit* (Paris: Gallimard, 1973, p. 106n.). Is not Shelley's relationship in *The Triumph of Life* to those whom Harold Bloom calls Shelley's "precursors" analogous to this? Could not this "poem" be called a *nouvelle?*

The question has the following resonance: What is a *nouvelle*

---

my belly was bitter.") Necessary comparisons, effects of translation and superimprinting in *The Triumph of Life, La folie du jour,* and *L'arrêt de mort* (among others). E.g., because of the *vision* ("And I had a vision. . . ." *"Kai eidon. . . ."*) that brings all these texts together on Patmos. (Hölderlin is there, with lots of people.) But also because of the imperative "Come" that forms their regular scansion. "Pas," because of the "Come," as a superimprinting of Revelation. Tremendous problems of

when it no longer relates, no longer is related as the *récit* of an event of life-after-life, nor simply produces it, but when its relationship to this "event" (living on) is the uncanny one that we are tracking down here under the titles *L'arrêt de mort* or *The Triumph of Life?* Living on comes about at "dawn," with the sunrise, for the one who says "I" and must not say anything. ("As for the rest, I don't want to say anything"; "[. . .] I, whom thoughts which must remain untold/ Had kept as wakeful as [. . .].") All the outpouring of light and solar glory at the beginning of *The Triumph* is here concentrated at the moment of J.'s resurrection: "J.'s waking took place at dawn, almost with the sunrise, and the dawn light charmed her." If we had the time and space here, we would have to summon up the paternal figure of the sun ("the Sun their father") that dominates the opening of *The Triumph,* until the arrival, with the moon, of "the ghost of her dead Mother," with the figure effaced, deliberately struck with insignificance, by J., the figure of her mother, the "queen mother," a mere walk-on, almost a supernumerary, a figurant, a figureless figure, the vanishing origin of every figure, the bottomless, groundless background against which J.'s life fights, and from which it is snatched away, at every moment. Since we shall never have time and space enough for this mother, here is one passage, one of her regular, stealthy passings through the text, a few lines after J.'s "waking" at "dawn":

> Apparently the morphine had not affected her spirits at all: someone who is saturated with drugs can seem lucid and even profound, but not cheerful; well, she was extremely and naturally cheerful; I

---

translation. The translators should read—and quote—all these texts in Hebrew and Greek. What happens when *eidos* is translated as "vision"? And the words *erkhou* and *hupage* by "come" and sometimes by "go"? The *va* and *viens* ["go" and "come"; cf. *va-et-vient,* "interrelationship"] of *Thomas l'obscur* (in two versions). Direct the entire reading of *L'arrêt de mort* toward the end, when Jesus says: " 'I am Alpha and Omega, the beginning and the end, the first and the last [*prōtōs kai eskhatos, ē arkhē*

remember that she poked fun at her mother in the kindest manner, which was unusual. When I think of all that took place before it and after it, the memory of that gaiety should be enough to kill a man. But at the time, I simply saw that she was gay, and I was gay, too.

   During that whole day she had almost no attacks, though she talked and laughed enough to bring on twenty. She ate much more than I did [. . .].

There is a great deal to be said about this gaiety, about the quality of experience thus designated to describe what is proper to an act or instance of living on, the levity of its affirmation, of the *yes, yes, yes to yes* without self-recollection, the *yes* that, saying and describing nothing, performing only this affirmation of the *yes* saying *yes to yes, must not even* [*ne doit même pas*] have, and know, itself [*s'avoir et se savoir*]. But this "need not" [*ne pas devoir*] or "must not" [*devoir ne pas*] is also an interdiction that interposes an unconscious between the event and the very experience of it, between the living-on and the present, conscious, knowing experience of what thus comes about [*arriver*]. I—the one who says me, that is to say, me—do not know what has happened, what will have happened [*arriver*] to me. *J. must not know* [*ne doit pas savoir*] *what has happened to her.* This *ne . . . pas* is to be understood any—and every—way that you wish; it is re-cited here in every way, every mode, every mood. The narrator's fright:

   "Why," she said coldly, "are you staying *precisely* tonight?" I suppose she was beginning to know as much as I did about the events of the early morning, but at that moment I was frightened at the

---

*kai to telos*].' . . . . 'Surely I come quickly [*Nai, erkhomai takhu*].' . . . . And the Spirit [*pneuma*] and the bride [*numphē*] say, 'Come,' " and so on. By way of the whole bibliography and sigillography of· the *seven seals.* And of Blanchot's eschatology, in *Le dernier homme* ("Often what he told of his past was so obviously taken from books that, immediately put on guard by a sort of suffering, people went to great lengths to avoid hearing him. This is where his desire to speak faltered most

thought that she might discover what had happened to her; it seemed to me that would be something absolutely terrifying for anyone to learn who was naturally afraid of the night.

It is thus not sure that she knows what has happened to *her,* that is, her coming back to life; in any event she *shouldn't* know, she should *not know,* she must not have known, she should not have known, found out. . . . Here "know," *savoir,* means "discover," "learn"; these are the narrator's words. Now, what the narrator is frightened of is the possibility that J. might have "learned" or "discovered" from *him*—from his more or less irrepressible *récit,* from an account that he was unable to contain at the time of the event itself—the triumph of life that had happened, that had come, to her. He is frightened at the thought that he might have let something slip, might have violated the interdiction that forbids the *récit* of the event, already a past event, which has never been *present* (because she regains her breath before he has finished speaking her first name, telling her in effect "Come," "Come again," "Come back") and which in itself belongs to the order of the *récit.*

This frightening thing that has come about without ever presenting itself, this event that is ineffable at the very moment it is seen, seen without there being anything to see except a look or *vision* ("her eyelids [. . .] opened to reveal something terrible which I will not talk about, the most terrible look [. . .]"), this terrible thing, the terribleness of the thing [*la chose*] is not only ineffable, unnarratable: it is interdictory, it forbids telling and even seeing ("[. . .] I had seen and taken by surprise something

---

strangely. He did not have a clear idea of what we call the seriousness of facts. The truth, the precision of what must be said, astonished him. [. . . .] 'What do they mean by "event"?' I read the question in his movement of retreat. [. . . .] She called him 'the professor.' [. . . .] He spoke to no one. I don't mean that he didn't speak to *me,* but it was someone other than me who would listen to him. [. . . .] Is he still coming? Is he going away already? [. . . .] The joy of saying yes, of

I shouldn't have seen"). But the interdiction is violated by itself ("I shouldn't have . . ."). It begins the *arrêt* of the *récit,* in other words paralyzes it but also sets it in motion with a single *pas* [step, "not"]. The interdiction trangresses itself and produces the *pas* that crosses it: the *récit.* The *récit* that tells "what happened" without having been present, and that tells it to the very "subject" to whom it happened and who is not supposed to know —this impossible *récit* is surpassed, overrun, *débordé,* by its own *arrêt de mort.* What must remain beyond its reach is precisely what revives it at every moment. The forbidden thing forbids. That which forbids (that which is forbidden) happens, comes about, without attaining, without happening in or to, the *récit.* And J. must not find out from the "I" what thus happens without happening to her, the "subject" of the whole thing, of *la chose.*

Perhaps *"chose"* has always designated, in philosophy, that which does not come about [*n'arrive pas*]. Things come about, but *la Chose,* in its determination as *hupokeimenon* or *rēs,* is the substance to which "accidents" happen and to which predicates attach, but which cannot itself be the accident or predicate of something else. *La chose n'arrive pas à autre chose. La chose,* when defined as the *hupokeimenon,* is that to which the *sumbebēkos* or accident happens, but which, being a thing, *chose,* does not happen, does not come about. To this extent and in this sense at least, the history or possibility of narrative is not essentially constitutive of *la chose.* Nor of *la chose* as *aisthēton* or as *hulē,* to use the three determinations whose history—or fable—Heidegger

---

affirming endlessly. [. . . .] He had to be in excess [*en surnombre*]: one more, just one too many. [. . . .] I am constantly spared thinking: he, the last one, still would not be the last. [. . . .] Even a God needs a witness. [. . . .] But with me there, he would be alone, more than any other man, without even himself, without that last one that he was— thus the very last." It should all have been quoted, at length.) or of Nietzsche's (for example "Ödipus. Reden des letzten Philosophen mit

offers us in "The Origin of the Work of Art." Here, *la Chose* is "terrible" because in its very not-happening it happens (comes about) to the "Come," in its *pas de chose* [no thing, thingly step, thingly "not"]: proceeding, progression [*procès*], as *arrêt de mort* that cannot be decided, neither life nor death, but rather LIVING ON, the very progression that belongs, without belonging, to the progression of life and death. Living on is not the opposite of living, just as it is not identical with living. The relationship is different, different from being identical, from the difference of distinctions—undecided, or, in a very rigorous sense, "vague," *vagus*, evasive, *évasé* [splayed, bevelled], like a bevelled *edge* [*bord*]. I shall quote a passage in which "living, living on" is defined precisely as a "vague objective," at the exact moment when this comma between the two verbs is the mark of the uncertainty of a transition or opposition between them: neither conjunction, nor disjunction, nor equation, nor opposition, but merely punctuation marking a pause before the desire for an *arête*, an *arrêt*, a "firm decision," is expressed. I quote this passage also because of the proximity of a "triumph." This is one of the times that she "triumphs," absolutely, intransitively:

> The pain near her heart did not go away, but the symptoms died down and she had triumphed once more. The treatment was discussed again: she wanted it very much, either in order to get it over with or because her energy could no longer be satisfied with a vague objective—living, living on [*vivre, survivre*]—but needed a firm decision on which she could lean heavily.   [translation modified]

---

sich selbst. Ein Fragment aus der Geschichte der Nachwelt": "The last philosopher, that's what I call myself, for I'm the last man. No one speaks to me but me alone, and my voice comes to me like the voice of a man dying. . . ." To be quoted in its entirety.). But I shall reread that elsewhere. This, too, is a "fragment." Insaturable context. And how could what I am writing here "concern" *The Triumph of Life*, which I read in a "foreign" language, and of which I lack so many contextual

This *vivre, survivre* delays at once life and death, on a line (the line of the least sure *sur-*) that is thus one neither of clear-cut opposition nor of stable equivalence. "Living, living on" differs and defers, like "differ*a*nce," beyond identity and difference. Its domain is indeed in a narrative formed out of traces, writing, distance, teleo-graphy. Tele-phone and tele-gram are only two modes of this teleography in which the trace, the grapheme in general, does not come to attach secondarily to the telic structure but rather marks it *a priori*. Differ*a*nce—*arrêt de mort* or triumph of life—defers (differs like) the narrative of (from) writing. We notice this, as it "re-marks itself," (for example) in the immediate context of the passage that I just quoted on the "triumph" and "living, living on." The narrator has just recounted, written, what J. had written to him. ("During the beginning of my stay in Arcachon, J. wrote to me at fairly great length, and her handwriting was still firm and vigorous.") The narrator is always away (at a distance, *tele-*); he always returns from afar and finally remains at a distance. What does she write him? "She told me the doctor had just had her sign a paper in case an accident should occur. So the treatment, which consisted of a series of shots—one each day, given to her at home—was about to begin." The doctor, the one who has thus condemned her and in effect signed her death warrant by prescribing this treatment, the author of the *arrêt de mort,* asks her, the condemned woman, to release him from his responsibility as a doctor, with a signature subscribing to the *arrêt de mort*. The narrator has already signed her death warrant, subscribed to it, by telling J. that she is condemned to die, that the doctor has given her up. In the case of the paper,

---

features? On what conditions, however. . . ? *20–27 February 1978.* Last judgment. Resurrection of the dead. Ghosts, *Doppelgänger*. (Nietzsche: I am a *Doppelgänger,* in *Ecce Homo*. The event—which *"sur-vient"* ["takes place," "occurs"; lit., "comes on"]—how will they translate this word?—consists in nothing, nothing but coming about, going on, and being gone.) Apocalypse, eschatology, the "last War," the "context" of *L'arrêt de mort*. "Come" is said to the event that comes about. An

she must surrender, with a piece of writing signed and counter-signed, thus "giving herself death," risking death in an effort to live on. This gesture is confirmed by the demand formulated else-where in the text: "If you don't kill me, you'll kill me." Now, this treatment itself, as prescribed or ordered by the doctor, will be deferred in turn, postponed, for a reason that is still unre-vealed, after a "crisis" and more than one *telephone* call. The day before the treatment was to begin, the paper having been signed,

> she felt a violent, stabbing pain near her heart and had such a severe attack [*crise*] of choking that she had them telephone her mother [—she does not do the telephoning herself, she *has* it done: one more relay along the way—] who then called the doctor. This doctor, like all fairly prominent specialists, was not often willing to go out of his way. But this time he came quite quickly, no doubt because of the treatment he was supposed to begin adminis-tering the next day. I don't know what he saw: he never talked to me about it. To her, he said it was nothing, and it is true that the medicine he prescribed for her was insignificant. But even so, he decided to postpone the treatment several days.   [translation mo-dified]

Since it is at this point that she "triumphed once more," the sus-picion arises that there is perhaps a connection between the start of the treatment and the death sentence, because she triumphs when the treatment is postponed. But because she also demands death and gives it to herself, all these propositions on the triumph and the *arrêt* are reversed at every turn.

Such would be the truth beyond truth of living on [*la sur-vérité*

---

apocalyptic superimprinting of texts: there is no paradigmatic text. Only relationships of cryptic haunting from mark to mark. No palimp-sest (definitive unfinishedness). No piece, no metonymy, no integral corpus. And thus no fetishism. Everything said here about double in-vagination can be brought to bear—a labor of translation—on what is worked out in *Glas,* for example, on the subject of fetishism, as the argument of the *gaine* ["sheath," "girdle"; cognate of "vagina"] (to be

*du survivre*], the hypertopia of these proceedings [*de ce procès*]. *La Chose* takes place without taking place [*a lieu sans avoir lieu*]: a *non-lieu* in the proceedings, a *non-lieu* at the "end" of the proceedings beyond even acquittal, debt, the symbolic, the judicial. (The *non-lieu* is the strange judgment in French law that is worth *more* than an acquittal: it fictively annuls the very proceedings of indictment, arraignment, detention, and trial [*"cause"*], even though the proceedings have taken place; the transcript of them remains, and the certification of the *non-lieu*.) The unnarratable event of J.'s coming back to life holds the *récit* breathless for an interminable lapse of time that is not merely the time of what is narrated: the one who narrates [*le récitant*] (between the narratorial voice and the narrative voice) is also, first, *one who lives on.* This living on is also phantom revenance (the one who lives on is always a ghost) that is noticeable (re-markable) and is represented from the beginning, from the moment that the posthumous, testamentary, scriptural character of the narrative comes to unfold. The narrator has spoken of the doctor's sentencing J. to death, of the way in which he himself has told her about it, of the "several sentences" that she "wrote down" and "wished to keep secret." ("I still have them. [. . . .] No mention of me. I could see how bitter she had felt when she heard me agree to her suicide.") And here he is, sentenced himself by the same doctor, and thus living on, in the "supernumerary" "remains" of a life:

> Her doctor had told me that from 1936 on he had considered her dead. Of course the same doctor, who treated me several times, once told me, too, "Since you should have been dead two years

---

translated "vagina"? On the *gaine,* see *Glas,* p. 257; see also, on the subject of fetishism, "against" Hegel, Marx, and Freud, pp. 253 and 235. Freud: the fetish erects itself like a "monument," a *"stigma indelebile,"* a "sign of triumph"). *L'arrêt de mort* and fetishism. ("In her nightly terror, she wasn't superstitious at all; she faced a very great danger, one that was nameless and formless, altogether indeterminate, and when she was alone she faced it all alone, without recourse to any trick or fetish"

ago, everything that remains of your life is a reprieve [*est en sur-nombre*, is supernumerary]." He had just given me six more months to live and that was seven years ago. But he had an important reason for wishing me six feet underground. What he said was only an expression of his desire, only suggested what he wanted to happen. In J.'s case, though, I think he was telling the truth. [translation modified]

This does not rule out the possibility that J.'s death sentence is also an expression of the *narrator's* desire.

The reprieve in which each moment of life is *extra*, super-numerary (the supernumerology—1936, two years, six months, seven years, six feet—with which everything is accounted for and all these accounts are settled), this living *on*, establishes this *récit*, this former *récit*-less "*récit*" (now the erasing of the designation "*récit*" is part of the *récit* of *L'arrêt de mort*), in truth beyond truth [*la sur-vérité*], the supplement of truthless truth.

Why truth beyond truth? At the moment when the narrator has said, "I was frightened at the thought that she might discover what had happened to her; it seemed to me that would be some-thing absolutely terrifying for anyone to learn who was naturally afraid of the night," he suspects himself of letting himself say what must not be said (that is to say, as always, the only thing to be said), the thing that would (absolutely) frighten, *la chose effrayante*. This is the beginning of what I shall call, using a figure justified elsewhere ("Pas"), the stairway [*escalier*] or es-calade of truth, one truth about another, one truth *on* (top of) another, one above or below the other, each step more or less

---

[translation modified].) Similarly, everything said here about double in-vagination can be brought to bear—a labor of translation—on what is said in "La double séance" about the *hymen* (as syllepsis) and the pane of glass [*vitre*]. A discussion, still to come, of the *vitrifying* structure of writing and desire in *L'arrêt de mort* (". . . I saw her again, through a store window. When someone who has disappeared completely is sud-denly there, in front of you, behind a pane of glass, that person becomes

true than truth. This is not a matter of impersonal or objective truth, of veracity, of telling the truth that is equivalent to the thing in question. Nor of the relationship between truth and interdiction (the truth that must not be told), a transgressive truth or a trangression of truth, truth as law or above the law.

From J. there is a *demand for narrative:* "Perhaps I did commit a grave error in not telling her what she was expecting me to tell her. My deviousness [*manque de franchise*] put us face to face like two creatures who were lying in wait for one another but who could no longer see one another" [translation modified]. He has not concealed from her the thing that he has not told her: she knew it well enough, in a way, to expect him to tell her. Not telling the truth, in this case, or rather being "devious," failing to be "frank," is not saying something (something that is, in a way, known) but simply not *saying,* not *admitting,* what is already revealed, not unveiling the revealed. One might then think that truth is here in the act of *saying,* of *reciting,* and not in the relationship of veracity between what is said or experienced and the saying of it, between the saying and the thing said, in this case between the narrative and what it narrates (its meaning [*sens*] or its referent): all of these distinctions are called into question in this entire hypertopia. But if we were to think of truth as involving solely the act of saying, we would still be consigning truth [*confier la vérité*] to the *present* of an act (saying, narrating, reciting) or indeed of a performative (a saying or reciting that produced, in the present, the referent of the saying or *récit,* the recited referent of the *récit,* its undeferred "referred"). However, this *present,* too, is borne away in the stairstep progression of truth (above and) beyond truth.

---

the most powerful sort of figure (unless it upsets you). [. . . .] The truth is that after I had been fortunate enough to see her through a pane of glass, the only thing I wanted, during the whole time that I knew her, was to feel that 'great pleasure' again through her, and also to break the glass. [. . . .] The strangeness lay in the fact that although the shop window experience I have talked about held true for everything, it was most true for persons and objects that particularly interested me.

The truth-beyond-truth of life-after-life: the truth that J., as she lives on, is not told, is not, as in most cases, that she has been given up, that she is sentenced to die, that the illness will not spare or pardon her, that she is *going* to die or even that she *has just* [*vient de*] died, but rather that she is not dead, that she died and has lived on. This is what is terrible in the thing: *la chose* as the event of living on, of life-after-life—but this event, this coming back to life, is never present. This is why it is truth-less, more or less than true. This truth-beyond-truth provides the narrator (himself condemned, sentenced, to live on and condemned by the double bind of an impossible demand) with a double "excuse":

1. "My excuse is that in that hour I exalted her far above any sort of truth and the greatest truth mattered less to me than the slightest risk of worrying her" [translation modified].

If we stopped here, if that were all, we could interpret this movement in banal terms: he prefers J.'s well-being in life, her peaceful tranquillity, to his own sincerity, his own relationship to truth. But this is precisely not all, and for this reason the excuse, at least the one that he has or that he gives to himself, is a double one: J. has access to, or rather only approaches, *aborde,* a truth that is superior to his, to the truth in the name of which he forbids himself to say that which is true.

2. "Another excuse is that little by little she seemed to approach a truth compared to which mine lost all interest."

The truth that she only approaches may be what she already knew yet wanted, he believes, to hear from him, but perhaps also a secret located *above* what he could have told her but has forbidden himself to: *la Chose effrayante,* life-after-life that has come

---

For instance, if I was reading a book that particularly interested me, I read it with vivid pleasure, but my very pleasure was behind a pane of glass: I could see it, appreciate it, but not use it up. In the same way, if I met someone I liked, everything nice that happened between us was under glass and thus preserved, but also far away and in an eternal past. Yet where unimportant people and things were involved, life regained its ordinary meaning and immediacy, so that though I preferred to keep

about or come on without coming to be here and now [*sans ar-river*], the approach of what has come to pass, is *past,* without hav-ing taken place in the present, replacing both life and death without "taking" a "place," in the time that elapses or does not elapse when a first name mobilizes and paralyzes the entire narra-tive, forbids the very step that it sets in motion, *fascinates* all the writing of *L'arrêt de mort*. It can also be read as a fascinating *treat-ment of* truth. In the unarrestable dissemination of its titles, the *arrêt de mort* is the truth *about* truth, *on* truth, truth*less* truth *on* truth, the *récit*-less *récit* of truth*less* truth *on* truth.

From beginning to end. Let's start now at the end, the very end, the end of the end, the end of what I shall call for the sake of convenience and without rigor the "second part" of the "book." But this second part is "whole," perfectly autonomous. True, if we accept the entire conventional system of legalities that organizes, in literature, the framed unity of the corpus (binding, frame, unity of the title, unity of the author's name, unity of the contract, registration of copyright, etc.), *L'arrêt de mort* (in each of its versions) is *a single book,* signed by *a single author,* and made up of two narratives, two *récits,* in the first person, following in a certain order, and so forth. And everything that can call into question, in the text, this conventional system of legalities, also presents itself in its framework [*cadre*]. Within this framework, the strange construction of the double narrative is held together at an invisible hinge, a double inner edge [*bord*] (the space be-tween the last sentence of the first *récit* and the first of the sec-ond). There is no absolute guarantee of the unity of the two *récits,* and even less of continuity from one to the other, or even that the

---

life at a distance . . ." [translation modified]. ". . . And perhaps I would have known something about its [*ses*] intentions which even it [*elle*] could never have known, made so cold by my distance that it was put under glass . . .") and in *La folie du jour* (it is glass that has almost cost him his eyesight) or in "Une scène primitive" (". . . through the window-pane [. . .] (as if through the broken window) . . ."). Will they translate *verre* and *vitre* with *glas?* Something else that escapes

narrator who says "I" in each is the same. And even if, to increase
the undecidedness, he starts by saying, "I will go on with this
story," there is no thread that continues from one story to the
other, no temporal link, no character, no situation, or anything
of the sort. And "this story" can refer, with its demonstrative, to
a completely different story as well as to the one that has just
ended with an "I stop" "at the moment" when "what is extraordinary begins." This undecidedness is never resolved. The double
*récit* is constructed so as to preserve the undecidedness and to hold
in suspension the demand for narrative that, as in *La folie du jour,*
demands unity from a narrator capable of remembering and of
gathering (himself) together, telling "exactly" what has happened. Among other things, we can always wonder, against the
law (of the registration of copyright, with all its implications, for
example of the fixed identity of the author as a "real" signatory,
the bearer of a single patronymic name), whether the time of the
"second" *récit* does not come, will not have come, before that of
the "first." Thus the title *L'arrêt de mort* (one more supplementary
meaning) can refer also to the *arrêt de mort* in the *récit,* almost at the
"center" of it. J.'s life after the death sentence, then death, then
life-after-life, then death, seem in fact to be succeeded by the
long-awaited entrance of Nathalie—a first name that refers to the
Nativity with the resonance of good news, tidings we have already heard. Isn't Nathalie the triumph of life? This reading of
the *arrêt de mort* at the middle of *L'arrêt de mort* is powerfully
called for by the crater of the double inner edge: the "first" *récit*
stops at the moment the *arrêt de mort* has done its work, but this
suspension also marks the moment when "what is extraordinary"

---

usage, using up, use-value. The wearing away, the using up, of what is
out of use. Surplus-value and process of fetishization. The "under-glass"
quality of the text in translation, and thus of every mark. How can a
translation be signed? How can a proper name be translated? Is there,
from that moment on, such a thing as a proper name? And the "yes" in
translation. People who get married abroad (*oui . . . oui . . .*) [in the
French text: *"yes, yes"*]: all the guarantees in the transferring of marriage

in the *arrêt de mort* begins: "What is extraordinary begins at the moment I stop. But I am no longer able to speak of it." What is extraordinary begins where the "I" stops, where the narratorial voice stops, at the *"arrête"* of the voice. Let us recall *Le pas au-delà:* " 'Speak on the arrête—*the line of instability—of the spoken word.' As if it were present at the exhaustion of dying: as if night, having started too early, at the earliest moment of day, doubted that it would ever come to night."* The line of this cutting edge, this "arrist," this *arrête,* passes "between" the two *récits* of *L'arrêt de mort.* Indeed, the double *récit* revolves (in the turning of a version or a revolution) around *la raie de mort* [*raie:* line, stripe, parting, ridge], death crossed out, blocked, held in check, signed, sealed, sentenced.

The truth beyond truth of living on: the middle of the *récit,* its element, its ridge, its backbone [*arête*]. There is only one blank space in the typography of the book, between the two *récits.* Before, in the first version, there were two. By erasing, by doing away with the second blank space, in the second version—the blank space that separated the two *récits* from the sort of epilogue that was in danger of being meta-narrative and pretending to gather together the two *récits*—by making this change, Blanchot has given the "middle" space an even more remarkable singularity. This is not the only effect of this change, but it counts.

Now, immediately after this blank space, at the bottom of one page and at the top of another, after the absolute interruption, the connectionless connection [*rapport sans rapport*], after J.'s second death, after the narrator has said, "What is extraordinary begins at the moment I stop. But I am no longer able to speak of

---

certificates. Fundamental irresponsibility for a translated text. The ideal thing is translation into a foreign writing system (Japanese, for example, for a European). But that's valid in "my" language, too. An impossible contract. Two unrelated processions. *27 February–6 March 1978.* Don't forget that N. (Nathalie) is a translator. ("She translated writings from all sorts of languages. . . .") The narrator notes: "That was an aspect of her character which helped to mislead me about her."

it," on the next page, the facing page, the other shore, truth enters—thematically, and by name. As if the veil of an interdiction were finally going to be lifted—any minute now, once more.

"I will go on with this story, but now I will take some precautions. I am not taking these precautions in order to cast a veil over the truth. The truth will be told, everything of importance that happened will be told. But not everything has yet happened. [*Mais tout ne s'est pas encore passé.*]"

Not everything has yet happened. This is difficult to understand. When does this refer to? Whatever the answer to this question, the *récit* of *this* story, the one that begins here, will not recount a past event. It will not report, will not relate (a *rapport sans rapport*) something that remains prior to and thus outside the writing, the *récit* or, as we can now say, the series. *L'arrêt de mort* is in series.

Not everything has yet happened. The coming of the thing, of *la chose,* its event or advent, will be also the coming of the thing to the *récit,* subsequent to the narration, at least to its beginning, and will thus be a *récit*-effect. Thus the *récit* will be the cause—as well as *causa, chose* [thing, mere tool]—of what it seems to recount. The *récit* as the cause and not as the relating of an event: this is the strange truth that is announced. The *récit*'s the thing. But we must beware: this formula, *"la chose est le récit,"* implies no performative presentation or production. What we have here is not that conclusion, readily drawn these days, using a logic of truth as presentation substituted for a logic of truth as representative equivalence, according to which new logic the narrative is the very event that it recounts, the thing presenting itself and the

---

All these texts, it should now be clear, involve law and transgression, and the order that is *given,* and the sort of order that can be obeyed only by transgressing it beforehand. Read yesterday, among some graffiti: "do not read me." I continually ask what *must* be done or not be done (for example in reading, writing, teaching, and so on) to find out what the place of that which takes place, is constructed upon (for example the university, the boundaries between departments, between one discourse

text presenting itself—presenting *itself*—by producing what it says. If there is performance here, it must be dissociated from the notion of presence that people always attach to the performative. What is here recited will have been that non-presentation of the event, its presence*less* presence, as it takes place place*less*ly: the "-less" or "without," and the *pas,* without *pas,* without the negativity of the *pas.*

I said that "truth" appeared, at least in name, in the middle, at the beginning and at the end. And that I was going to begin at the end to recount it in turn. But how are we to decide, to fix [*arrêter*] the end of such a text? Its unfinishedness is structural; it is bound to itself in the shifting binding of the *arrêt.* I shall proceed a bit arbitrarily, as for every *arrêt,* for time is short, and I hope you will forgive me. We always ask to be forgiven when we write or recite. For here I am recounting. And so I shall choose the episode of the key.

There is a key in the *récit:* a "Yale" key. Like all keys, it locks and unlocks, opens and closes. This key has been stolen and concealed by N. (Nathalie). The terrifying scene that this episode will have occasioned seems to form a pendant-piece, in this second *récit,* to the scene of J.'s return to life in the first. But superimposing is something you can never be sure about, and above all we cannot strictly speaking call either of these a "scene": in neither does *la Chose* present itself, nor does anything else make itself visible—or if so, it forbids one to speak of it. This is, this will be, the moment in which "I" says "Come." This time "I" does not utter the "Come" in the conditional or virtual form or mood, or as a quotation, as in the three occurrences that I have

---

and another, and so on). Today, respecting (up to a certain point) the contract or promise that binds me to the authors of this book, I have felt it best to confine myself to the problem of the "must" [*"il faut"*] and its transgression (in the realm of reading, writing, the institution of the university, and so on—all domains that defy delimitation) from the standpoint of translation (*Über-setzung, Über-tragung,* trans-ference, and so forth). What *must not* be said, today, if we are to follow the dominant

cited, quoted, elsewhere ("Pas"), and "I" is addressing himself here not to the merely grammatically feminine, the feminine gender of "thought" or "speech," *la pensée* or *la parole,* or to a neuter (beyond sexual difference), but rather, *it seems,* in the present, indeed, to a woman. (True, this woman is no one: "I can say that by getting involved with Nathalie I was hardly getting involved with anyone: that is not meant to belittle her; on the contrary, it is the most serious thing I can say about a person.")

I must assume that you are familiar with the text. In the course of an air raid during the Second World War, in an underground shelter in the metro (already what you would call a crypt), he tells her for the first time *in French,* in his language, things that he usually tells her in a fictive way or mood [*mode*], playfully, without any commitment, in her language, a *Slavic* language, for example proposing marriage to her. As long as they spoke to each other in the language of the other [*la langue de l'autre*], it was *as if* speech were *irresponsible.* But this irresponsibility already commits the speakers and, as we shall see, the return to the mother tongue does away with commitment as well as seals it. It spells the *arrêt* of commitment. The commitment thus *arrêté,* both in one's own language and in the language of the other, is indeed the *hymen.*

> For quite some time I had been talking to her in her mother tongue, which I found all the more moving since I knew very few words of it. [. . .] She [. . .] would answer me in French, but in a different French from her own, more childish and talkative, as though her speech had become irresponsible, like mine, using an

system of norms of this domain? I do not say it; I say what must not be said: for example, that a text can stand in a relationship of transference (primarily in the psychoanalytical sense) to another text! And, since Freud reminds us that the relationship of transference is a "love" relationship, stress the point: one text loves another (for example, *The Triumph of Life loves,* transferentially, *La folie du jour,* which in turn . . .). It's enough to make a philologist laugh (or scream), and Freud

unknown language. And it is true that I too felt irresponsible in this other language [*langage*], so unfamiliar to me [. . .]. So I made the most friendly declarations to her in this language [*langage*], which was a habit quite alien to me. I offered to marry her at least twice, which proved how fictitious [*fictif*] my words were, since I had an aversion to marriage (and little respect for it), but in her language [*langue*] I married her, and I not only used that language lightly but, more or less inventing it, and with the ingenuity and truth of half-awareness, I expressed in it unknown feelings which shamelessly welled up in the form of that language and fooled even me, as they could have fooled her.

But *tromper,* "fooling," for words that express in the language of the other a "truth of half-awareness," is also *tromper la surveillance* (as we say in "my" language, French), eluding the watchful eye of some monitor, in order to tell the truth. All the more so since the language of the other, as the language of truth, is never just the language of the other. Since it is "of the other," I invent it at every moment ("more or less inventing it"), I speak it for the first time, as if at the moment of its initial establishment, of the first contract by which I adapt and adopt [(*m'*)*approprie*] the language. At the same time, in the mythic time of this "at the same time" of the language of the other and my establishment of it, I make the contract *and* exempt myself from it. All *at once.* I am "irresponsible" *and* absolutely committed in the establishment of the language of the other. Is it not significant that the "at once," the "at the same time," of this double bind, is the occasion of the *hymen,* its chance and its law?

The words spoken in the language of the other are "true,"

---

himself, who, however, did speak of transference as a "new edition" (in the metaphorical sense, of course, of *Übertragung!*). On what conditions is this transferential magnetization possible between what are called textual bodies? This strange question has, perhaps, long engaged (or long committed) me. Engaged me in what must not be. . . . [*Dans ce qu'il ne faut pas.*] How are you going to translate that? What must not be done, in the realm of translation, transference, or the aforementioned

commit the speaker, are binding, in legal proceedings, in accordance with a contract that is all the more inflexible since the words belong to the language of the other. The paradox of the heteronomous dissymmetry that is due to the apparently formal element in the language before any consideration of context: the obligation is binding to whatever extent the words of the obligation are "fictitious," "fictive." There is commitment only in the language of the other, which I speak, of necessity, irresponsibly and fictively, in expropriation, but the language of the other is more contractual, contracts more, is closer to the conventional, fictive origin, to the extent that I invent it and thus adopt, appropriate it, mythically, in the present act of each spoken word. The language of the other lets the spoken word have the word, and commits us to keep our word. In this sense, there is "language of the other" whenever there is a speech-event. This is what I mean by "trace."

I must now propose a long reading. We have here the passage from the language of the other to *my* language, the *mother* tongue, the theme of which should also be related to the figure of the mother as figurant, walk-on, extra, super, in this *récit* and in certain others. Here, a sudden intrusion, the event that comes to pass in the metro when I say to the other, in my language this time, what was reserved for the other language, truth as fiction which commits and provokes—*la Chose,* the theft of the little "Yale" key. This comes immediately after the passage that I just quoted.

> They did not fool her at all; I am sure of that. And perhaps my frivolity, though it made her a little frivolous too, aroused disagreeable thoughts more than anything else, not to speak of one other

---

comparative literature: for example, relating in a monstrous association the "phenomenon," "occurrence," "surrection" of *"rose"* in *The Triumph of Life* (so many times "arose," "rose," "I rose," "I arose") to—not the resurrection—but the *"rose"* of resurrection in *L'arrêt de mort*. This is what would not be serious, sober, even if effects of homonymic transference are at play already and of necessity within Shelley's poem, which is, moreover, full of colors and embroidered flowers. The last word that

thought about which I cannot say anything. Even now, when so many things have become clear, it is difficult for me to imagine what the word marriage could have wakened [*faire naître*] in her. She had once been married, but that business had left her only the memory of the unpleasant details of the divorce. So that marriage was not very important to her either. And yet why was it that the only time, or one of the only times, she answered me in her own language, was after I had proposed marriage to her: the word was a strange one, completely unknown to me, which she never wanted to translate for me, and when I said to her: "All right, then I'm going to translate it," she was seized by real panic at the thought that I might hit on it exactly, so that I had to keep both my translation and my presentiment to myself.

The interdiction remains: there is "one other thought about which I cannot say anything," and the only "answer," *"réponse,"* that she gives to his proposal of marriage is neither "yes" nor "no" but an untranslatable word: not only in a foreign language but also "strange" and unknown to him. The risk of his perhaps being able to translate it nevertheless, makes its untranslatability more an interdiction than an impossibility. If he translated it, there would be an answer, the "response" of a *sponsa* (fiancée, a promise made), and this possibility is maddening for her. It is this understanding of a "yes" (which must be untranslatable and unquotable, must remain outside the language, strange and foreign), this understanding between them, which, along with "madness" and "insane words," will make her flee, will interrupt the *hymen* even as it consummates it in the confusion of their tongues.

---

J., the woman who "lives on," has spoken, was not *la Chose* but *la Rose,* "the perfect rose," *"la rose par excellence."* Not the sand-rose, even though the woman who lives on called for it twice at the moment when her pulse "scattered like sand." Twice, at the moment of her double death, of her double *arrêt de mort,* she says, "Quick, a perfect rose." Reread *in extenso.* For example: "Another excuse is that little by little she seemed to approach a truth compared to which mine lost all inter-

It is possible that the idea of being married to me seemed like a very bad thing to her, a sort of sacrilege, or quite the opposite, a real happiness, or finally, a meaningless joke. Even now, I am almost incapable of choosing among these interpretations. Enough of this. As I said, I was deluding myself much more than I was her with these words, which spoke within me in the language of someone else [*la langue d'une autre*]. I said too much about it to her not to feel what I was saying; inwardly I committed myself to honoring these strange words; the more extreme they were, I mean alien [*étrangers*] to what might have been expected of me, the more true they seemed to me because they were novel, because they had no precedent; the more I wanted, since they could not be believed, to make them believable, even to myself, especially to myself, putting all my effort into going farther and farther and building, on what might have been a rather narrow foundation, a pyramid so dizzying that its ever growing height dumbfounded even me. Still, I can put this down in writing: it was true; there cannot be any illusions when such great excesses are involved. My mistake in this situation, the temptations of which I see most clearly, was much more the result of the distance I imagined I was maintaining from her by these completely imaginary [*fictifs*] ways of drawing close to her. Actually, all that, which began with words I did not know and led me to see her much more often, to call her again and again, to want to convince her, to force her to see something other than a language in my language [*autre chose qu'un langage dans mon langage*], also urged me to look for her at an infinite distance, and contributed so naturally to her air of absence and strangeness that I thought it was sufficiently explained by this, and that as I was more and more attracted by it, I was less and less aware of its abnormal nature and its terrible source.

---

est. Towards eleven o'clock or midnight she began to have troubled dreams. Yet she was still awake, because I spoke to her and she answered me. She saw what she called 'a perfect rose' [*une rose par excellence*] move in the room. During the day I had ordered some flowers for her that were very red but already going to seed, and I'm not sure she liked them very much. She looked at them from time to time in a rather cold way. They had been put in the hall for the night, almost in front of her

No doubt I went extremely far, the day we took shelter in the metro. It seems to me that I was driven by something wild, a truth so violent that I suddenly broke down all the frail supports of that language [*langue*] and began speaking French, using insane words that I had never dreamt of using before and that fell on her with all the power of their madness. Hardly had they touched her when I was physically aware that something was being shattered. Just as that moment, she was swept away from me, borne off by the crowd [*foule*], and as it hurled me far away, the unchained spirit of that crowd struck me, battered me, as if my crime had turned into a mob [*foule*] and was determined to separate us forever.

Shall we leave this text on its own power?

We should neither comment, nor underscore a single word, nor extract anything, nor draw a lesson from it. One should not, one should refrain from—such would be the law of the text that gives itself, gives itself up, to be read [*qui se donne à lire*]. Yet it also calls for a violence that matches it in intensity, a violence different in intention, perhaps, but one that exerts itself against the first law only in order to attempt a commitment, an involvement, with that law. To move, yieldingly, towards it, to draw close to it fictively. The violent truth of "reading."

This is what is happening right here. With great violence, I draw three motifs from the quotation.

1. The fiction of the foreign language is intended to keep a distance, indeed infinite distance, within all the rapprochement, proximation, *propriation,* appropriation. *Pas d'Ent-fernung:* dis-tance. The *pas* is less susceptible of definition by words like "fiction,"

---

door, which remained open for some time. Then she saw something move across the room, at a certain height, as it seemed to me, and she called it 'a perfect rose.' I thought this dream image came to her from the flowers, which were perhaps disturbing her. So I closed the door. At that moment she really dozed off, into an almost calm sleep, and I was watching her live and sleep when all of a sudden she said with great anguish 'Quick, a perfect rose,' all the while continuing to sleep but

"language," "language of the other," than it is itself capable of remarking on them, drawing our attention to them [*il . . . les donne . . . à remarquer*].

2. Where does this "truth" come from, the "truth so violent" of "I" 's repatriation in his own language? From the fact that the reappropriation does not take place and that he discovers the language of the other in his "own" language, French, in the utterly new words that he speaks in it. (Between the two experiences or the two events or the two languages, the relationship is once more one of double invagination.) Just as in the previous experience, when he was speaking Nathalie's language, but this time within his language, his "mother" tongue, he initiates, discovers, *establishes,* creates; he speaks in words that are "novel," that have "no precedent." If he begins "speaking French," he does so "using insane words that I had never dreamt of using before." Hence their madness, madness for both him and her. We can also say that these "French" words are *untranslatable* for him, absolutely familiar and absolutely foreign. He speaks his mother tongue as the language of the other and deprives himself of all reappropriation, all specularization in it. The effect of commitment, of breaking and entering, of heteronomous expropriation, gives truth this over-violence: within my "mother" tongue I have broken all the safety-devices ("I suddenly broke down all the frail supports of that language"), everything that authorizes awareness or consciousness and the illusion [*leurre*] of appropriation with respect to language. Will it be said that by letting the trace of the other involve or commit me in this linguistic expropriation I am breaking with what is maternal in the mother tongue? Or on the

---

now with a slight rattle. The nurse came and whispered to me that the night before that word had been the last she had pronounced: when she had seemed to be sunk in complete unconsciousness, she had abruptly awakened from her stupor to point to the oxygen balloon and murmur, 'A perfect rose,' and had immediately sunk [*et aussitôt avait sombré*] again./ This story chilled me." *6–13 March 1978*. *"et aussitôt"*: to translate this, like everything said above about the *"et,"* the translators will

contrary with the paternal law that kept me away from what was maternal? You will find that I have rung some changes on these questions elsewhere.

3. The *hymen s'arrête:* it comes about *and* is immediately forbidden. It is the double-bind structure of this event: its "madness." The interruption of the *hymen*—which is nothing other than its coming to be, its event—does not arise from any decision. No one has the initiative. As soon as the words have "touched" her, she is "swept away from me, borne off by the crowd": she does not leave, nor do I, and this "sweeping away" consigns what it carries off, to *dispersion* (the event, the *coup*—blow, stroke, "suddenly"—the pulse once more "scatters like sand") and to *anonymity.* All the same, the crowd (dispersion and anonymity) brings in no verdict of acquittal. The crime has taken place (and every *hymen* intervenes, like a crime, "between perpetration and the memory of it": here I draw a veil over "La double séance"), and its dissemination dissolves or absolves it in the crowd only by multiplying it incalculably ("as if my crime had turned into a mob and was determined to separate us forever"). And my crime is that I loved her, proposed marriage to her, this *alliance*—but in a language [*langue*] that I have never been able to reappropriate or even understand, whether it be her (Slavic) language, a foreign language, or insane words (themselves foreign) in "my" language. My crime is that I proposed marriage to her in language [*langage*] that could commit me only if it was the other's, thus only if I did not understand it as mine and if it thus did not commit me, if even as it bound me, was binding upon me, it set me free. But this is always the case, always "normal": a language

---

have to consult (or refer the reader to) the Greek "at the same time," *hama,* and *en tō ephexēs* ("immediately") as they are treated in "Ousia et grammè." What is a *reference,* a reference to a thing, to a text, to one text, to the other? What is this word "reference"? And the reference of a certain "perfect rose"? The absolute crypt, unreadability itself. And yet the "references" call for an "infinite finite analysis," an infinite-finite reada-translata-bility. Do not go on about the symbolism of the flower

[*langue*] can never be appropriated; it is mine only as the language of the other, and vice versa. The essential irresponsibility of the promise or the response: this is the crime of the *hymen*. The violence of a truth stronger than truth. The crime of the *hymen* takes place without taking place and repeats itself endlessly, by the throng [*en foule*], like sand, like the *arrêt de mort:* interminable proceedings.

What happens then? There's no justifying this trip, nor this series of leaps and omissions (and I am referring to writing as well as to reading). He has lost her and is looking for her. First, although "at her house [*chez elle*], no one had answered the telephone," he goes there, thinking "that she was not answering it" on purpose. But even at the door there is no answer: it is "deaf." Yet "every time I had gone, she had been there" in that room. (The last words of *L'arrêt de mort:* "and to that thought [*et à elle*] I say eternally, 'Come,' and eternally it is there [*elle est là*].") In this room he cannot even "make out the trail [*trace*] she had left in passing through" or wait for her, thus "replacing her." Replacing *her:* the woman named Nathalie, the first name that celebrates the birth of Christ, as we have noted, but also the first name of the woman who gave birth, in the story, to Christiana, whom at this moment "I cursed [. . .] for being [away] in the country, where she could not stop her mother from getting lost." Feeling "lost" himself rather than uneasy for Nathalie's sake, he is like "a wanderer in search of nothing." Has she drowned herself? No, suicide horrifies her. Then comes the moment when he stops [*arrête*] wandering. He reaches [*arrête*] a sort of decision, coolly arrived at, that one is tempted to compare to the moment

---

(have done so elsewhere, at length, precisely about the rose). "Symbol" of life (the rosiness of cheeks, imitated by make-up in *L'arrêt de mort*), "symbol" of death (funeral flower) or of love, the rose is also the paradigm of that which never has to account for itself ("die Rose ist ohne warum," "the rose has no why or wherefore"), the enigmatically arbitrary that signifies the non-significance of the arbitrary, of the thing with no why or wherefore, without origin and without end. (See "Le

in the "first" *récit* when he (the same one, another) returns, then calls her back to life, then "gives" her death: "[. . .] reason returned to me, at least a fairly cool and lucid feeling which said to me: the time has come, now you have to do what has to be done." His resolution is purely formal in nature. In any case, we are told nothing of its content: what you have to do is do what has to be done. *Il faut "il faut":* he gives himself this pure order or prescription at the same time that he receives it. He will return home, but home is not home, for two reasons. First, he lives in hotels, has no place of his own. Second, because there are two places, two hotel rooms: one, in an almost empty hotel with no owner present (it's wartime, and he's been called up), a room in which "I had nothing [. . .] but some books" and where "I almost never went," and went "at night [only if] it was really necessary"; the other, in the hotel on the rue S., where "I had asked N. never to go." She called him there one morning and "what I said," his *"réponse,"* makes him hate the place. As he goes back there on this particular evening, he notes that "the strange thing" is that he does not think at all that she might be waiting there. He doesn't feel like sleeping in either place, so he tries to get a room in "a rather shady hotel," but since that hotel is full, he returns to the one on the rue d'O., the one where he "almost never [*presque pas*]" stays. His room there is like a crypt: with the elevator out of order, it is reached by way of a *stairwell* [*escalier*] with "a cold smell of earth and stone." The cryptic topology of this dark room, this obscure chamber, has the resonance of a certain triumph of life. It is a *for intérieur* [usually "conscience," "inner tribunal," "heart of hearts"] without intimacy, an enclave

---

'sans' de la coupure pure" and all of the reading, in a seminar at Yale on *La chose,* of Heidegger's text on "Die Rose ist ohne warum." To be continued elsewhere, as is what concerns Ponge's rose.) If the rose is not a thing, and not *la Chose* either. Understand the perfect *rose* not as a thing but as a word, breath, a word breathing its last: adjective, noun (common or proper), immediately nominalizable predicate (*rose, la rose, le rose, Rose* ["pink" (adj.), "rose" (n.), "pink" (n.), "Rose"]). The first

larger than its inhabitant but which this inhabitant nevertheless
carries within him; he haunts rather than inhabits it. The relationships of inclusion or inherence that link the part to the
whole, cannot be fixed, defined, *arrêtés,* in terms of boundaries.
The part includes the whole, and life triumphs over life. "Everything about that room, plunged in the most profound darkness,
was familiar to me; I had penetrated it, I carried it in me, I gave
it life, a life which is not life, but which is stronger than life and
which no force in the world could ever overcome." This camera
obscura is a secret; no one goes there, and he keeps the key in his
wallet. Hence the transgression that follows, the theft of a key
and a letter, a crypt broken into, desecrated—and a representa-
tionless scene of *la Chose:* this scene is what I was coming to.

[. . .] The elevator was not working and in the stairwell, from the
fourth floor on up, a sort of strange musty smell came down to me,
a cold smell of earth and stone which I was perfectly familiar with
because in the room it was my very life. I always carried the key
with me, and as a precaution I carried it in a wallet. Imagine that
stairwell plunged in darkness, where I was groping my way up.
Two steps from the door I had a shock [*je fus frappé par un coup*]:
the key was no longer there. My fear had always been that I would
lose that key. Often, during the day, I would search my wallet for
it; it was a little key, a Yale key, I knew every detail of it. That
loss brought back all my anxiety in an instant, and it had been
augmented by such a powerful certainty of unhappiness that I had
that unhappiness in my mouth and the taste of it has remained
there ever since. I was not thinking anymore. I was behind that
door. This might seem ridiculous, but I think I begged it, en-

---

word of the first scene of the first act of a play (Genet's *Paravents,* for example; see *Glas*), it retains, out of context, the reserve of all those powers (*Rose!*) of a name beyond names, the reserve that it still retains when
it becomes the last word (*par excellence*) of the last act: of the dead
woman and of death, of *la Chose par excellence.* Rose: rose: "rose": I, a
rose, rose. Its own subject and predicate, a tautology into which the
other, however, has intruded, a flower of rhetoric without properties,

treated it, I think I cursed it, but when it did not respond, I did something which can only be explained by my lack of self-control: I struck it violently with my fist, and it opened immediately.

I will say very little about what happened then: what happened had already happened long ago, or for a long time had been so imminent that not to have revealed it, when I felt it every night of my life, is a sign of my secret understanding with this premonition. I did not have to take another step to know that there was someone in that room. That if I went forward, all of a sudden someone would be there in front of me, pressing up against me, absolutely near me, of a proximity that people are not aware of: I knew that too. Everything about that room, plunged in the most profound darkness, was familiar to me; I had penetrated it, I carried it in me, I gave it life, a life which is not life, but which is stronger than life and which no force in the world could ever overcome. That room does not breathe, there is neither shadow nor memory in it, neither dream nor depth; I listen to it and no one speaks; I look at it and no one lives in it. And yet, the most intense life is there, a life which I touch and which touches me, absolutely similar to others, which clasps my body with its body, marks my mouth with its mouth, whose eyes open, whose eyes are the most alive, the most profound eyes in the world, and whose eyes see me. May the person who does not understand that come and die. Because that life transforms the life which shrinks away from it into a falsehood.

I went in; I closed the door. I sat down on the bed. Blackest space extended before me. I was not in this blackness, but at the edge of it, and I confess that it is terrifying. It is terrifying because there is something in it which scorns man and which man cannot endure without losing himself. But he must lose himself; and who-

---

with no proper meaning, a repeated self-quotation. "A rose is a rose is a rose": in *L'entretien infini,* Blanchot says that this line of Gertrude Stein's disturbs us because it is "the locus of a perverse contradiction" (see the passage that follows, p. 503). When speaking of the "narrative voice," he mentioned a "shrewd perversity." Here the translators might amass references—to the Mystic Rose in *Miracle de la Rose* and in *Glas,* to the same Mystic Rose in "The Secret Rose" by Yeats, whose "Second Com-

ever resists will founder, and whoever goes forward will become this very blackness, this cold and dead and scornful thing in the very heart of which lives the infinite. This blackness stayed next to me, probably because of my fear: this fear was not the fear people know about, it did not break me, it did not pay any attention to me, but wandered around the room the way human things do. A great deal of patience is required if thought, when it has been driven down into the depths of the horrible, is to rise little by little and recognize us and look at us. But I still dreaded that look. A look is very different from what one might think, it has neither light nor expression nor force nor movement, it is silent, but from the heart of the strangeness its silence crosses worlds and the person who hears that silence is changed. All of a sudden the certainty that someone was there who had come to find me became so intense that I drew back from her, knocked violently into the bed, and immediately saw her distinctly, three or four steps from me, that dead and empty flame in her eyes. I had to stare at her, with all my strength, and she stared at me, but in a strange way, as if I had been in back of myself, and infinitely far back. Perhaps that went on for a very long time, even though my impression is that she had hardly found me before I lost her. At any rate, I remained in that place for a very long time without moving. I was no longer at all afraid for myself, but for her I was extremely afraid, of alarming her, of transforming her, through fear, into a wild thing which would break in my hands. I think I was aware of that fear, and yet it also seems to me that everything was so entirely calm that I could have sworn there was nothing in front of me. It was probably because of that calm that I moved forward a little, I moved forward in the slowest possible way, I brushed against the fireplace, I stopped again, I recognized in myself such great patience, such

---

ing" should also be quoted—to Rilke, of whom Blanchot is a prodigious reader—to all his "rose" 's and all his "roses" (a formidable *anthology*, from which, because space is limited and for the sake of translation, I shall extract here only this line, from "Les roses," a poem written by Rilke *in French:* "Rose, toi, ô chose par excellence complète. . . ." Read and translate in full.), to Kierkegaard, of whom Blanchot is a prodigious reader ("The seal is yours, but I keep it. But you also know

great respect for that solitary night that I made almost no movement; only my hand went forward a little, but with great caution,
so as not to frighten. I wanted most of all to go towards the
armchair, I saw that armchair in my mind, it was there, I was
touching it. In the end I got to my knees so that I would not be
too large, and my hand slowly crossed through the dark, brushed
against the wooden back of the chair, brushed against some cloth:
there had never been a more patient hand, nor one more calm, nor
more friendly; that is why it did not tremble when another hand, a
cold hand, slowly formed beside it, and that hand, so still and so
cold, allowed mine to rest on it without trembling. I did not
move, I was still on my knees, all this was taking place at an infinite distance, my own hand on this cold body seemed so far away
from me, I saw myself so widely separated from it, and pushed
back by it into something desperate which was life, that all my
hope seemed to me infinitely far away, in that cold world where
my hand rested on this body and loved it and where this body, in
its night of stone, welcomed, recognized and loved that hand.

Perhaps this lasted several minutes, perhaps an hour. I put my
arms around her, I was completely motionless and she was completely motionless. But a moment came when I saw that she was
still mortally cold, and I drew closer and said to her: "Come." I
got up and took her by the hand; she got up too and I saw how tall
she was. She walked with me, and all her movements had the same
docility as mine. I made her lie down; I lay down next to her. I
took her head between my hands and said to her, as gently as I
could, "Look at me." Her head actually did rise between my hands
and immediately I saw her again three or four steps from me, that
dead and empty flame in her eyes. With all my strength, I stared
at her, and she too seemed to stare at me, but infinitely far behind

---

that in a sealing ring, the letters are reversed; thus the word 'yours,' by
means of which you certify and validate possession, reads 'mine' from
my side. Thus I have sealed this packet and should wish you to do the
same with this rose before putting it in the temple of archives"; the
reversal "yours"/"mine" takes place, of course, only in Danish)—to so
many others. *L'arrêt de mort* as another *Roman de la rose* (we know that
this text, too, presents considerable problems of the unity or duality of

me. Then something awoke in me, I leaned over her and said,
"Now don't be afraid, I'm going to blow on your face." But as I
came near her she moved very quickly and drew away (or pushed
me back).    [translation modified]

(Quoting or not quoting is always equally unjustifiable, in the
eyes of the law that concerns me here. What must we do to allow
a text to live? Are we to take it—and how—or merely to "brush
against" it? Say to it, "Come"? Isn't that what one always does
"at home," i.e., in accordance with the violent law of one's own
*economy,* here of mine? But we have just seen how what properly
belongs to an economy, someone's own economy, is anonymously
dedicated, divides itself and submits to the other who was waiting there for him already, without waiting for him, and how he
said "I remained [*je restai*]," then "I stopped [*je m'arrêtai*]
again." The rest has just been read [*vient d'être lu*].)

The "Come" that has just rung out will be quoted, after a time
in which we are told of "the obstacle which must be overcome"
and of what is said to have "triumphed over an immense defeat,
and is even now triumphing over it, and at each instant, and
always, so that time no longer exists for it." In the interval between the first occurrence, event, coming of the "Come" in the
story and the first quotation of it, an interval that I'll leave for
you to read, that I'll let you read (it's like letting someone, or
something, live), he sees her "in the morning," like J., in the
room and "quite gay" [translation modified]. This is a time of
coldness beyond cold. A semblance of "natural life" [translation
modified] has returned. "Naturally, what I had to do was live

---

the corpus and of the "I," the narrator or the author). And to place here
this rose on the most abyss-like of crypts, these "discovered fragments"
by Bataille, on Laure (just published by Jérôme Peignot, Laure's
nephew): "Walking through the streets, I discover a truth that will not
leave me in peace: that sort of painful contraction of my whole life that
for me is related to Laure's death [in October 1938, dates found at the
beginning of *L'arrêt de mort*] and to the sparse autumn sadness, it also

with her, in her apartment: I had to take my revenge on that door." And here is the quotation of the "Come," "single" in its serial repetition:

> [. . .] I felt determined to transform the most simple details of life into so many insignificant words, that my voice, which was becoming the only space where I allowed her to live, forced her to emerge from her silence too, and gave her a sort of physical certainty, a physical solidity, which she would not have had otherwise. All this may seem childish. It does not matter. This childishness was powerful enough to prolong an illusion that had already been lost, and to force something to be there which was no longer there. It seems to me that in all this incessant talking there was the gravity of one single word, the echo of that "Come" which I had said to her; and she had come, and she would never be able to go away again.

"Come": a single word, unique, and yet, in and of itself, entwined, interlaced, in a series. Truth beyond truth inscribes its own effacement there, in the middle of and on the invaginated boundaries of the *récit,* of these crypts, death- or bridal chambers that bring about [*donnant lieu à*] this double *récit,* this *arrêt de mort* which is finally only its own homonym. After the theft of the key—the event of a *hymen* that brings at once alliance and separation, when "as I came near her she [. . .] drew away" ("joined: separated"—*L'attente l'oubli*), in the crypt—*another arrêt de mort* punctuates the *récit.* Each time beyond decision, in a serial repetition that does not change the uniqueness of the event. Hence the extraordinary lightness, slightness, the indifferent dis-

---

for me the only way to 'crucify' myself. [. . . .] 11 October. As Laure was dying, I found in the then ruined garden, among the dead leaves and wilted plants, one of the prettiest flowers I've ever seen: a rose, 'autumn-colored,' barely opened. Distracted as I was, still I picked it and took it to Laure. Laure was then lost in herself, lost in an undefinable delirium. But when I gave her the rose, she emerged from her strange state, smiled at me, and spoke one of her last intelligible sentences: 'It's

tractedness, the strange or insignificant coldness that is allied, in narrative affect, with a bottomless sorrow and mourning beyond measure. At the very moment when unhappiness is "immense," one must not "have faith," he says, "in dramatic decisions. There was no drama anywhere. In me it had in one second become weaker, slightly distracted, less real. [. . .] I knew that if I did not immediately again become a man carried away by an unbridled feeling I was in danger of losing both a life and the other side of a life." Thus we come to the other *arrêt de mort,* and the other theft: in the wallet, she had found not a letter but a card, and an address, the address of a sculptor who would make a cast of her head and her hands—enough to turn her into an effigy.

(Before reading this passage, let us recall the "first" *récit,* the "stillness of a recumbent effigy," the narrator's request for permission to "have [J.] embalmed." Earlier he "had sent a very beautiful cast of J.'s hands to [. . .] a professional palm reader and astrologer." To embalm, to make a death mask or cast, is indeed to set about the *arrêt de mort* in its double triumph, and indeed the chambers of this desire are in a sort of "funeral home." This comes about (again) in series in the two *récits.* There is an *arrêt* between the two deaths, and thus hypertopia: between the two deaths in each *récit,* and between the two *arrêts de mort* from one *récit* to the other. Two *récits* in one, one *récit* in two, synonymous, homonymous, anonymous. He (the narrator, whose identity is doubly problematic: he had no name, and there is no guarantee that he does not have two, from one half-*récit*—or half-mourning—to the other) loves them. He loves them . . . dead. He loves (by) seeing them. He loves (by) seeing them dead.

---

gorgeous,' she said to me. Then she brought the flower to her lips and kissed it with a mad passion as if she wished to hold on to everything that was slipping away from her. But it lasted only an instant: she threw down the rose the way children throw down their toys and became once more alien to everything that came near, breathing convulsively. 12 October. [. . . .] Laure's dying was almost finished when she raised with a weary movement one of the roses that had just been

But when he sees them they die—when he sees them, and when they see him with that terrible look of theirs, see him as their death—with these looks, they die, are dead. Die, are dead, when he loves them—die, are dead, of this love. Moreover, he can love, desire, only behind a pane of glass, he says elsewhere. One imagines a glass coffin: this is one thematic of this *récit*—and of others—which I reserve here. But each woman is also the double, death mask, cast, ghost, body at once living and dead, of the other. Separated: joined. There are two of them, absolutely different, absolutely *other*, infinitely separated by the *arrêt de mort* between two heterogeneous *récits*. They are each bound to "me" (to the one who says "I" in each instance and who is not necessarily the same, who is perhaps not the same precisely because he, the same in name or first name, is linked, bound, in accordance with a double *hymen* and twice says "yes," twice "Come") in accordance with a double vow. By the same double token [*coup*], himself by the same token double, "I" becomes two, absolutely foreign to himself, divided, partitioned in his crypt: he belongs to two different *récits*, two different vows; he has another, a woman, dictate to him what he says and tell him what has to be done—another, a woman, who *inspires*. Everything is decided, we have seen, in the moment of an insufflation in which we no longer know who has the absolute initiative. Even the mouth of one of those women, "open to the noise of agony [*agonie*], did not seem to belong to her, it seemed to be the mouth of someone I didn't know, someone irredeemably condemned, or even dead." Interruption, this connectionless connection [*rapport sans rapport*] of the *arrêt*, passes not only between J. and N. but also, with the same interminable

---

spread before her, and she cried out almost in a voice absent and infinitely pained: 'The rose!' (I believe those were her last words.) [. . . .] At that same moment I was recalling what I had felt that very morning: 'Take a flower and look at it until you and the flower are in harmony. . . .' That was a *vision*, an *inner vision* maintained by a silently felt necessity." *20–27 March 1978*. Resurrections. Easter week. The translators should refer to the end of my apocalypse (*Glas*), entirely con-

stroke, inside me, the ego, the henceforth insideless insides of the *récitant*. But if the two women are different, utterly other "in relation to" [*par rapport à*] one another, each one *is* the other. Each one signifies and preserves [*garde*] the other. Each one remains— the other. For and by the other. Each sings the other's *arrêt de mort*. One dies *while* the other lives, lives on, comes—again. "While": "as": "when": "in order that": "because": "as soon as": this is the timeless time of the "and," of the "and immediately" that recurs, that comes back, so often in the *récit* to describe the *simul* without causality, without absolute synchrony, without order. For the narrator: the death of one is what keeps the other under guard—preserves the other, preserves [him] from the other. Thus in the time of the "and" they must—*il faut*—they must both die so that, each time, the other will live. One dies *and* the other lives: an "immediately" that weds symbiosis to synthanatosis in a triumph without identity, without identical- ness. In a double signature, he himself signs *their arrêt de mort,* at their request, their demand, he says, in order to preserve them, keep them, embalm them, encrypt them . . . *and his arrêt de mort,* with and in the same hand. What binds him to each of the two dead women (alliance, ring, vow, *hymen,* double affirmation, yes, yes, come, come: come back, come again—"come," again), each of these two revenants, living on as ghostly fiancées—this bond is double not because it commits him twice, attaches him to two women, to two identities: this *hymen* is a "double bind" each time, because each of these bonds that bind is, in itself, double. It signifies, desires, *arrête* life death, the life the death of the other so that the other lives *and* dies, the other of the other—

---

cerned with the paschal conjunction. The Christ-like figure again, of the "who?," of the X. of *L'arrêt de mort,* over whom "it's about time we raised a cross," says the doctor who condemns him. The translators will have to refer here to what is said about chiasmus, about χ (*chi*) and the *ichthus* in "+ R (par dessus le marché)" (in reference to Adami) and in Hillis Miller's article "Ariadne's Thread" (*Critical Inquiry,* volume 3, number 1). There is another X., in *L'arrêt de mort,* the creator of that

who *is* without being the *same*. For there is an other of the other, and it is not the same: this is what the order of the symbol seeks desperately to deny. The double bond to each woman *signifies* to each woman the *arrêt de mort* (death *and* life-after-life/life-after-death) so that the other's *arrêt de mort* will be possible (so that she will live on and cease to live). The *arrêt de mort*—what is designated by the title of the book and of the "totality" of a *récit* that is never gathered together to form one *récit* and that thus questions even the unity of its "title," as well as the unity of the narrator—the *arrêt de mort* would thus follow this "double bond" whose terrifying *figura*, figure, face, traverses the *récit* that is forbidden, inter-dicted in the quasi-middle of it, over above beyond its double inner border.

But there are enough signs that make it possible to read [*donnant à lire*] one *récit* in the other, and the double overrun of these two inner borders, so that *double invagination* is here no longer simply a formal structure. It is related in an essential way to the double bind that ties the "narrator" to each of these two women—related in an essential way to the triumph of life or to the *arrêt de mort* interrupted in the "middle," the "middle" "of it," *at the very place* where the *relationship* of the "book" *to itself,* in its fragile binding, is formed, the *relationship* of the "I" *to himself,* his alliance with himself, his ring, his anniversary, the *alliance* that joins him to himself. This *very* place, the very *same* place, being the place, the locus, of interruption, is also the place where double invagination gathers together what it interrupts in the strange *same*ness of this place. The *arrêt de mort* calls forth what it forbids: the death of the other whom it is supposed to preserve.

---

"process which is strange when it is carried out on living people, sometimes dangerous, surprising, a process which . . . Abruptly [. . .]." X. is the name of the sculptor, the one who, *par excellence,* fixes life death [*arrête la vie la mort*]. *Arrêt* without *Aufhebung:* of translation. Economy. Temptation, but it's impossible, to recount the history of *this* text (countless episodes: for example the Yale Seminar in 1976, Venice, the lecture in Belgium—the feminist leader, a prodigious reader of

One *récit* (one woman) makes the other die and live in a movement that is unarrestable and unnarratable. By the same (double) token, activity *comes down to* [*revient à*] passivity, making a person die *comes down to* letting a person die, making a person live *comes down to* letting a person live. But in going from "making" to "letting," we are no longer passing from one opposite to the other, not passing into passivity. The passivity of "letting" is different from the passivity of couples and pairs, e.g., the pair active/passive.

Each woman lives off and dies of the other, preserves the other and loses the other, preserves and loses the other's narrator. The word "and" is to be understood in each case as a conjunction that does not join logically, for example in contradiction, nor according to chronology, succession or absolute simultaneity, nor according to some fundamental ontology. This "and" must be understood, if possible, as it appears in the story, where it seems to be unreadable in terms of any of the *conjunctions* that I have just mentioned. And the conjugality of the double bind between the two women and the narrator (if there is only one narrator), joins or weds this "and" to itself *as* an *arrêt de mort*. (One example, although we could give a long series of them: "I called to her by her first name; and immediately—I can say there wasn't a second's interval—a sort of breath came out of her compressed mouth [. . .] ." "[. . .] And to that thought [*et à elle*] I say eternally, 'Come,' and eternally it is there.") This "and"-, "and immediately"-writing, as it annihilates time in the ring of eternal return, yokes affirmation to itself in its *récit,* in the being-at-the-same-time of the other beyond time, in the accompaniment of

---

Blanchot, who realizes, after the fact, that it was hard for her to bear that a "man" should have dared the "mad hypothesis" of the *hymen* between the two women; she used the most academic criteriology against me, demanded "proof," and so on—reading "Morella," the thought of that Miss Blind bent over the corrections of *The Triumph,* hesitations about the title—I had first thought of "Living On—in Translation" and "Translations"—my calculations about the English—how will they

that which is not accompanied—this "and"-writing returns, recurs, regularly when the narrative voice is (lets itself be) heard in
Blanchot's text—in all the other texts signed by him. It is like a
silent gliding, the elusiveness of a cause that does not accompany
its effect, of a before and an after that are indistinct in the soft,
light step [*pas*] of a movement. And, unceasingly, *sans arrêt,
arrête,* and *arrête* nothing.

Each woman lives off and dies of the other, and the same for
the other, each preserving the other's narrator, and they lose him
immediately. What do they preserve him from? From loneliness
*with* the other, from the single vow with the other. But in each
case there is a double vow, a single, unique vow, as they sign the
narrator's *arrêt de mort*: he can live in accordance neither with the
single nor with the double alliance. He is, moreover, one who is
"living on" in each of the stories, each time promised (given up,
condemned) by a doctor to imminent death, like *another* anonymous Christ (X., *chi,* chiasma, raising "a cross over him"). I have
already quoted the "first" *récit*; this is from the "second": "He [an
editor] thought I was nearing my end, he telephoned the doctor,
who also gave me up for lost [*m'enterrait*] every few weeks, and
got this opinion from him: 'X.? My dear sir, it's about time we
raised a cross over him.' A few days later, the doctor told me this
as though it were an excellent joke." Later, in the course of a
story about blood that should be analyzed: "The doctor put me in
his clinic; he thought I was dying." A couple of pages later: "The
night before, I had been on the point of dying."

The two women, like the doctor, sign his death warrant, and
he signs theirs, but always in a countersignature, because the

---

render the *il faut* or perhaps the *faut-il* that is the imprint of prescription in "Living On"?—the Paris Seminar in 1974 or 1975 on "Die
Aufgabe des Übersetzers," what my friend Koitchi Toyosaki said to me
yesterday, the article in *La part du feu* entitled "Traduit de" [it begins
thus: "In *For Whom the Bell Tolls,* Robert Jordan, discovering the importance of the moment that he is in the process of living, repeats to himself in a variety of languages the word 'now.' Now, *ahora, maintenant,*

death that is "given" is always requested, demanded, by the one who receives it and immediately gives it to himself or herself, in order to sign it, with/from/in the hand of the other.

And thus we see . . . another *hymen*.

Among these three survivors, as they live on, there can be an *arrêt* only of death. No [*pas d'*] infidelity, more than one fidelity. Three, to lose: lost. He, the sole narrator, in his improbable and divisible identity, can live neither the single nor the double alliance, and he preserves himself, makes/lets one woman preserve him from the other, using one terror to avoid the other, and the double *récit,* as we have perhaps seen adequately, insures the possibility of the impossible *arrêt de mort.* Nothing seems capable of surpassing this terrifying, triumphant affirmation—unless it comes to hold in store/check something even worse [*garder du pire*]. Unless there is something even worse—and thus more desirable, more madly terrifying—for the narrator: the *hymen* between the two women. What if the structure of the *récit,* the interruption between the two stories, guaranteed at first the non-meeting of J. and N.? And what if it were this—that the two women love each other and approach one another, before him and without him—what if it were this *hymen* that the *arrêt de mort* was both to forbid, as absolute terror, and thus, since every *arrêt de mort* calls forth what it suppresses, to make/let it live, be readable, die [*donner à vivre, à lire, à mourir*] in the unconscious, imperceptible structure of this *récit?* I am speaking here of the fascination of one woman by the other, across the uncrossable glass partition that separates the two stories. They do not know each other, have never met; they inhabit two utterly foreign worlds.

---

*heute.* But he is a bit disappointed [. . .]"}, the five pages in *L'amitié* entitled "Traduire" [last words: ". . . with this conviction that to translate is, ultimately, madness."], and so on), but I count the words and I give up. Economy. Political. . . . If there is something that arrests translation, this limit is not due to some essential indissociability of meaning and language, of signified and signifier, as they say. It is a matter of *economy* (economy, of course, remains to be *thought*) and retains

They telephone each other ("Come") across the infinite distance of a no-connection [*d'un sans rapport*]. The narrator is between them, saying "I," with an "I" identical *and* other, from one *récit* to the other. In him, before him, without him, they are the same, the same one, "two images superimposed on one another," a "photographic" superimposing; they are utterly different, completely other, and they unite and call to each other: "Come." Of course, nothing on the manifestly readable surface of the *récits* makes it possible to sustain such a mad hypothesis. How could the character from one story desire, marry, fascinate, etc., the character from another story? And if we wished to consider *L'arrêt de mort* a single *récit,* joined to itself by the supposed identity of the character who says "I," how could we fail to see that J. and N., in the story, have no connection, no relationship with each other, do not meet, just as the two series of events in which they are involved never intersect? Of course. No normal category of readability, then, could give credence to the mad hypothesis according to which the double invagination that attracts us in this *récit* could make it possible to read [*donner à lire*] the unreadable *hymen* between the two women: one *with(out)* the other. I am speaking here neither of an intention nor of a construction on the part of the "author"—which does not mean that the interruption between author and narrator, or indeed between the two women, is simple: it is as ambiguous as the interruption of every *arrêt de mort.* As ambiguous, moreover, as the dis-tance of *differ*a*nce* (*Ent-fernung*): from one *récit* to the other, they—the two women, the two voiceless voices, tele-phone one another: Come. And the relationship, the connection, between the two *récits* would be tele-graphic in nature. Furthermore, I am speaking here neither

---

an essential relationship with time, space, counting words, signs, *marks*. The unity of the word is not to be fetishized or substantialized. For example, with more words or parts of words the translator will triumph more easily over *arrêt* in the expression *arrêt de mort*. Not without something left over, of course, but more or less easily, strictly, closely, tightly. Beware of the "new mode of expression" of the "totally new

of an intention nor of a construction on the part of the
"narrator"—which does not mean that the interruption between
narratorial voice and narrative voice, the two voices, the two
women, one *without* the other, is simple: it remains as improbable
as the interruption of every *arrêt de mort.* And yet something like
X-ray analysis or "blood" *[sang]* analysis can make readable
*[donner à lire]* that which is unreadable in this narrative body. (A
moment ago I drew (on) the "blood" that circulates in one of the
two stories, the "mysterious" blood, "so unstable that it was as-
tonishing to analyze," the "madness of blood" in which the narrator seeks "hope of escaping the inevitable.") The readability of
unreadability is as improbable as an *arrêt de mort.* No law of
(normal) reading can guarantee it in its *legitimacy.* By normal
reading I mean every reading that insures knowledge transmitta-
ble in its own language, in a language, in a school or academy,
knowledge constructed and insured in institutional constructions,
in accordance with *laws* made so as to resist (precisely because
they are weaker) the ambiguous threats with which the *arrêt de
mort* troubles so many conceptual oppositions, boundaries, borders. The *arrêt de mort* brings about the *arrêt* of the law. The
double invagination of this narrative body in deconstruction overruns and excedes not merely the oppositions of values that make
the rules and form the law in all the schools of reading, ancient
and modern, before and after Freud; it overruns a delimitation of
the fantasy, a delimitation in the name of which some would here
abandon, for example, the mad hypothesis to "my" fantasy-
projection, to that of the one who says "I" here, the narrator, the
narrators, or me, who am telling you all this here. This unreadability will have taken place, as unreadable, will have become

---

language" and the like. Economy: stricture and not *coupure,* rupture. It
is always an *external* constraint that arrests a text in general, i.e., *anything,* for example life death. What is arrested here: the authenticity
(*Eigentlichkeit*) of a being-for-death. Think exteriority from the angle of
this economy of the *arrêt. Arrêt:* the greatest "bound" energy, "banded,"
*bandeé,* tightly gathered around its own limit, retained, inhibited

readable [*se sera donné à lire*] right here, as unreadable, from the very bottom of the crypt in which it remains. It will have taken place where it remains: that's the proof. From here on it's up to you to think what will have taken place, to work out both the conditions for its possibility and its consequences. As for me, I must break off here, interrupt all this, close the parenthesis, and let the movement continue without me, take off again, or stop, arrest itself, after I simply note this: in everything that happens, it's as if the narrator desired (in other words forbad)—from the moment he comes to say "I" onward—one thing: that the two women should love one another, should meet, should be united in accordance with the *hymen*. Not [*pas*] *without him, and immediately without him.* That they, these two other women, others of the other, should not merely resemble each other but should be the same: this is what he desires, what he would die of, what he desires like the death that he would "give" himself. This is absolute terror: the bottomless boundless abyss of that which is single, unique—the other death, laughable, the most simply insignificant death, the most fatal. And immediately *la Chose* is its double. It remains [*reste*] its double. But now we shall be able to make out the *arrestance* of this *reste*.)

> At about ten o'clock Nathalie said to me:
> "I telephoned X., I asked him to make a cast of my head and my hands."
> Right away I was seized by a feeling of terror. "What gave you the idea of doing that?" "The card." She showed me a sculptor's card which was usually with the key in my wallet.

Should we say that he gave her the idea of or the desire for the death mask, as he had wished to embalm the other woman, in

---

(*Hemmung, Haltung*) *and immediately* disseminated. Sand. Empty, unloaded, discharged, of itself, spontaneously. In the trance of the *trans-*. On the word *transe,* the translators should quote *Glas,* at great length (e.g., p. 30). Trans/partition. *Trépas* [death: *trans-* + *passus*]. "Trespassing." To be related, without translation, to all the "trans-" 's that are at work here. I hope that they will not believe that, escorted by this mob, this

order to preserve both of them, to keep them alive-*and*-dead, living on? Yes *and* no. Yes, because it is indeed thanks to him, next to him, *on* him, that she *finds* this "idea," this direction, this destination, this address. No, because she *finds* them only by *stealing* them from him, from a place where he was hiding them, in a crypt, a crypt next to his body, clinging to his skin, the wallet, an object that is detachable from him, neither clothing nor itself a body, a safe containing other detachable objects, a card, keys, and the like. These detached objects are of a particular nature: they operate, orient, open, close; they make something readable or keep it secret. They, like the wallet that contains them, are not objects or simply things. "It seems to me you don't always behave very sensibly with that wallet," he tells her.

At this point the exchange of a "yes" takes a particular form and responds to specific demands (" 'Say yes,' and I took her by the hand [. . .]," then "I nodded [*je fis signe que oui*]. I was still holding her hand [. . .]") in the course of a scene that I cannot quote here. Then—as "yes" responds to nothing, nothing but the other "yes," itself—then the "terrible thing," the "victory over life," the "will to triumph" [*l' "intention triomphale"*], "glory," the "madness of victory" will all be evoked, named; then, too, will come the cry of "yes, yes, yes!"

> She looked so human, she was still so close to me, waiting for a sort of absolution for that terrible thing which was certainly not her fault.
>
> "It was probably necessary," I murmured.
>
> She snatched at these words.
>
> "It was necessary, wasn't it?"
>
> It really seemed that my acquiescence reverberated in her, that it had been in some way expected, with an immense expectancy, by

---

procession of doubles, ghosts, *transes, folies du jour,* manic jubilations and triumphs, I have produced here an underground or shady translation of *The Triumph,* and for example of "The crowd gave way, & I arose aghast/ Or seemed to rise, so mighty was the trance,/ And saw like clouds upon the thunder blast/ The million with fierce song and maniac dance/ Raging around; such seemed the jubilee. . . ." I have amassed

an invisible responsibility to which she lent only her voice, and that now a supreme power, sure of itself, and happy—not because of my consent, of course, which was quite useless to it, but because of its victory over life and also because of my loyal understanding, my unlimited abandon—took possession of this young person and gave her an acuity and a masterfulness that dictated my thoughts to me as well as my few words.

"Now," she said in a rather hoarse voice, "isn't it true that you've known about it all along?"

"Yes," I said, "I knew about it."

"And do you know when it happened?"

"I think I have some idea."

But my tone of voice, which must have been rather yielding and submissive, did not seem to satisfy her will to triumph.

"Well, maybe you don't know everything yet," she cried with a touch of defiance. And, really, within her jubilant exaltation there was a lucidity, a burning in the depths of her eyes, a glory which reached me through my distress, and touched me, too, with the same magnificent pride, the same madness of victory.

"Well, what?" I said, getting up too.

"Yes," she cried, "yes, yes!"

"That this took place a week ago?"

She took the words from my lips with frightening eagerness.

"And then?" she cried.

"And that today you went to X.'s to get . . . that thing?"

"And then!"

"And now that thing is over there, you have uncovered it, you have looked at it, and you have looked into the face of something that will be alive for all eternity, for your eternity and for mine! Yes, I know it, I've known it all along."

I cannot exactly say whether these words, or others like them, ever reached her ears, nor what mood led me to allow her to hear

---

references (to "things" and "texts," they would say) but in truth what I have just written is without reference. Above all, to myself or to texts that I have signed in another language. Precisely *because of* this jubilant multiplicity of self-references. "In order to come into being as text, the referential function had to be radically suspended" (Paul de Man, "The

them: it was a minor matter, just as it was not important to know if things had really happened that way. But I must say that for me it seems that it did happen that way, setting aside the question of dates, since everything could have happened at a much earlier time. But the truth is not contained in these facts. I can imagine suppressing these particular ones. But if they did not happen, others happen in their place, and answering the summons of the all powerful affirmation which is united with me, they take on the same meaning and the story is the same. It could be that N., in talking to me about the "plan," wanted only to tear apart with a vigilant [*jalouse*] hand the pretences we were living under. It may be that she was tired of seeing me perserve with a kind of faith in my role as man of the "world," and that she used this story to recall me abruptly to my true condition and point out to me where my place was. It may also be that she herself was obeying a mysterious command, which came from me, and which is the voice that is always being reborn in me, and it is vigilant too, the voice of a feeling that cannot disappear. Who can say: this happened because certain events allowed it to happen? This occurred because, at a certain moment, the facts became misleading and because of their strange juxtaposition entitled the truth to take possession of them? As for me, I have not been the unfortunate messenger of a thought stronger than I, nor its plaything, nor its victim, because that *thought,* if it has conquered me, has only conquered through me, and in the end has always been equal to me. I have loved it and I have loved only it, and everything that happened I wanted to happen, and having had regard only for it, wherever it was or wherever I might have been, in absence, in unhappiness, in the inevitability of dead things, in the necessity of living things, in the fatigue of work, in the faces born of my curiosity, in my false words, in my deceitful vows, in silence and in the night, I gave it all my strength and it gave me all its strength, so that this strength is too

Purloined Ribbon," in *Glyph 1.* Quote in full.). Transreference. How can one sign in translation, in another language? Living on—in/after whose name, in/after the name of what? How will they translate that? Of course, I have not kept my promise. This telegraphic band produces an untranslatable supplement, whether I wish it or not. Never tell what

great, it is incapable of being ruined by anything, and condemns us, perhaps, to immeasurable unhappiness, but if that is so, I take this unhappiness on myself and I am immeasurably glad of it and to that thought I say eternally, "Come," and eternally it is there.

---

you're doing, and, pretending to tell, do something else that immediately crypts, adds, entrenches itself. To speak of writing, of triumph, as *living on,* is to enunciate or denounce the manic fantasy. Not without repeating it, and that goes without saying.

# 4

## GEOFFREY H. HARTMAN

# Words, Wish, Worth: Wordsworth

### I

Thinking of walking with Dora in the English countryside, Wordsworth is waylaid by a Miltonic image from *Samson Agonistes* that makes his twelve-year-old daughter an Antigone leading the blind Oedipus:

> *"A LITTLE onward lend thy guiding hand*
> *To these dark steps, a little further on!"* *

Wordsworth suffered from severe eye-strain and feared to go blind. The fact is alluded to when he calls himself "not un-menaced" (9), but this merely qualifies a surprise he insists on: the usurpation of that text on his voice, and the anticipatory, proleptic nature of the thought. He records an involuntary thought having to do with privation, and which implies a halted traveler. He looks forward to the pleasure of walking with Dora, and instead of an easy progression from thought to fulfillment, from innocent wish to imaginative elaboration, something interposes darkly and complicates the sequence. The movement of fantasy is momentarily blocked; it no longer rises as easily and naturally as dawn but must precipitate itself as a Morning Voluntary: "From thy orisons / Come forth; and while the morning air is

---

* See p. 215 below for the entire text of the poem, preceded by a bibliographical note.

yet / Transparent as the soul of innocent youth, / Let me, thy happy guide, now point thy way . . ." (20–23).

Yet this active gesture or call—a kind of antistrophe to the opening invocation which had blocked him, for it restores an image of the poet as "natural leader"—this excursive voice is soon halted once more by images which revive, thematically now, and from within the wishful narrative, the anticipatory, even vertiginous power of imagination:

> Let me, thy happy guide, now point thy way,
> And now precede thee, winding to and fro,
> Till we by perseverance gain the top
> Of some smooth ridge, whose brink precipitous
> Kindles intense desire for powers withheld
> From this corporeal frame; whereon who stands
> Is seized with strong incitement to push forth
> His arms, as swimmers use, and plunge—dread thought,
> For pastime plunge—into the "abrupt abyss,"
> Where ravens spread their plumy vans, at ease!
>
> [23–32]

What happens here seems ordinary enough because it does not inspire an ecstatic utterance. There is no address to Imagination, as in *Prelude* VI: "Imagination—here that Power . . . That awful Power rose from the mind's abyss. . . ." But imagination, of course, has already risen from the "abrupt abyss" in the form of a voice, the quotation from *Samson Agonistes*—echoing back to *Oedipus at Colonus*—which opens the poem. It disturbs the course of time and nature, not only by foreshadowing a Wordsworth who is old and blind but also by reversing the roles of child and father. Though Wordsworth tries to normalize this sense of reversal (4–10), the disturbance lingers on, and his mood soon rises again to a prophetic pitch ("Should that day come"). At that point the halted voice turns deliberately outward and imports sounds from nature in order to restore its faith in natural continuity:

Should that day come—but hark! the birds salute
The cheerful dawn, brightening for me the east;
For me, thy natural leader . . .

[12–14]

The sun always rises, eventually, for Wordsworth. But the phantoms of imagination—glimpses of glory or privation, ancestral voices, blind thoughts—continue to cast over the cheerful scene a mingled light. Wordsworth's steps remain devious and halting, "dark steps," uncertain of a progress he affirms. Nature proves to be a temple (35 ff.) or school of awe, and the poet is drawn as if compulsively toward some "abrupt abyss," or "center whence those sighs creep forth / To awe the lightness of humanity" (*Ode to Lycoris*).

It is a sighing yet awe-inspiring voice which opens this poem. If Wordsworth's poetic thought has a beginning, it is in such a voice, or the visionary stir produced by it. We can give the voice a context, of course, yet we cannot humanize it completely. As its "invisible source" "deepens upon fancy" (*Ode to Lycoris*), the poet may associate it with oracular cave or Egerian grot or some other omphalos or sacred place. What is "a little further on" if not a *templum:* a destined or clearly demarcated spot, the locus of a death, and perhaps an exaltation? The opening quotation, like the poem as a whole, borders on that space: we hear a voice that is scarcely human speaking in words that are all too human. An afflicted man, part beggar, part prophet, looks from the extreme edge of his mortal being toward justification.

These liminal words, then, are close to being final words. They overshadow the poem and compel Wordsworth to an interpretive or reflective, rather than freely fictive, response. There cannot be many poems that begin with a quotation and develop against or in the shadow of it. Perhaps every poem does so, in the sense that the effaced or absorbed memory of other great poems motivates its own career. But not as directly as here, where the very status of poetry is challenged, since it seems to be neither oracular-visionary speech nor a purely reflective, mediated kind of language. It is both, undecidably: the poet is Major Man, free of guidance, and the source rather than dupe of oracles, but also one who continues to live in this problematic area of divine intimations.

There is indeed something oracular (inaugural may be the proper word) about the beginning of the poem. It is as if Wordsworth's spirit had been unconsciously playing at Sybilline leaves with Milton or the Classics. It is not the first time, of course, that the poet's voice is usurped by a visionary reflex or "trick of memory." Yet here the quasi-oracular source proves to be, via Milton, from the Classics, and is not only a passage but also a passage-way he must negotiate: the words perplex the poet like a dark omen whose psychic antecedents remain as obscure as the cry recorded in "Strange fits of passion."

Through the "dark passage," then, of a text surfacing in his mind, Wordsworth struggles to find a "passage clear" (52) that would lead him and Dora to a sublimer scene. That scene may possibly be the Alps (34–39) which he will visit on an anniversary trip in 1820, and toward which his thought turns after the war with France. But a repetition of the wish to guide Dora evokes at the end "heights more glorious still" and "shades more awful" (53f.) that seem to lie beyond nature. If Wordsworth is repeating his Alpine journey of 1790 in the spirit, he foresees a still further journey, until the image of blindness, so charged yet absurd at the beginning, reveals its truth at the close. For each new journey could increase his sense of loss. *Tintern Abbey* already suggests that loss and the need for borrowed sight: "and in thy voice I catch / The language of my former heart, and read / My former pleasures in the shooting lights / Of thy wild eyes." In the present poem we are "a little further on." There is no repetition in a finer tone but rather a "mournful iteration"—a phrase even more telling if it contains a pun on *iter,* the Latin word for journey.

# II

*. . . the childhood shows the man
As morning shows the day.*

MILTON, *Paradise Regained*

Interpreters have commented adequately on the poet's return to
Nature or memories of childhood and somewhat on his return to
the writers of Reformation England. Equally remarkable is his
regression, after 1801, to the Classics. It begins with a renewed
interest in the poets of the Reformation, who were also poets of
the Renaissance—who managed, that is, to revive the Classics as
well as Scripture.

The Classical sources, though, are almost as dangerous as
Imagination itself. Do not brood "o'er Fable's dark abyss,"
Wordsworth solemnly cautions us in 1820. It may be like the
abyss from which imagination springs in *Prelude* VI, or the
"abrupt abyss" that kindles in us "intense desire for powers
withheld" (27). The voice of Samson-Oedipus, rising so forcefully
from the mind's abyss, could represent the felt though repressed
power of pre-Christian literature: a power which, like Imagination,
points to the possibility of unmediated vision. Samson-Oedipus
himself, at this juncture in the drama, approaches divine status.

"A little onward" starts with a private psychic event, a well-
known text flashing on the poet's mind, yet ends with a peroration that shows unmistakably how intensely Wordsworth felt
about both Classical wisdom and Scripture. The peroration combines two inherited notions: that of the Book of Nature which
lies open to all eyes, and that of the Reformers "opening" the
Book of God for all to read:

> Now also shall the page of classic lore,
> To these glad eyes from bondage freed, again
> Lie open; and the book of Holy writ,
> Again unfolded, passage clear shall yield. . . .
>
> [49–52]

Wordsworth stops short of suggesting that the Classics are a kind of scripture, but he extends a principle shared by Milton, the Reformers, and the great scholars of the Renaissance, that we must go directly to the sources. Only then does reading lead to inspiration. When freed like Holy Writ from false mediation, classic lore may open itself to the private conscience as forcefully as at the beginning of this poem.

Wordsworth's movement toward the Classics is virtually as daring as his movement toward childhood. To reintegrate the Classics is not unlike reintegrating a childhood conceived as the heroic age of the psyche. But the association between childhood and early literature is not the usual primitivistic one. That would be impossible with the Classics which are called such because they appear to us incredibly mature. The reason for linking the Classics with youth or childhood is that pagan fable, rhetoric and history, were the literary staple of the young poet. Though trivialized by school routine and eighteenth-century usage, Wordsworth's republican sympathies and Milton's example kept them alive. And when childhood comes back, they come back. Commenting in the 1840's on the *Ode to Lycoris,* composed within a year or so of "A little onward," Wordsworth remarks: "Surely one who has written so much in verse as I have done may be allowed to retrace his steps in the regions of fancy which delighted him in his boyhood, when he first became acquainted with the Greek and Roman poets. . . . Classical literature affected me by its own beauty. But the truths of scripture having been entrusted to the dead languages, and these fountains having been recently laid open at the Reformation, an importance and a sanctity were at that period attached to classical literature that extended, as is obvious in Milton's *Lycidas,* for example, both to its spirit and form in a degree that can never be revived."

Yet the insistence of the Classics is not explained so easily, even if the poet himself could fall back on associationist psychology. There is very little urbane classicism in Wordsworth; and nothing, or almost nothing, of hellenistic "beauty" as Winckelmann conceived of it, and which affected so many European and

English writers. I would guess that Keats and Shelley were less radical in their understanding of the Classics than Wordsworth, though they were also less defensive. In Wordsworth's recollection of Classical texts there is often something involuntary, a sympathy not agreed to, or painfully hedged about. His difficult reserve has a pathos of its own that seems to go beyond the ordinary type of Christian scruple. Milton and Milton's use of the Classics recall to him a more absolute beginning: a point of origin essentially unmediated, beyond the memory of experience or the certainty of temporal location. A "heavenly" origin, perhaps, in the sense of the myth (already a mediating device) that the *Intimations Ode* presents, and which makes a heuristic use of Plato's notion of preexistence. This recession of experience to a boundary where memory fades into myth, or touches the hypostasis of a supernatural origin—as well as complete respect for that boundary—is what preoccupies the psyche of the poet. Only that boundary, uncertain as it is, separates in his mind childhood, the Classics, and divinization. The Classics, then, reach beyond religious or temporal mediation toward a dubious and dangerous point where "all stand single" (1850 *Prelude* III. 189).

The scene from Sophocles has, of course, a near-Christian pathos: humiliation precedes exaltation. Yet in terms of the poem, the reversed roles of daughter and father is what is most affecting, and it may carry us back to a famous text from Wordsworth's own poetry. Did he not write at the very onset of his reviving passion for the Classics, "The Child is Father of the Man?" And does this not disorder our temporal and genealogical perspective? If the thought becomes an axiom for modern developmental psychology, and for the poet himself the stone that marks a boundary he will not cross, it remains as scandalous a paradox as ever founded a poetry of experience.

The riddling image is part of an "extempore" lyric of 1802, "My heart leaps up when I behold / A rainbow in the sky." It affirms what Wordsworth calls "natural piety." Piety comes from a sphere of virtues associated with Classicism, and "natural piety" suggests something inborn, a gift of nature which should protect

nature. In 1816 "natural piety" is still there, in the image of Antigone as a "living staff" helping her father; and though the
poet's heart sinks rather than leaps up when the image of the
blind Oedipus comes into his mind, at least there is a strong "extempore" response: a negative leaping rather than none. That leap
could well go "beyond" or "outside" (ex) time: it points to a
more absolute power to begin, or to posit a beginning—as in
the poem of 1816. What seems to have changed, or intensified
into a haunting symbol, is the poet's fear that the time may come
when, blind or not, he will be spiritually blind to nature, autonomous even beyond his desire.

This fear is no late birth, however: it can be found in Wordsworth's earliest poetry, pervades *Tintern Abbey* and the blind
beggar episode of *Prelude* VII, and is inevitably mingled with
thoughts of Milton, or what would happen to his own "genial
spirits" were they to "find no dawn" (cf. *Paradise Lost* III. 24).
Until nature blanks out under the influence of imagination, or of
"The prophetic spirit . . . Dreaming on things to come,"
Wordsworth invokes no mediation except nature. And even
when obliged to recognize the future necessity of a wisdom that
is "blind" in the sense of being purely an inner light, he still
portrays it as dependent on nature as Oedipus is on Antigone.

"The Child is Father of the Man"—Antigone leading her father, or childhood nature returning upon the poet to guide him,
are different emblems of one truth. Childhood, or its continuous
role in the growth of the mind, is the truth Wordsworth discovers, and in the light of which he rejects all heroic and clas-
sicizing themes; but what is rejected returns and discovers itself
as a yet deeper childhood, capable of reaching through time and
renewing itself in the poetic spirit. If that is not the Wordsworthian Enlightenment, it must be the Wordsworthian
Renaissance.

# III

Wordsworth's poetry often describes a flashing on the inward eye.
An after-image or memory surprises the mental traveler. A wish

that has formed, sometimes unconsciously, or at least so naturally that no thought is taken of it, is suddenly made conscious by being defeated, crossed, or fulfilled in an unexpected way. The emphasis is on the strange fulfillment rather than on defeat; but precisely because of that, every anticipatory movement of the mind is attended by "anxiety of hope" (1805 *Prelude* XI. 372). The wish, whether active fantasy or vague daydream, tends toward fulfillment. Wordsworth screens, therefore, even the most innocent "leaping up" of eye and heart. Many of his poems, in fact, are simply reflections on "wayward" motions of the mind. The result is a consciously minor poetry, depressed yet psychically fascinating, which enacts that very distrust of *enthusiasm* limiting the greater part of eighteenth-century verse.

That the flash should take the form of a quotation clarifies further Wordsworth's relation to eighteenth-century verse: that is, to post-Miltonic or post-visionary writing. How much of it tends toward the condition of quotation, attenuated allusion and paraphrase! It has been argued that the sonnet by Gray severely criticized in the Preface to *Lyrical Ballads* should be read with quotation marks around its phraseology. Gray, it is suggested, knew the inadequacy of those words in the face of death. But what of the "sad incompetence of human speech" (1850 *Prelude* VI. 593) in the face of imagination? The visitings of imaginative power in Wordsworth put quotation marks even around nature. Thus the lines from *Samson Agonistes* that usurp the beginning of Wordsworth's poem are a fulfillment of literary velleities: they exalt the "borrowed voice" of eighteenth-century poetry. They give the glory to Milton, and to an imagination as privative as it is prophetic.

To represent Wordsworth as a Jonah evading the divine Word, or a privative imagination, may seem melodramatic. There is here no city, no Nineveh to prophesy against. But there is Wordsworth's knowledge that the imagination may not be on the side of nature. The voluntary or involuntary utterances that rise in him are not allowed to gain even an artificial ascendancy. He both acknowledges and refuses their vehicular, visionary power. Quotation or exclamation marks keep them in quarantine: no easy, integrating path leads from the absolute or abrupt image to the meditation that preserves it. Wordsworth does not solicit metaphors for poetry.

"A little onward" remains a *conspicuously* secondary response. The gambit offered by imagination is declined, and so, ultimately, is the opening toward a radical Classicism. Though the poem implies the wish, "Where Imagination was, the Classics shall be," Milton and Scripture and perhaps the strength of the Classics themselves interfere, and the wish becomes, "Where Imagination was, quotation shall be." An unmediated psychic event turns out to be a mediated text: words made of stronger words, of the Classics and the Bible, and suggesting even by their content the need for mediation. Wordsworth records scrupulously an inward action: *the incumbent mystery of text—as well as sense—and soul.*


# IV

The relation of "text" and "soul" is the province of a theory of reading. Although there have been many attempts (from I. A. Richards through Norman Holland, Stanley Fish and Wolfgang Iser) to understand the reading experience, and to draw a theory from actual or reported acts of reading, the matter is usually studied in divorce from the history of interpretation. Even when history enters, it does so as the social record of *Rezeptionsgeschichte* or as the structural record of the particular work's "indeterminacy," and not in connection with great movements in theology or political philosophy.

However, we must be able to talk of the reader both intrinsically, or as he is in himself, and historically, as someone set concretely in a changeable field of influence. Many contemporary thinkers are therefore not satisfied with viewing reading as a "practical" matter to be corrected or improved by some sort of training. They see it rather as a vital "praxis" imbued with theory, or ideological values. The rise of Protestantism, for ex-

ample, is not irrelevant to the reading experience, in Wordsworth's time or now. The claim that Scripture contemplated by
faithful minds would prove inspiring—that a priestly or institu-
tionally sanctioned hermeneutic was not a necessary mediation—
is at least analogous to our modern prejudice in favor of "critical"
reading and against methodological machinery. There has been,
of course, a recent revival of methodology, due to the parascien-
tific disciplines of structuralism and semiotics, on the one hand,
and increasing interest in medieval (Christian or Jewish) allegorical exegesis, on the other. But this has merely sharpened the
conflict between two types of reading: the direct or "inner light"
approach, inherently critical when applied to secular works, because it pits the wit ("ingenium," "natural light," "good sense")
of the reader against a text considered as potentially crucial or influential; and the learned, scientific, or philosophical approach,
which sees all works, secular or sacred, as deeply mediated constructs, not available to understanding except through a study of
history or of the intertextual character of all writing.

Wordsworth's poem suggests that we must read the writer as a
reader. The writer is a reader not only in the sense that he must
have read to write, and so is "mediated," however original his
work. He is a reader because of his radically responsive position
vis-à-vis (1) texts, and (2) an inner light—or inner darkness—
that enables his counter-word, the very act of interpretation itself. Reading is a form of life whether or not correlative, as in
Wordsworth, to a specific theology. But if we take Wordsworth's
poem of 1816 as paradigmatic, it suggests that when a theology
exists, even should that theology affirm direct inspection and the
efficacy of a principle of inner light, it requires historical study to
be appreciated. So that the conflict between direct and mediated
types of reading continues to operate.

The complexities do not end here. For there is, of course, a
metaphor in the concept of "inner light." Though it plays an important role from Augustine through Descartes, assumes a salient
position in the Reformation, and is continued in such derived
formulations as Heidegger's *"Lichtung,"* one wonders why the

correlative metaphor of "inner voice" was not found to be as appropriate.*

The emphasis on "light" rather than "voice" may be an unconscious and simple falsification. But it may also point to the repression of the oracular or enthusiast element in the reader. That is certainly the case in England where a conservative or Catholic protestantism is especially sensitive to the un-English nature of any ideology of inner voice. T. S. Eliot, whose poetry pastures on voices of all sorts—aurality being an essential aspect of its aura— still tries to disqualify, and savagely, the concept of inner voice as politically and religiously subversive. He attacks Middleton Murray who had claimed that "The English writer, the English divine, the English statesman, inherit no rules from their forebears; they inherit only this: a sense that in the last resort they must depend on the inner voice." Eliot smells a Romantic, populist and even daemonic heresy in this. "My belief is that those who possess this inner voice. . . . will hear no other. The inner voice, in fact, sounds remarkably like an old principle which has been formulated by an elder critic in the now familiar phrase of 'doing as one likes.' The professors of the inner voice ride ten in a compartment to a football match at Swansea, listening to the inner voice, which breathes the eternal message of vanity, fear, and lust."

I have quoted this skirmish to show how easily the idea of inner light when reconnected with that of inner voice becomes ideologically sensitive again. The metaphor is an explosive one. Yet we must honor the fact that Wordsworth's poem of 1816 begins with an "inner voice" usurping his voice. That inner voice also proves to be a text. It is the textual voice of Milton evoking the agony of Samson for whom the sun is dark, and "silent as the moon." It seems like a giant and awkward step to go from this to the Snowdon episode at the end of *The Prelude,* where the "voice of waters" roars up to the "silent light" of the moon. The circum-

---

*But see my discussion of "voice" in Heidegger, on pp. 206–7 below.

stances on Snowdon are, Wordsworth explicitly states, unusually awful and sublime (1805 *Prelude* XIII. 76); perhaps, then, the inner rising of Milton's voice, as in the poem of 1816, was more usual.

In any case, this silencing of light—the removing, by a kind of negative metaphor, of sound from light, or the addition to light of a now separated sound—is more than a figurative depiction of blindness. It occurs (very subtly circumstanced) in the opening stanzas (1, 2) of the *Intimations Ode*—and there too sound returns. Though no overt reversal (as on Snowdon) is found in the *Ode*'s third stanza, there is a feeling of discovery and relief. An inner source opens: it is as if Wordsworth, in the absence of "a sound-like power in light" (Coleridge), had uttered internally the wish "Let there be light," or more precisely, "Let there be sound, and light from sound." Not so much *son et lumière,* but the illumination that sound is. The reader's fiat, "Let the sources be opened," and the poet's "Now also shall the page . . . Lie open," begin to coincide when we shift to the "oracular cave" of the ear: "Strict passage, through which sighs are brought,/ And whispers for the heart, their slave" (*On the Power of Sound,* ll. 6–8).

## V

These lines, however, when followed by "And shrieks, that revel in abuse / Of shivering flesh" etc., suggest something quite specific, which explains why the ear's "oracular cave" is "dread . . . to enter" (ll. 5–6). Wordsworth evokes sounds of lust or passion ("How oft along thy mazes, / Regent of sound, have dangerous Passions trod," ll. 81–82), with a reserve that intensifies rather than veils the affect. One cannot separate in his description love-ecstasy from religious ecstacy or martial frenzy. We are in the realm of the passions, perhaps of their tenuous sublimation; and it is the stricken ear rather than stricken eye that leads us there, via resonances of other great Music Odes of the eighteenth century, including Collins's *The Passions, an Ode for Music.*

The "dread" is more than an abstract anxiety, then: the

"strict" of "strict passage" points at once to the ineluctable modality of hearing, its "constricted" nature which overdetermines sounds that all pass through the same narrow channel, and to the burden on heart and conscience, on moral response, which is imposed. The "incumbent mystery of sense and soul" includes the charged relation of "passion" to voice and hearing. "Strange fits of passion have I known: / And I will dare to tell, / But in the lover's ear alone, / What once to me befell."

"The sounding cataract haunted me like a passion," also foregrounds the word. These uses share an ambiguity: "passion" seems to mean a passionate utterance, as when someone is said to "fall into a passion." The word joins emotion and motion of voice. The "power in sound" takes a form that is vocal as well as verbal, like song—except there is no song, only a movement of voice heard internally, or in revery, or one that [vexes] its own creation" (1805 *Prelude* I. 47). Perhaps the term "lyrical ballad" indicates this excess of voice-feeling over the articulate word. The "power in sound" is the severe music of the signifier or of an inward echoing that is both intensely human and ghostly.

"Passion," in any case, is generally used in this meaningful way. Wordsworth begins *The Prelude* with an extempore effusion whose special character he then points out. He calls it, in fact, a "passion" (1805 *Prelude* I. 69) and even within the extempore passage the word is not unambiguous ("Pure passions, virtue, knowledge, and delight,/ The holy life of music and of verse" [1805, I. 53–54]). Wordsworth's narrative can almost be said to begin with "an Ode, in passion utter'd" (1805, V. 97), which the poet holds to our ear.

This intricate press of meanings in "passion" emerges explicitly later in *The Prelude:*

> whatsoe'er of Terror or of Love
> Or Beauty, Nature's daily face put on
> From transitory passion, unto this
> I was as wakeful, even, as waters are
> To the sky's motion; in a kindred sense

Of passion was obedient as a lute
That waits upon the touches of the wind.
                    [1805, III. 132–38]

Here the word is first used in its conventional sense (equivalent to elevated if volatile mood), then "in a kindred sense," that of passively evoked spontaneous utterance, as of the wind harp. A passion like that had inaugurated *The Prelude*. "O there is blessing in this gentle breeze" shows the poet responsive to "the touches of the wind." He expresses an aeolian mystery to which we now turn, that purifies the ear by its gentle touch, and removes us from heavy to lighter breathing.

# VI

*. . . my ear was touched*
*With dreams and visionary impulses.*

WORDSWORTH, *To Joanna*

To what extent is poetry the working through of voices, residues as explicit and identifiable as the usurping passage from Milton, or as cryptically mnemonic as rhythm and dream phrase? Freud insists that direct speech, when it occurs in dreams, is something previously heard, however radically the dream-work may change its context. Ideas of the inspired poet or the dictating muse also point to this realm where words are as ineluctable as images: we cannot choose but hear.

The poet, a famous definition holds, dreams with his eyes open, yet this latent pressure of voices or texts suggests he dreams with open ears. "The winds come to me from the fields of sleep" (Wordsworth, *Intimations Ode*). The winds must carry intimations, but do they come from fields in the poet's dreams, fields that are asleep because their virtue lies unregarded, wintry fields now moving towards new life, or fields elysian? What aeolian mystery is here? The context of the line in Wordsworth's *Ode* yields nothing but the surround of sound: trumpeting cataracts, mountain echoes, the shouts of a shepherd boy. These sounds open his ears, as if a luster that had faded from the eye could be restored through aural intimations: winds, words, echoes. The ear, naturally dark, searches a darkness that has befallen sight. "To the open fields I told / A prophecy" (1805 *Prelude* I. 59–60) reverses gratefully, or gives back amply, what has been received: the breeze, the winds, their words, now come from within the poet himself.

> Visionary Power
> Attends upon the motions of the winds
> Embodied in the mystery of words.
> There darkness makes abode, and all the host
> Of shadowy things do work their changes there. . . .
> [1805 *Prelude* V. 619–23]

Between the visionary power ascribed to words and the working dark of aural experience there must be a relation. Very often ears become eery in Wordsworth. "With what strange utterance did the loud dry wind / Blow through my ears!" (1805 *Prelude* I. 347–48). "At that time," Wordsworth adds, "I hung alone," just like an aeolian or abandoned harp, the poet's ears being the wind instrument. The actual context is his hunting for ravens' eggs, when he finds himself on a "perilous ridge" between earth and sky, "ill sustain'd" and "almost suspended by the blast." Sense itself, the direct referential meaning, is "almost suspended" by a curious verse-music that then leads into the simile: "The mind of Man is fram'd even like the breath / And harmony of music" (1805 *Prelude* I. 351–52). We hear, as well as see, the "motion mov'd" and the "louds" in "clouds." We wonder if ears and eyes have not opened beyond the "open fields."

Yet Wordsworth's prophecy to the fields is never formalized as a visionary distortion of words and world. The words remain familiar, and what their motion opens up is still fields and clouds. That there is referentiality, that we find some stability in this world, is the end that is praised. The means are troubling, however, that move the poet toward this happy end. "Ah me!" he sighs, enumerating the "discordant elements" that have inter-fused in his mind. Nature's means are visitations both gentle and severe, but even the gentle ones are described in terms that con-tain power. From earliest infancy Nature "doth open up the clouds, / *As at the touch of lightning*" (1805 *Prelude* I. 363 ff., my italics). That phrase approaches paradox, like "blast of harmony" (1805 *Prelude* V. 96).

Is there an equivalent in sound to this "touch of lightning?" A flash of sound, or thunder touch? I think this is what the poem of 1816 shows when it begins with the voice of Milton's Samson. Here too referentiality is maintained, in the sense that the usurp-ing voice is referred to a specific text. It is not a floating, ghostly intrusion: a hollow voice from some mysterious spot in the land-scape of the mind. The intertextual referent delimits the ghost-liness as we see *through* the text. Milton's voice opens up an ear in Wordsworth not blinded (darkened beyond memory) by that rev-elation.

We are close now to understanding Wordsworth's style: more precisely, the relation between textuality and referentiality. The poet's words are always antiphonal to the phoné of a prior experi-ence. Or, the prior experience is the phoné.

> [I] Have felt whate'er there is of power in sound
> To breathe an elevated mood, by form
> Or image unprofaned; and I would stand
> Beneath some rock, listening to sounds that are
> The ghostly language of the ancient earth,
> Or make their dim abode in distant winds.
> Thence did I drink the visionary power.
>                   [1805 *Prelude* II. 324–30]

By phoné I mean voice or sound before a local shape or human source can be ascribed. Wordsworth's antiphonal style—his ver-sion of "ecchoing song"—limits by quotation or self-institutionalizing commentary a potentially endless descent into the phantom ear of memory. We almost forget that, in the poem of 1816, something has reached through historical and personal time to claim a second embodiment. The moment is comparable in its very difference to when Milton falls into Blake's left tarsus and inspires a Christian pseudopod that marches on (*Milton*, Plate 15). The Miltonic voice becomes Blake's phantom limb. Yet Wordsworth's footing is radically different from Blake's: it has nothing of the confidence of "And did those feet in ancient times / Walk upon England's pleasant green." Wordsworth's voice has lost, or is always losing, its lyric momentum; formally it is hesitant, disjunctive, "dark steps" over places in nature or scripture aware of the "abrupt abyss" that may, again, open up.

It is Wordsworth's own writ, his own poem, that should be disclosed, yet by a fate for which the word Oedipal is appropriate, an oracular "Discourse of the Other" interposes, one that involves the relation of child and parent, or younger poet and elder. Reacting to these inner "passions" Wordsworth projects nature as something that speaks "rememberable things," as something that textualizes a phantom voice: perhaps "the ghostly language of the ancient earth," perhaps the language of dream image and phrase. The result is lyric poetry precariously extended, even *The Prelude*'s stumblingly progressive form: a lengthened night music, the residue of a long day's night.

# VII

*O first-created beam, and thou great Word,*
*Let there be light*

MILTON, *Samson Agonistes*

In Wordsworth trembling ears and enlightened ears go together. The path toward enlightenment leads through dark passages filled with strange sounds. To characterize what is heard as a "ghostly language" is already to humanize it by a metaphorical act that engages the drift of the entire *Prelude*. "My own voice cheered me," the poet says candidly at the outset, because it is a voice rather than the mutterings, sobbings, yellings and ghostly blowing echoes that are his ear-experience. When he adds, "and, far more, the mind's / Internal echo of the imperfect sound" (1850 *Prelude* I. 55–56) he suggests not only his hope for a perfected voice, his "cheerful confidence" that he will advance beyond the prelusive strains of this perambulatory pastoral (*paulo majora canamus*), but also his hope that he will master the echo-sphere—darkly numinous after-effects evoking the "dim abode" of a visionary geography which "unknown modes of being," "mighty Forms that do not live / Like living men" (1805 *Prelude* I. 425 f.) inhabit. Poetry is echo humanized, a responsive movement represented here in schematic form.

This progress toward a language which is human and timely, a word that dwells with and between men, remains uncertainly fulfilled. For the "power in sound" cannot be humanized by a sheer act of will or the arbitrariness of metaphorical speech. And the doctrine of the Logos ("In the beginning was the Word"), which evokes a parallel enlightenment ("A Voice to Light gave Being" is Wordsworth's allusion to it in *On the Power of Sound*), remains caught up in mystery. The Logos dwells with God and when it comes to men is not understood. The Light to which it gives Being lights a darkness that is uncomprehending. In the vision on Snowdon, however, which is the finale to *The Prelude*, Wordsworth recovers the "fellowship of silent light / With speaking darkness." The poet ascends the mountain and brings back the word. Yet even here sound does not come first but in the form of an antiphonal response from the abyss. What Wordsworth brings back, then, is a second that becomes a first: an antiphony that reverses the priority of "silent light" and shows itself to be coeval, even ante-phonal. The poet brings the speaking darkness to light; he transforms the power in sound into enlightened sound.

Thus Snowdon is a vision of mastery, though a peculiar one. The power in sound and the power in light, or ear and eye, or nature and mind, are asymmetrical elements that struggle toward what Wordsworth calls "interchangeable supremacy," "mutual domination." There is no single locus of majesty or mastery: it is doubled and troubled by shifts in the poet's interpretation of what he experienced. Though light begins by usurping the landscape (both internal and external), sound roars up in reclamation; and no cosmological or ontological position is reached that would resolve the conflict. Wordsworth's manuscript revisions also suggest radical metaphoricity rather than mastery: power is not unified or localized as the property of one place, organ or element; it is as "homeless" as the "voice of waters" itself. He may insist in the commentary (1850 *Prelude* XIV. 63 ff.) that what he saw was the "type" of a "majestic intellect," yet the most striking feature or "soul" (1805 *Prelude* XIII. 65) of the vision is an instance of *timely utterance* (*Intimations Ode,* l. 23).

I borrow this phrase to characterize the voice of waters roaring to the sky and into the poet's moonstruck mind. The force of their utterance replaces timelessness with timeliness. And what we hear, as these not-so-still and not-so-small voices break in, proves timely in three ways: they release the poet from a fixation, they make him stand in time once more, and their delayed response (their seeming untimeliness) is what endows them with timely, that is, antiphonal effect. They seem to make literal the logos-power as Wordsworth conceives it: "A Voice to light gave Being; / To Time. . . ."

## VIII

On Snowdon hearing replaces a state of non-hearing as a "voice" is disclosed. To say the voice is intelligible or that what is heard is readable would move beyond Wordsworthian premises, even if we accept the conjunction of ideas of time and voice in "timely utterance." For this phrase tells us nothing specific about what was uttered or whether what was uttered had an intelligible, that is, human language content.

I want to insist, however, that the reversal of "powers" on Snowdon includes the poet as reader of a prior and sacred text. There is a "first" text to which his stands as a "second," but this relation is reversible and the later utterance achieves its own firstness. What Wordsworth has done is to raise the antiphonal cues in his precursor text(s) to a new, a "second" power. He has created his own text by a verbal geometry that extends the lines of force in a prior scripture. The scripture in this case is Scripture.

For the "timely utterance" of the voice(s) heard on Snowdon parallels principally the *Let there be light* of Genesis, the first divine utterance that emerges from the brooding over chaos, and creates at once language and light. Light is uttered, and with light, time (the division of day and night), and with light and time the Word that the Gospel of Saint John rightly extracts from that fiat as having been "with" God. But in Wordsworth, and it constitutes a reversal, the breaking through of speaking darkness to silent light presupposes a separate fiat that had been overlooked and which rises up to claim equality or primordiality. It is as if the instancy of light—"For instantly a light upon the turf / Fell like a flash" (1850 *Prelude* XIV. 38–39)—had satisfied one wish in the psyche, but had roused another, which then suggests an infinite repetition (*Prelude* XIV. 71). *Let there be light* is the first wish, not consciously voiced by Wordsworth, but recalled into existence by the effect, *And there was light.*

Perhaps the very fact that light was given without a conscious or wishful motion of the voice raised in the poet the question of the status of voice. Prevenient light elides or usurps the consciousness of voice; the flash is there, magically, before one is aware of having wished or asked for it. There is, likewise, no explicit reflection that precedes the poet's consciousness of the voice of waters. Instead of *Let there be voice,* which must have been doubly intense if unuttered in Wordsworth, because the voice of that wish was elided both by the prevenience of light and the silent sky, we find that *And there was light* is followed as suddenly by *And there was voice.*

Thus two things are silenced in the episode: voice (temporarily) and the wish or fiat-form itself. Another way of putting it is to say that "Let there be" as a primordial wish, and "Let there be" as a primordial speech act (*voicing* desire) converge in the vision;

that this convergence is felt to be dangerous; and that an unauth-
orized or ur-fiat is repressed. Instead of the voice of Wordsworth's
wish only the responsive or antiphonal word is given, and not so
much as a word but as the image of a voice; and this pattern is
continued in Wordsworth's commentary on the vision, which
again prevents the coming to conscious voice of a primordial and
wishful calling. Though this calling is suggested (1850 *Prelude*
XIV. 93–99) and even viewed as the basis of poetic power, it appears in the main angelic and soothing, as if it took away rather
than imposed the consciousness of human autonomy, creative or
wilful. The 1805 *Prelude* talks of "peace at will" (XIII. 114), an
ambiguous formulation that while it stresses a "sovereignty
within," calming the will at will, also suggests an ultimate re-
nunciation of sovereignty ("Let Thy will be done"). The 1850 version clarifies that pacific urge:

> Hence, amid ills that vex and wrongs that crush
> Our hearts—if here the words of Holy Writ
> May with fit reverence be applied—that peace
> Which passeth understanding, that repose
> In moral judgements. . . .
>                                   [XIV. 124–28]

Yet Nature, however strong its presence, does not extinguish
the creative principle in the poet. The after-thought, by interpreting the spectacle on Snowdon as a grand emblem of responsive verse—as a magnified Davidic psalm, caught at the
source, at psychogenesis—allows Wordsworth to authorize himself in a movement analogous to the responsive *And God saw
. . . that it was good.* In his commentary Wordsworth blesses his
own vision.

# IX

*There darkness makes abode*

WORDSWORTH, *Prelude* V

Is there in Wordsworth a silenced ur-fiat? Considered in itself "Let there be" mingles desire and speech in a way that defeats ontological or even grammatical specification. "Let there be" . . . what? Can an *object* be supplied that really completes the fiat: that makes it a sentence? "Let there be" is so basic a "passion" that to add the word "voice" as its object sentences it to redundance, while all other objects delimit it. One feels that not an object of desire is called for but "something evermore about to be" (1850 *Prelude* VI. 608); and that the mood of the phrase at once goads and restrains the reality-hunger of an infinite will desiring omnipotent and manifest fulfilments. Yet fulfilment cannot be separated from responsiveness if "Let there be" asks for a response which is the object still to be created. Creation and response merge, even as imagination (infinitely wishful brooding) and intellectual love (socializing and excursive thought) cannot stand "dividually."

To separate out the verbal form of "Let there be" has its own precariousness: it is a peculiar form and if sounded reflexively could lead to self-cancelling equivocations. Perhaps it is enough to suggest that Wordsworth was haunted by the fiat as such, and sought to convert a divine or wilful imperative into a responsive or timely utterance—picking up toward this cues from sacred texts: from Genesis, Psalms, and *Paradise Lost* as a creation epic.

I leave moot the questions of whether there is a semiotic way of describing the demand-and-response structure of this word (the fiat) that is also a wish. What we do know is that as a word-wish it is always queered on its way to an utterance that might bring fulfilment. Utterance itself, that is, blocks or delays the wish or alters it. At once fiat and fit (read: "Strange fiats of passion have I known"), the status of the word-wish remains unresolved.

Every "passion" of words, then, is under the shadow of being a "strange fit"—or not fit at all, because the correspondence (the expected harmony) between word and wish has been disturbed. The blocking of the wish in utterance is also explicit at the beginning of "A little onward." The most intriguing episode of this kind, however, happens to be associated with Snowdon by continguity and theme: it occurs during the poet's experience of creative power on Salisbury Plain and is recorded in the penultimate book of *The Prelude* (1850, XIII. 279–349). Wordsworth describes himself falling into a revery or trance about the British past while traveling solitary over the desert-like plain:

> Time with his retinue of ages fled
> Backwards, nor checked his flight until I saw
> Our dim ancestral Past in vision clear;
> Saw multitudes of men, and here and there,
> A single Briton clothed in wolf-skin vest,
> With shield and stone-axe, stride across the wold;
> The voice of spears was heard, the rattling spear
> Shaken by arms of mighty bone, in strength,
> Long mouldered, of barbaric majesty.
> I called on Darkness—but before the word
> Was uttered, midnight darkness seemed to take
> All objects from my sight; and lo! again
> The Desert visible by dismal flames;
> It is the sacrificial altar, fed
> With living men—how deep the groans! the voice
> Of those that crowd the giant wicker thrills
> The monumental hillocks, and the pomp
> Is for both worlds, the living and the dead.

"I called on Darkness" is a fiat-style wish followed by immediate fulfilment. And it is as dramatic an episode of omnipotence of voice as Wordsworth's poetry affords. As a "fit," moreover, it is strange enough. Fulfilment comes in a peculiar and perhaps unexpected manner, "before the word / Was uttered." This may indicate nothing more than instantaneity. The 1805 version omits the phrase. But it may also indicate that, had it been uttered, the wish might have been blocked or tangled up in sublime feel-ings—as when an unconscious wish, hinging on the idea of Crossing the Alps, becomes conscious during the composition of the Simplon Pass episode in *Prelude* VI.

Or Wordsworth's utterance was not in time, and the darkness that came was not the darkness called. Unless he yielded to the horror encroaching on him during his trance, unless he became its accomplice (which is a possible interpretation), one could have expected him to wish for blankness, that is, a blanketing sort of darkness. But if his call was not uttered in time the darkness which came may have been the one that was to be averted, and he found himself in the grip of a vision of human sacrifice. (One darkness forestalls another, as one type of light another for the travelers who set out to see the sun rise from Snowdon.)

Equally remarkable is (1) that the episode shows a decreating rather than creating word, and (2) that whereas on Snowdon a timely utterance revealed "speaking darkness," here the poet speaks the darkness. Instead of uttering the primal fiat which conflates light and the word, Wordsworth may have approached an "unutterable" fiat conflating darkness and the word. This would explain the blocking or eliding of wish or fantasy (any "Let there be") in Wordsworth. The fiat is waylaid on its way to utter-ance because the poet is anxious lest he speak the opposite of a creating word—an untimely or "apocalyptic" word. He fears that "Let there be voice" will conflate with "Let there be darkness" to produce a "speaking darkness" and a flight of time (1850 *Prelude* XIII. 318–20) that may continue unchecked.

As Wordsworth, then, approaches the Apocalyptic there is his concern that "the furnace shall come up at last" (Christopher Smart). And that is what happens on Salisbury Plain almost as literal vision:

> and lo! again
> The Desert visible by dismal flames;
> It is the sacrificial altar, fed
> With living men—how deep the groans! . . .
> [1850 *Prelude* XIII. 329–32]

"The Desert visible . . ." is a version of Milton's hell, "No light/ But rather darkness visible." The "dismal flames," moreover, lead us back to the theme of voice, its mystery and efficacy. Druidic sacrifice is portrayed as the efficacious sacrifice of human voices:

> . . . how deep the groans! the voice
> Of those that crowd the giant wicker thrills
> The monumental hillocks, the the pomp
> Is for both worlds, the living and the dead.
> [1850 *Prelude* XIII. 332–35]

It is as if the assumption of visionary status by the poet (see 1850, XIII. 300ff.) must revive voices like these, ancestral, fearful, unenlightened. The tale punishes the teller: it is the price he pays for aspiring to potency of voice. That groaning or speaking darkness seems but an extension of his own voice which also spoke darkness.

Snowdon at once deepens and modifies dread of voice. It suggests that the *shift* from speech-act to spoken, from visionary voice to visionary text, is part of a vast metaphoric activity identifiable with creative power itself. To become "A power like one of Nature's" (1850 *Prelude* XIII. 312) is to produce such "mutations" or "transformations": "to one life impart / The functions of another, shift, create. . . ." Creativity appears as metaphoricity, and lodges in such shifts from voice to image and vice-versa.

The blocked or elided fiat in Wordsworth may therefore be described as a "mutation" that is muted. The fiat, whether considered as a primal text or as a primordial speech-act, expresses metaphoricity by lodging it in the formulaic and performative utterance of a sacred voice. Yet on Salisbury Plain, Snowdon, and in the poem that provided our starting point, the fiat is merely a "dark passage." Metaphoricity cannot terminate in the "dark deep thoroughfare" (1805 *Prelude* XIII. 64) of such texts, each of which discloses a radical shift that recovers from the primal fiat the image of a voice that called on darkness: whether to delimit it, or to honor its prior claim.

# X

*. . . divine respondence meet*

SPENSER, *The Fairie Queene*

The phrase "timely utterance" can be applied both to the fiat ("Let there be . . .") and to such ordinary wishes as "Let me, thy happy guide, now. . . ." Whatever the difference in imaginative intensity between extraordinary and ordinary wishes, there is a common link which extends also to the simplest form that wishing takes: "Good morning," or "This morning gives us promise of a glorious day." Greetings and blessings of this kind maintain their connection with the highest, most elaborate verbal forms: for example, with Milton's *On the Morning of Christ's Nativity,* which is but another "Good Morning" or "timely utterance." The poet, in the prologue to the hymn, puts the question to himself whether his voice can join the angel quire and honor the greatness of the event. "This is the month, and this the happy morn." He should, he must respond; and in Wordsworth, where ritual occasions are not so manifest, where a "living calendar" replaces that of fixed feasts, the burden of responsiveness is more continual, indefinite, self-imposed.

But if the poet is always under this obligation of "timely utterance," if "Let there be verse" is always incumbent, then the power of imagination cannot be only a blessing. It may come to vex its own creation (1805 *Prelude* I. 47). The creative will, or the wish to respond with timely utterance, and even to renew time by means of it, may become wilful and turn against what it wishes to bless; and "thereof come[s] in the end despondency and madness" (*Resolution and Independence*). The imagination may feel like Hamlet: "The time is out of joint. O cursed spite / That ever I was born to set it right."

The problem of response, in the case of Wordsworth, is not made easier by his understanding of the "power in sound." Ultimately or primordially this is the fiat power. It is not, then, only a matter of response but also of demand and potency. The fiat as a wish does not take the form of a blessing except retrospectively: it is a compelling call, a force exerted to make something, even time itself, conform. "There was a time, when. . . ." Then let that time come again.

It may be an innocent wish when Wordsworth looks forward to walking with his daughter in the English countryside. But his looking forward is also a looking back at scenes involved with memories and associations: he attempts to recapture the time that was, to read in Dora's eyes as in Dorothy's (*Tintern Abbey,* 11. 117 ff.). The utterance that darkens his wish, the usurping memory of Milton's text, is an obscure judgment on him which he answers in verses more reflective than imperious, verses that merely gain time by a characteristic *whiling.* His poem to Dora becomes a lingering, wayward iteration, a thrice-wishful journeying to transform a failed "Good Morning" into a blessing of what caused it to fail: that disconcerting and usurping Miltonic quotation. For the close of the poem joins together not only Dora's and William's hands but also Classical and Scriptural sources of inspiration. Text calls unto text, and Milton's assumption of the Classical tradition is involved. The bar, at least the literary bar, between Classical and Christian has been removed.

But what of the bar between father and daughter? Dora has entered her twelfth year, she is on the threshold of puberty. The Oedipal situation is there, whether or not it prompts those opening words from the literary unconscious. The displacements are complex yet it would not be difficult to understand them as an elaborate disguise of the incest wish. Dora emerging into womanhood may be assuming in the poet's mind a supportive role not unlike Dorothy's. The "guiding hand," by a crude if powerful reduction, would then point to a wished-for touch; the "intense desire for powers withheld" to what is repressed or prohibited; the final "hand in hand" to a union that looks beyond earthly and kinship bars (lines 43–48 would imply that the father prefers his daughter to withdraw as a nun rather than emerge from her orisons / horizons, cf. *Hamlet,* act 3, sc. 1). Through this Oedipal reading the timely utterance points to a transcendence or transgression of time, even as we recover the life-situation it responds to. The wish reveals a double structure of sublimative and regressive motivation; and the poet's voice darkens understandably as it verges on the unutterable blessing that consecrates union with Dora.

# XI

*Why then I'le fit you.*

Hieronymo, in Kyd's The Spanish Tragedy

It would be hard to distinguish, therefore, the wish for a "Now" from the wish for a "Thou" in the "timely utterance" of poetry. We have been concerned to reveal the structure, or phenomenology, of the word-wish in the form of the fiat, and also in the form of blessing (or curse). But "Now" and "Thou," those mutually echoing words, also play their part. I have elsewhere described their contribution to a "western," or residually epiphanic, style; and a full account would have to include their transmission through the predication language of both Classical and Christian hymnology.

Some theology is indispensable here. So Jacques Lacan, for instance, has tried to understand the "imperative Word" as it founds or maintains us in time. His theory of symbolic mediation, based at once on Freud and semiotics, views symbols as enveloping "the life of man in a network so total that they join together, before he comes into the world, those who are going to engender him 'by flesh and blood'; so total that they bring to his birth, along with the gifts of the stars, if not with the gifts of the fairies, the shape of his destiny; so total that they give the words that will make him faithful or renegade, the law of the acts that will follow him right to the very place where he *is* not yet and even beyond his death; and so total that through them his end finds its meaning in the last judgement, where the Word absolves his being or condemns it—unless he attain the subjective bringing to realization of being-for-death." Through such a theory we touch again the lost imagination of theology, or what used to go under the name of a "theology of the poets." Carlyle does not do better in *Sartor Resartus*.

To many contemporary thinkers theology remains a junkyard of dark sublimities. Littered with obsolete and crazy, or once powerful now superstitious ideas, it emits at best no light but rather darkness visible. The contemporary mind prefers a semiotic theory of symbolic mediation, however complicated by Freudian insights. Yet there has been a discernible movement of recovery, to which, in addition to Lacan, such different rabbis as Gershom Scholem, Owen Barfield, Walter Benjamin, Erich Auerbach (on "figura") and Kenneth Burke (on Augustinian "logology") have contributed.

The most effective *countertheological* movement at present is Jacques Derrida's post-Heideggerian analysis of voice, or "timely utterance." It focusses on the deceptive relation between speech acts and being-in-time. Utterance discloses the relation of human wishes to existence yet also complicates rather than resolves wishing, for the latter does not disappear into time. It reveals, through such phenomena as texts, an "untimely," that is, residual and deferred element. The eclipse of voice by text is valorized, in the wake of Heidegger's analysis of temporality and of the "call" (*Ruf*) or "voice" (*Stimme*) of conscience. Heidegger describes conscience as a mode of discourse not dependent on vocal utterance, but which "in calling gives us to understand" (*Being and Time*, paragraphs 55ff.). This silent discourse (Derrida will see it as characteristic of textuality) reveals that the "voice" of conscience, or the guilt and care inherent in human nature, are not echoes of prior events, that is, prehistorical or pretemporal constitutions. They are characteristics of *Dasein*, human existence in time, and are inauthentically interpreted by theological, historical and psychologistic positivisms.

Though Heidegger, then, cannot avoid the metaphor of "voice," he effectively cancels its divine or psychogenetic status. His analysis of the discourse of conscience is of something that "speaks silence," that mutes the directly communicative, affective or performative, word. According to Heidegger even inner speech, or the dialogue of self with self, may be an evasion of human responsibility. (We can think of the clammy intimacy of certain novels or interior monologues, which evade guilt by means of their contagious, all-embracing confession.) Structures of congruence or correspondence, which substitute harmony for hierarchy—demand satisfied, expectation fulfilled, or the desired convergence of voice and act in utterance—reveal not truth but rather untruth: the failure to "overhear" oneself, or an erroneous "mishearing" (mistaking of the self, *Sichverhören*) which shows we cannot seize ourselves in time. We have no authentic way of passing judgment on ourselves. We must continue to live, *unpurged by voice, ours or another's,* in guilt or debt or responsibility. We live with these death-feelings, then, toward a death that resolves them.

The prematurity of voice—its pathos of presence, its peculiar, proleptic ecstacy, its capable self-exculpation—is exposed also by Derrida's technique of "deconstruction." Yet the greatest deceit voice has practiced is to represent itself as repressed by the written word. Derrida argues that it is writing that really suffered the repression, by being considered a mere reduction or redaction of the spoken word. So the interpreter zealously redeems the buried voice of the text instead of understanding how texts eclipse voice and speak silence. There is no authentically temporal discourse, no timely utterance, except by resolute acts of writing. It is in writing that the "subjective" attains, to quote Lacan's paraphrase of Heidegger, a "bringing to realization of being-for-death." Writing, as an individual or collective process, defers utterance of the definitive *parole* or password—from generation to generation.

Against Husserl, Heidegger, and a certain kind of philosophical technique, I hope to have shown that it is not necessary to bracket "natural experience," psychology, or ordinary language, in order to disclose the structure of "timely utterance." (Derrida's bracketing, his parenthesis style, is both more sly and obvious: every referent or "thing" is deferred, and this movement of *différance,* identified with writing, discloses no "thing.") By starting with a simple if miscarried wish, a given of human nature as uni-

versal as can be found, it was possible to trace the complex inter-
actions of poetry with that wish. I had no recourse to a special
interpretive system like psychoanalysis, although taking a wish
as my starting point, and recognizing its devious connexions to
voice and time, were prompted by that movement. Yet I did not
try and reduce the wish to something prior or deeper; and I made
no decision, in particular, on the priority of wish to word. The
notion of word-wish, and of its prototype in the fiat, may be
useful for a future reflection on the relation of wish, speech act
and text, especially when the text is poetic or visionary. But
again, while appreciating the area of concern focussed on in
speech act theories, I have not depended on them.

Wordsworth wrote in his famous "spousal verse" published as a
Prospectus to the uncompleted *Recluse:*

> . . . my voice proclaims
> How exquisitely the individual Mind
> (And the progressive powers perhaps no less
> Of the whole species) to the external World
> Is fitted:—and how exquisitely, too—
> Theme this but little heard of among men—
> The external World is fitted to the Mind. . . .

Annotating this Blake commented: "You shall not bring me
down to believe such fitting & fitted I know better & Please your
Lordship." Blake is not wrong. He sensed the debt this passage
owed to the theological and rhetorical principle of accommo-
dation. God's truth, any great truth, must be accommodated—fitted—to human understanding. Like Heidegger, Blake
rejected this principle (or idiom) which claimed to redeem what
the former calls "natural experience" and the latter "natural
man." But their rejection is itself strongly redemptive: it rids us
also of a condescending view of human power ("bring me down,"
"Please your Lordship") implied by the need to accommodate
truth to human perception. We might put it this way: fitting has
to do with tailoring, not with creating.

Yet the content of the passage in Wordsworth is creation: "the creation (by no lower name / Can it be called) which they [the Mind and the external World] with blended might / Accomplish." Wordsworth's "fitting and fitted" tries to respect the "blended might," that is, the "interchangeable supremacy" or "mutual domination"—the mobile, responsive, reciprocal factor—in the fiat; and he goes so far as to say, in verses introducing the visionary experience on Salisbury Plain (but more apt for what follows on Snowdon), that there is a creative passion in both nature and the mind:

> I felt that the array
> Of act and circumstance, and visible form,
> Is mainly to the pleasure of the mind
> What passion makes them; that meanwhile the forms
> Of Nature have a passion in themselves,
> That intermingles with those works of man
> To which she summons him. . . . .
>
> [1850 *Prelude* XIII. 287–93]

Strange fit of passions, indeed! The poet like the prophet, he continues, has a peculiar faculty, "a sense that fits him to perceive/ Objects unseen before" (1850, XIII. 304–05). Though the meaning of "fits" is plainly enough "accommodates," can we avoid hearing "that causes fits to fall on him, like on prophets of old, visions that make him perceive . . . ?" That the word "fit" should become so divided against itself, capable of expressing both responsive adaptation and imaginative frenzy, points to the problem of all poetry with a creative or visionary claim. The fiat, its pressure on vision and utterance, can become a fit nothing could modify. Against that possibility Wordsworth writes, wishfully perhaps, yet consuming nothing but the voice of his wish.

## XII

I end by returning to a beginning: that of *The Prelude*. This poem opens like "A little onward" with a quotation. But the poet quotes himself, not Milton; and the "passion" expressed is that of poetry as it seeks to be an extemporaneous response to "present joy." The Wordsworthian text inspires itself before our ears: made of nothing more than a breeze, a feeling, a minimalist impulse ("saved from vacancy"), it is shadowy and insubstantial without being overtly visionary. The fifty-odd verses of this prelude to *The Prelude* are but a recovered or extended breathing ("I breathe again!" 1805, I. 19), and can be compressed into a sentence made of their first and last lines:

    1   Oh there is blessing in this gentle breeze
    54  The holy life of music and of verse.

What does it amount to? The breathing apostrophic O, the facticity of "There is" (cf. *"Es gibt,"* or the balladic "There is," "It is"), the sense, in this present, of not being able to distinguish between the pure movement of a voice that blesses and the prompting impulse, so that voice and blessing, voice and wish, become as one, the wish being for voice and voice elaborating the wish—it adds up to nothing progressive, to nothing but a new, confident, even self-originating textuality. The text is built almost *ex nihilo,* yet exposes in its course (it finds, as it goes on, feeding-sources in the Classics, Scripture, and Milton) the problematic of giving and receiving, of nourishing and being nourished, of self-tasking and being tasked, which is the dilemma of emergent maturity (the growth of the poet's mind) as well as a point at issue between Coleridge (the friend addressed) and Wordsworth.

If, in the event, Wordsworth fails to make a "present joy" the "matter" of his song, it is because a "present," in the sense also of "gift" (cf. the virtual pun in Milton's "Say heavenly Muse, shall not thy sacred vein / Afford a present to the infant God?"), proves to be an effect of grace and not of work, of divine rather than human and self-inaugurated power. The question is again that of achieving a "timely utterance" rather than an involuntary or self-provoked one. Is there a present (time) that is a present (gift) without detracting from the mind's reciprocal, reciprocating power?

Poetry, in Wordsworth, names that ideal moment of "blended might" or "interchangeable supremacy." Yet despite "Eolian visitations" (1805 *Prelude* I. 104), the poet's time may not have come. In Milton's *Nativity Ode*, the time is given ("This is the month, and this the happy Morn") and justifies the poet who joins his voice to the sacred quire. In *Lycidas*, however, the occasion though solemn is less compelling: there is doubt expressed in "forced fingers rude" and "season due": perhaps *Lycidas* is a pretext for a questionable trial of strength (cf. 1850 *Prelude* I. 94ff. "my soul / Once more made trial of her strength. . . ."). It is not a "timely-happy" moment and Milton calls for "lucky words."

Compared to *The Prelude*, "A little onward" begins with an *untimely* utterance. Though the latter is still in the form of a quotation that represents a direct movement of speech, the words seem to have come, extempore, to the wrong voice and confuse the speaker's relation to time. Elsewhere too Wordsworth records utterances which make it hard for him to read the time. "The clock / That told, with unintelligible voice, / The widely parted hours," as he watches (outside Gravedona) the "dull red image of the moon" from "hour to hour . . . as if the night / Had been ensnared by witchcraft" (1850 *Prelude* VI. 700–22), almost literalizes that kind of experience. Has he called on darkness without knowing it? He seems to have become, like Hamlet, "cursed" in a time out of joint.

Indeed, there are Shakespearian as well as Miltonic echoes evoked by this sense of the untimely event. A famous "spot of time" (1805 *Prelude* XI. 345–89) recounts how the young Wordsworth climbed a crag overlooking the meeting-point of two highways to watch for the horses that would take him home for the Christmas vacation. There he waits "in anxiety of hope," a single sheep on his right hand and a whistling (1850: blasted) hawthorn on his left. He is, as it were, at the crossroads of a stark clock. He strains his eyes, watching the mist advancing on the line of each of those two roads in "indisputable shapes"—an episode followed shortly by his father's untimely death. "You come most carefully upon your hour," one guard says to the other near the beginning of *Hamlet* as they wait for the "questionable shape" of Hamlet's father's ghost. The boy's wish, innocent enough, that the time pass quickly, that he see what is to come, darkens retrospectively into a sense of his transgressive relation to time, associated with Shakespearean complexities. One event follows another too fast, like the marriage the funeral in *Hamlet*. The boy's father dies; and the boy feels obscurely that he called on darkness without knowing it, that he cursed the time which now curses him. It is "desire," i.e., the omnipotence of thoughts or imagination, that is corrected. "How awful is the might of souls / And what they do within themselves" (1850 *Prelude* III. 180f.). Such childhood experiences provide a basis for the poet's sublimely absurd invocation of the Child as "Mighty Seer" in the Great Ode.

Perhaps the strangest of these episodes is a poem composed "almost extempore" in the groves of Alfoxden and included in *Lyrical Ballads* of 1798. This poem, *The Idiot Boy*, finds its climax in an "answer" to a "question" which the mother puts to Johnny after his abortive night ride. " 'Tell us Johnny, do, / Where all this long night you have been, / What you have heard, what you have seen.' " But the poet himself had already given up this wish for a story. "O reader! now that I might tell / What Johnny and his horse are doing! / What they've been doing all this time. . . ." He cannot tell; he feels unable to pursue a "delightful tale" (despite some speculation on his part), because what may have happened is inward to the idiot boy. We, the reader, learn nothing of all that adventure except the women's anxiety as Johnny fails to return—an anxiety linked to the clock ("The clock is on the stroke of twelve, / And Johnny is not yet in sight")—and the few words Johnny utters:

> 'The Cocks did crow to-who, to-who
> And the sun did shine so cold.'

Is this not the very type of an "untimely utterance," this quotation which is "all his travel's story," and which hovers undecidably between mournful and gleeful iteration?

In a peculiar and moving comment on idiots Wordsworth remarked that their life was with God. We are bound to ask, after our lengthy analysis of "A little onward," where the life of such a poem is. For it is both a minor *poem* and a considerable *text*. In this case, the order of poetry and the order of texts seem to diverge. It is just possible, of course, that the distinction will prove false. We may have to conclude either that such poems are weak, and redeemed only by the responsive interpreter, or that they have the sort of strength we are not yet fit to perceive: that our present image of great poetry stands in the way of their peculiar textual quality. Eventually there might be a new convergence, and certain of Wordsworth's minor poems might be seen for what they are, and accorded the esteem that accrues, say, to Milton's minor pieces.

Time will tell. Yet time, precisely, is at issue. The life of Wordsworth's lines is often uneasy and as if somewhere else: still to be manifested by the action of time or the utterance of future readers. One could apply to Wordsworth what he says of the idiot boy: "You hardly can perceive his joy." We should not forget that Wordsworth's greatest poem remained hidden, and that its power and authority (in the light of which we *now* read everything else) was but alluded to in the rest of his oeuvre. At its curious worst this allusive manner can produce the stylization we find in ll. 34–39 of "A little onward" (referring to the Alps); but there is also a general effect of indirect or inner reference. Keeping *The Prelude* in reserve, almost like God his own Son, Wordsworth reposed on a text-experience whose life remained with God. He delayed becoming the author of a poem so original that it could not be accommodated to known forms of Christianity. In what he does publish, then, the relation of author to poem is often the strangest mixture of knowingness and childlikeness—it is, in short, a divine idiocy. The intertextual glitter of Milton, his blended might of Scripture and Classical lore, is but an undersong to Wordsworth's intratextual strain that repeats something already begotten in himself.

## TEXT OF POEM
## AND BIBLIOGRAPHICAL NOTE

For the text given below, see E. de Selincourt, *The Poetical Works of William Wordsworth*, vol. 4 (Oxford: Clarendon Press, 1947), pp. 92–94 (by permission of Oxford University Press). In his Notes to the same volume de Selincourt lists other echoes of Milton (p. 422). There are also curiously inwrought allusions to scenes involving the blinded Gloucester in Shakespeare's *King Lear*. I discuss these in "Diction and Defense in Wordsworth," *Psychiatry and the Humanities*, ed. Joseph H. Smith, vol. 4 (New Haven, 1980). Coleridge's fragmentary *The Wanderings of Cain* (composed in 1798, during the ferment leading to *Lyrical Ballads*) had already imitated that pathetic "A LITTLE further. . . ." The allusion to Antigone is reinforced by the original version of line 11, which reads in all editions up to 1850, "O my Antigone, beloved child!" rather than "—O my own Dora, my beloved child!" The only extended discussion of the poem so far is by Leslie Brisman in *Milton's Poetry of Choice and Its Romantic Heirs* (Ithaca, 1973), chapter 5. Brisman emphasizes not only the debt to Milton but also how "Wordsworth achieves some of his finest moments by turning to Milton" and "takes the Miltonic sublime 'a little onward.' " He seeks to modify Harold Bloom's insistence on the sublime but restrictive shadow Milton throws on later poetry. On Wordsworth and voice, the most detailed studies have been by John Hollander: "Wordsworth and the Music of Sound," in *New Perspectives on Coleridge and Wordsworth*, ed. G. H. Hartman (New York, 1972) and his Churchill College Lecture, *Images of Voice* (Cambridge, England, 1970). Cf. also my *The Fate of Reading*, pp. 195f. and 288–92. Derrida's response to Heidegger on the issue of voiceless voice, conscience and writing is most succinctly set forth in *De la grammatologie* (Paris, 1967), pp. 31ff. For the quotations from Eliot in section IV, see his "The Function of Criticism" (1922), and for the quotation from Lacan in section XI, see his "Discours de Rome" (1953), "The function and field of speech and language in psychoanalysis," *Ecrits: A Selection* (New York, 1977), p. 68. With regard to the Oedipal interpretation of the poem ventured in section X, cf. my "The Voice of the Shuttle," in *Beyond Formalism* (New Haven, 1970), which tries to link a theory of life to a theory of literary condensation. The forbidden convergence of life-lines through the incest wish (more properly phrased, through a desire for union despite kinship bars) elides temporal

and historical structures; and poetry's "timely utterance" allows time for
that wish to be gratified in the very lineaments of delay.

> "A LITTLE onward lend thy guiding hand
> To these dark steps, a little further on!"
> —What trick of memory to my voice hath brought
> This mournful iteration? For though Time,
> The Conqueror, crowns the Conquered, on his brow
> Planting his favourite silver diadem,
> Nor he, nor minister of his—intent
> To run before him, hath enrolled me yet,
> Though not unmenaced, among those who lean
> Upon a living staff, with borrowed sight.
> —O my own Dora, my belovèd child!                    10
> Should that day come—but hark! the birds salute
> The cheerful dawn, brightening for me the east;
> For me, thy natural leader, once again
> Impatient to conduct thee, not as erst
> A tottering infant, with compliant stoop
> From flower to flower supported; but to curb
> Thy nymph-like step swift-bounding o'er the lawn,
> Along the loose rocks, or the slippery verge
> Of foaming torrents.—From thy orisons              20
> Come forth; and while the morning air is yet
> Transparent as the soul of innocent youth,
> Let me, thy happy guide, now point thy way,
> And now precede thee, winding to and fro,
> Till we by perseverance gain the top
> Of some smooth ridge, whose brink precipitous
> Kindles intense desire for powers withheld
> From this corporeal frame; whereon who stands
> Is seized with strong incitement to push forth
> His arms, as swimmers use, and plunge—dread thought,   30
> For pastime plunge—into the "abrupt abyss,"
> Where ravens spread their plumy vans, at ease!
>
>     And yet more gladly thee would I conduct
> Through woods and spacious forests,—to behold
> There, how the Original of human art,
> Heaven-prompted Nature, measures and erects
> Her temples, fearless for the stately work,

Though waves, to every breeze, its high-arched roof,
And storms the pillars rock. But we such schools
Of reverential awe will chiefly seek                    40
In the still summer noon, while beams of light,
Reposing here, and in the aisles beyond
Traceably gliding through the dusk, recall
To mind the living presences of nuns;
A gentle, pensive, white-robed sisterhood,
Whose saintly radiance mitigates the gloom
Of those terrestial fabrics, where they serve,
To Christ, the Sun of righteousness, espoused.

Now also shall the page of classic lore,
To these glad eyes from bondage freed, again            50
Lie open; and the book of Holy writ,
Again unfolded, passage clear shall yield
To heights more glorious still, and into shades
More awful, where, advancing hand in hand,
We may be taught, O Darling of my care!
To calm the affections, elevate the soul,
And consecrate our lives to truth and love.

# 5

## J. HILLIS MILLER

# The Critic as Host

> *"Je meurs où je m'attache,"* Mr. Holt said with a polite grin. "The ivy says so in the picture, and clings to the oak like a fond parasite as it is."
> "Parricide, sir!" cries Mrs. Tusher.
>
> *Henry Esmond,* Bk. I, ch. 3

## I

At one point in "Rationality and Imagination in Cultural History" M. H. Abrams cites Wayne Booth's assertion that the "deconstructionist" reading of a given work "is plainly and simply parasitical" on "the obvious or univocal reading."[1] The latter is Abrams' phrase, the former Booth's. My citation of a citation is an example of a kind of chain which it will be part of my intention here to interrogate. What happens when a critical essay extracts a "passage" and "cites" it? Is this different from a citation, echo, or allusion within a poem? Is a citation an alien parasite within the body of the main text, or is the interpretive text the parasite which surrounds and strangles the citation which is its host? The host feeds the parasite and makes its life possible, but at the same time is killed by it, as criticism is often said to kill literature. Or can host and parasite live happily together, in the domicile of the same text, feeding each other or sharing the food?

Abrams, in any case, goes on to add "a more radical reply." If "deconstructionist principles" are taken seriously, he says, "any history which relies on written texts becomes an impossibility"

(p. 458). So be it. That's not much of an argument. A certain notion of history or of literary history, like a certain notion of determinable reading, might indeed be an impossibility, and if so, it might be better to know that. That something in the realm of interpretation is a demonstrable impossibility does not, however, prevent it from being "done," as the abundance of histories, literary histories, and readings demonstrates. On the other hand, I should agree that the impossibility of reading should not be taken too lightly. It has consequences, for life and death, since it is incorporated in the bodies of individual human beings and in the body politic of our cultural life and death together.

"Parasitical"—the word suggests the image of "the obvious or univocal reading" as the mighty oak, rooted in the solid ground, endangered by the insidious twining around it of deconstructive ivy. That ivy is somehow feminine, secondary, defective, or dependent. It is a clinging vine, able to live in no other way but by drawing the life sap of its host, cutting off its light and air. I think of Hardy's *The Ivy-Wife* or of the end of Thackeray's *Vanity Fair*: "God bless you, honest William!—Farewell, dear Amelia—Grow green again, tender little parasite, round the rugged old oak to which you cling!"

Such sad love stories of a domestic affection which introduces the parasitical into the closed economy of the home no doubt describe well enough the way some people feel about the relation of a "deconstructive" interpretation to "the obvious or univocal reading." The parasite is destroying the host. The alien has invaded the house, perhaps to kill the father of the family in an act which does not look like parricide, but is. Is the "obvious" reading, though, so "obvious" or even so "univocal"? May it not itself be the uncanny alien which is so close that it cannot be seen as strange, host in the sense of enemy rather than host in the sense of open-handed dispenser of hospitality? Is not the obvious reading perhaps equivocal rather than univocal, most equivocal in its intimate familiarity and in its ability to have got itself taken for granted as "obvious" and single-voiced?

"Parasite" is one of those words which calls up its apparent opposite. It has no meaning without that counterpart. There is no parasite without its host. At the same time both word and counterword subdivide. Each reveals itself to be fissured already within itself, to be, like *Unheimlich, unheimlich.* Words in "para," like words in "ana," have this as an intrinsic property. "Para" as a prefix in English (sometimes "par") indicates alongside, near or beside, beyond, incorrectly, resembling or similar to, subsidiary to, isomeric or polymeric to. In borrowed Greek compounds "para" indicates beside, to the side of, alongside, beyond, wrongfully, harmfully, unfavorably, and among. Words in "para" form one branch of the tangled labyrinth of words using some form of the Indo-European root *per.* This root is the "base of prepositions and preverbs with the basic meaning of 'forward,' 'through,' and a wide range of extended senses such as 'in front of,' 'before,' 'early,' 'first,' 'chief,' 'toward,' 'against,' 'near,' 'at,' 'around.' "[2]

If words in "para" are one branch of the labyrinth of words in "per," the branch is itself a miniature labyrinth. "Para" is a double antithetical prefix signifying at once proximity and distance, similarity and difference, interiority and exteriority, something inside a domestic economy and at the same time outside it, something simultaneously this side of a boundary line, threshold, or margin, and also beyond it, equivalent in status and also secondary or subsidiary, submissive, as of guest to host, slave to master. A thing in "para," moreover, is not only simultaneously on both sides of the boundary line between inside and out. It is also the boundary itself, the screen which is a permeable membrane connecting inside and outside. It confuses them with one another, allowing the outside in, making the inside out, dividing them and joining them. It also forms an ambiguous transition between one and the other. Though a given word in "para" may seem to choose univocally one of these possibilities, the other meanings are always there as a shimmering in the word which makes it refuse to stay still in a sentence. The word is like a slightly alien guest within the syntactical closure where all the words are family friends together. Words in "para" include: parachute, paradigm, parasol, the French *paravent* (windscreen), and *parapluie* (umbrella), paragon, paradox, parapet, parataxis, parapraxis, parabasis, paraphrase, paragraph, paraph, paralysis, paranoia, paraphernalia, parallel, parallax, parameter, parable, paresthesia, paramnesia, paramorph, paramecium, Paraclete, paramedical, paralegal—and parasite.

"Parasite" comes from the Greek *parasitos,* "beside the grain," *para,* beside (in this case) plus *sitos,* grain, food. "Sitology" is the science of foods, nutrition, and diet. A parasite was originally something positive, a fellow guest, someone sharing the food with you, there with you beside the grain. Later on, "parasite" came to mean a professional dinner guest, someone expert at cadging invitations without ever giving dinners in return. From this developed the two main modern meanings in English, the biological and the social. A parasite is "Any organism that grows, feeds, and is sheltered on or in a different organism while contributing nothing to the survival of its host"; or "A person who habitually takes advantage of the generosity of others without making any useful return." To call a kind of criticism "parasitical" is, in either case, strong language.

A curious system of thought, or of language, or of social organization (in fact all three at once) is implicit in the word parasite. There is no parasite without a host. The host and the somewhat sinister or subversive parasite are fellow guests beside the food, sharing it. On the other hand, the host is himself the food, his substance consumed without recompense, as when one says, "He is eating me out of house and home." The host may then become host in another sense, not etymologically connected. The word "host" is of course the name for the consecrated bread or wafer of the Eucharist, from Middle English *oste,* from Latin *hostia,* sacrifice, victim.

If the host is both eater and eaten, he also contains in himself the double antithetical relation of host and guest, guest in the bifold sense of friendly presence and alien invader. The words "host" and "guest" go back in fact to the same etymological root: *ghos-ti,* stranger, guest, host, properly "someone with whom one has reciprocal duties of hospitality." The modern English word "host" in this alternative sense comes from the Middle English (*h*)*oste,* from Old French, host, guest, from Latin *hospes* (stem *hospit-*), guest, host, stranger. The "pes" or "pit" in the Latin words and in such modern English words as "hospital" and "hospitality" is from another root, *pot,* meaning "master." The compound or bifurcated root *ghos-pot* meant "master of guests," "one who symbolizes the relationship of reciprocal hospitality," as in the Slavic *gospodi,* Lord, sir, master. "Guest," on the other hand, is from Middle English *gest,* from Old Norse *gestr,* from *ghos-ti,* the same root as for "host." A host is a guest, and a guest is a host. A host is a host. The relation of household master offering hospitality to a guest and the guest receiving it, of host and parasite in the original sense of "fellow guest," is inclosed within the word "host" itself.

A host in the sense of a guest, moreover, is both a friendly visitor in the house and at the same time an alien presence who turns the home into a hotel, a neutral territory. Perhaps he is the first emissary of a host of enemies (from Latin *hostis* [stranger, enemy]), the first foot in the door, followed by a swarm of hostile strangers, to be met only by our own host, as the Christian deity is the Lord God of Hosts. The uncanny antithetical relation exists not only between pairs of words in this system, host and parasite, host and guest, but within each word in itself. It reforms itself in each polar opposite when that opposite is separated out. This subverts or nullifies the apparently unequivocal relation of polarity which seems the conceptual scheme appropriate for thinking through the system. Each word in itself becomes divided by the strange logic of the "para," membrane which divides inside from outside and yet joins them in a hymeneal bond, or which allows an osmotic mixing, making the stranger friend, the distant near, the *Unheimlich heimlich,* the homely homey, without, for all its closeness and similarity, ceasing to be strange, distant, and dissimilar.

One of the most frightening versions of the parasite as invading host is the virus. In this case, the parasite is an alien who has not simply the ability to invade a domestic enclosure, consume the food of the family, and kill the host, but the strange capacity, in doing all that, to turn the host into multitudinous proliferating replications of itself. The virus is at the uneasy border between life and death. It challenges that opposition, since, for example, it does not "eat," but only reproduces. It is as much a crystal or a component in a crystal as it is an organism. The genetic pattern of the virus is so coded that it can enter a host cell and violently reprogram all the genetic material in that cell, turning the cell into a little factory for manufacturing copies of itself, so destroying it. This is *The Ivy-Wife* with a vengeance.

Is this an allegory, and if so, of what? The use by modern geneticists of an "analogy" (but what is the ontological status of this analogy?) between genetic reproduction and the social interchanges carried by language or other sign systems may justify a transfer back in the other direction. Is "deconstructive criticism" like a virus which invades the host of an innocently metaphysical text, a text with an "obvious or univocal meaning," carried by a single referential grammar? Does such criticism ferociously reprogram the *gramme* of the host text to make it utter its own message, the "uncanny," the "aporia," "la différance," or what have you? Some people have said so. Could it, on the other hand, be the other way around? Could it be that metaphysics, the obvious or univocal meaning, is the parasitical virus which has for millennia been passed from generation to generation in Western culture in its languages and in the privileged texts of those languages? Does metaphysics enter the language-learning apparatus of each new baby born into that culture and shape the apparatus after its own patterns? The difference might be that this apparatus, unlike the host cell for a virus, does not have its own pre-existing inbuilt genetic code.

Is that so certain, however? Is the system of metaphysics "natural" to man, as it is natural for a cuckoo to sing "cuckoo" or for a bee to build its comb in hexagonal cells? If so, the parasitical virus would be a friendly presence carrying the same message already genetically programmed within its host. The message would predispose all European babies or perhaps all earth babies to read Plato and become Platonists, so that anything else would require some unimaginable mutation of the species man. Is the prison house of language an exterior constraint or is it part of the blood, bones, nerves, and brain of the prisoner? Could that incessant murmuring voice that speaks always within me or constantly weaves the web of language there, even in my dreams, be an uncanny guest, a parasitical virus, and not a member of the family? How could one even ask that question, since it must be asked in words provided by the murmuring voice? Is it not that voice speaking here and now? Perhaps, after all, the analogy with viruses is "only an analogy," a "figure of speech," and need not be taken seriously.

What does this have to do with poems and with the reading of poems? It is meant as an "example" of the deconstructive strategy of interpretation. The procedure is applied, in this case, not to the text of a poem but to the cited fragment of a critical essay containing within itself a citation from another essay, like a parasite within its host. The "example" is a fragment like those miniscule bits of some substance which are put into a tiny test tube and explored by certain techniques of analytical chemistry. To get so far or so much out of a little piece of language, context after context widening out from these few phrases to include as their necessary milieux all the family of Indo-European languages, all the literature and conceptual thought within those languages, and all the permutations of our social structures of household economy, gift-giving and gift-receiving—this is an argument for the value of recognizing the equivocal richness of apparently obvious or univocal language, even of the language of criticism. Criticism is in this respect, if in no other, continuous with the language of literature. This equivocal richness, my discussion of "parasite" implies, resides in part in the fact that there is no conceptual expression without figure, and no intertwining of concept and figure without an implied narrative, in this case the story of the alien guest in the home. Deconstruction is an investigation of what is implied by this inherence in one another of figure, concept, and narrative.

My example presents a model for the relation of critic to critic, for the incoherence within a single critic's language, for the asymmetrical relation of critical text to poem, for the incoherence within any single literary text, and for the skewed relation of a poem to its predecessors. To speak of the "deconstructive" reading of a poem as "parasitical" on the "obvious or univocal reading" is to enter willynilly into the strange logic of the parasite, to make the univocal equivocal in spite of oneself, according to the law that language is not an instrument or tool in man's hands, a submissive means of thinking. Language rather thinks man and his "world," including poems, if he will allow it to do so.

The system of figurative thought (but what thought is not figurative?) inscribed within the word parasite and its associates, host and guest, invites us to recognize that the "obvious or univocal reading" of a poem is not identical to the poem itself. Both readings, the "univocal" one and the "deconstructive" one, are fellow guests "beside the grain," host and guest, host and host, host and parasite, parasite and parasite. The relation is a triangle, not a polar opposition. There is always a third to whom the two are related, something before them or between them, which they divide, consume, or exchange, across which they meet. The relation in question is always in fact a chain. It is a strange sort of chain without beginning or end, a chain in which no commanding element (origin, goal, or underlying principle) may be identified. In such a chain there is always something earlier or something later to which any link on which one focuses refers and which keeps the series open. The relation between any two contiguous elements in this chain is a strange opposition which is of intimate kinship and at the same time of enmity. It cannot be encompassed by the ordinary logic of polar opposition. It is not open to dialectical synthesis. Each "single element," moreover, far from being unequivocally what it is, subdivides within itself to recapitulate the relation of parasite and host of which, on the larger scale, it appears to be one or the other pole. On the one hand, the "obvious or univocal reading" always contains the "deconstructive reading" as a parasite encrypted within itself as part of itself. On the other hand, the "deconstructive" reading can by no means free itself from the metaphysical reading it means to contest. The poem in itself, then, is neither the host nor the parasite but the food they both need, host in another sense, the third element in this particular triangle. Both readings are at the same table together, bound by a strange relation of reciprocal obligation, of gift or food-giving and gift or food-receiving.

The poem, in my figure, is that ambiguous gift, food, host in the sense of victim, sacrifice. It is broken, divided, passed around, consumed by the critics canny and uncanny who are in that odd relation to one another of host and parasite. Any poem, however, is parasitical in its turn on earlier poems, or it contains earlier poems within itself as enclosed parasites, in another version of the perpetual reversal of parasite and host. If the poem is food and poison for the critics, it must in its turn have eaten. It must have been a cannibal consumer of earlier poems.

Take, for example, Shelley's *The Triumph of Life*. It is inhabited, as its critics have shown, by a long chain of parasitical presences—echoes, allusions, guests, ghosts of previous texts. These are present within the domicile of the poem in that curious phantasmal way, affirmed, negated, sublimated, twisted, straightened out, travestied, which Harold Bloom has begun to study and which it is one major task of literary interpretation today to investigate further and to define. The previous text is both the ground of the new one and something the new poem must annihilate by incorporating it, turning it into ghostly insubstantiality, so that the new poem may perform its possible-impossible task of becoming its own ground. The new poem both needs the old texts and must destroy them. It is both parasitical on them, feeding ungraciously on their substance, and at the same time it is the sinister host which unmans them by inviting them into its home, as the Green Knight invites Gawain. Each previous link in the chain, in its turn, played the same role, as host and parasite, in relation to its predecessors. From the Old to the New Testaments, from Ezekiel to Revelation, to Dante, to Ariosto, to Spenser, to Milton, to Rousseau, to Wordsworth and Coleridge, the chain leads ultimately to *The Triumph of Life.* That poem, in its turn, or Shelley's work generally, is present within the work of Hardy or Yeats or Stevens and forms part of a sequence in the major texts of Romantic "nihilism" including Nietzsche, Freud, Heidegger, and Blanchot. This perpetual re-expression of the relation of host and parasite forms itself again today in current criticism. It is present, for example, in the relation between "univocal" and "deconstructionist" readings of *The Triumph of Life,* between the reading of Meyer Abrams and that of Harold Bloom, or between Abrams' reading of Shelley and the one I am proposing here, or within the work of each one of these critics taken separately. The inexorable law which makes the "alogical" relation of host and parasite re-form itself within each separate entity which had seemed, on the larger scale, to be one or the other, applies as much to critical essays as to the texts they treat. *The Triumph of Life* contains within itself, jostling irreconcilably with one another, both logocentric metaphysics and nihilism. It is no accident that critics have disagreed about it. The meaning of *The Triumph of Life* can never be reduced to any "univocal" reading, neither the "obvious" one nor a single-minded deconstructionist one, if there could be such a thing, which there cannot. The poem, like all texts, is "unreadable," if by "readable" one means a single, definitive interpretation. In fact, neither the "obvious" reading nor the "deconstructionist" reading is "univocal." Each contains, necessarily, its enemy within itself, is itself both host and parasite. The deconstructionist reading contains the obvious one and vice versa. Nihilism is an inalienable alien presence within Occidental metaphysics, both in poems and in the criticism of poems.

## II

Nihilism—that word has inevitably come up as a label for "deconstruction," secretly or overtly present as the name for what is feared from the new mode of criticism and from its ability to devalue all values, making traditional modes of interpretation "impossible." What is nihilism? Here the analysis may be helped by a chain which goes from Friedrich Nietzsche to Ernst Jünger to Martin Heidegger.

The first book of Nietzsche's *The Will to Power,* in the ordering by his sister of the *Nachlass,* is entitled "European Nihilism." The beginning of the first section of this book is as follows: "Nihilism stands at the door: whence comes this uncanniest of all guests?" ( *"Der Nihilismus steht vor der Tür: woher kommt uns dieser unheimlichste aller Gäste?"*)[3]

Heidegger's comment on this comes near the beginning of his essay on Ernst Jünger's *Über die Linie.* The title of Heidegger's essay was later changed to *Zur Seinsfrage, The Question of Being.* Heidegger's essay takes the form of a letter to Jünger:

> It is called the "uncanniest" [*der "unheimlichste"*] because as the unconditional will to will, it wants homelessness as such [*die Heimatlosigkeit als solche*]. Therefore, it does not help to show it the door because it has long since and invisibly been moving around in the house. The important thing is to get a glimpse of the guest and to see through it. You [Jünger] write: "A good definition of nihilism would be comparable to making the cancer bacillus visible. It would not signify a cure but perhaps the presupposition of it, insofar as men contribute anything toward it." . . . Nihilism itself, as little as the cancer bacillus, is something diseased. In regard to the *essence* of nihilism there is no prospect and no meaningful claim to a cure. . . . The essence of nihilism is neither healable nor unhealable. It is the heal-less [*das Heil-lose*], but as such a unique relegation into health [*eine einzigartige Verweisung ins Heile*].[4]

For these three writers, link after link in a chain, the confrontation of nihilism cannot be detached from the system of terms I have been exploring. To put this another way, the system of terms involves inevitably a confrontation with the uncanniest of guests, nihilism. Nihilism is somehow inherent in the relation of parasite and host. Inherent also is the imagery of sickness and health. Health for the parasite, food and the right environment, may be illness, even mortal illness, for the host. On the other hand, there are innumerable cases, in the proliferation of life forms, where the presence of a parasite is absolutely necessary to the health of its host. Moreover, if nihilism is the "heal-less" as such, a wound which may not be closed, an attempt to understand that fact might be a condition of health. The attempt to pretend that this uncanniest of guests is not present in the house might be the worst of all illnesses, the nagging, surly, covert, unidentified kind, there as a general malaise which undermines all activities, depriving them of joy.

The uncanniest guest is nihilism, *"hôte fantôme,"* in Jacques Derrida's phrase, *"hôte qui hante plutôt qu'il n'habite,* guest *et* ghost *d'une inquiétante étrangeté."* Nihilism has already made itself at home within Occidental metaphysics. Nihilism is the latent ghost encrypted within any expression of a logocentric system, for example in Shelley's *The Triumph of Life,* or in any interpretation of such a text, for example in Meyer Abrams' reading of *The Triumph of Life* or in reversed form in Harold Bloom's reading. The two, logocentrism and nihilism, are related to one another in a way which is not antithesis and which may not be synthesized in any dialectical *Aufhebung.* Each defines and is hospitable to the other, host to it as parasite. Yet each is the mortal enemy of the other, invisible to the other, as its phantom unconscious, that is, as something of which it cannot by definition be aware.

If nihilism is the parasitical stranger within the house of metaphysics, "nihilism," as the name for the devaluation or reduction to nothingness of all values, is not the name nihilism has "in itself." It is the name given to it by metaphysics, as the term "unconscious" is given by consciousness to that part of itself which it cannot face directly. In attempting to expel that other than itself contained within itself, logocentric metaphysics deconstitutes itself, according to a regular law which can be demonstrated in the self-subversion of all the great texts of Western metaphysics from Plato onward. Metaphysics contains its parasite within itself, as the "unhealable" which it tries, unsuccessfully, to cure. It attempts to cover over the unhealable by annihilating the nothingness hidden within itself.

Is there any way to break this law, to turn the system around? Would it be possible to approach metaphysics from the standpoint of "nihilism"? Could one make nihilism the host of which metaphysics is the alien guest, so giving new names to both? Nihilism would then not be nihilism but something else, something without a melodramatic aura, perhaps something so innocent-sounding as "rhetoric," or "philology," or "the study of tropes," or even "the trivium." Metaphysics might then be redefined, from the point of view of this trivium, as an inevitable rhetorical or tropological effect. It would not be a cause but a phantom generated within the house of language by the play of language. "Deconstruction" is one current name for this reversal.

The present-day procedure of "deconstruction," of which Nietzsche is one of the patrons, is not, however, new in our own day. It has been repeated regularly in one form or another in all the centuries since the Greek Sophists and rhetoricians, since in fact Plato himself, who in *The Sophist* has enclosed his own self-deconstruction within the canon of his own writing. If deconstruction could liberate us from the prisonhouse of language, it would seem that it should have long since done so, and yet it has not. There must be something wrong with the machinery of demolition, or some inexpertness in its operator, or perhaps the definition of it as liberating is incorrect. The *fröhliche Wissenschaft* of Nietzsche, his attempt to move beyond metaphysics to an affirmative, life-enhancing, performative act of language, is posited on a dismantling of metaphysics which shows it as leading to nihilism by an inevitable process whereby "the highest values devaluate themselves." The values are not devaluated by something subversive outside themselves. Nihilism is not a social or psychological or even world historical phenomenon. It is not a new or perhaps cyclically reappearing phenomenon in the history of "spirit" or of "Being." The highest values devalue themselves. Nihilism is a parasite always already at home within its host, Western metaphysics. This is stated as a "point of departure" (*Ausgangspunkt*) at the beginning of *Zum Plan* ("Towards an Outline"), at the opening of Book I of *The Will to Power,* just after the sentence defining nihilism as "this uncanniest of all guests":

> . . . It is an error to consider "social distress" or "psychological degeneration" or, worse, corruption as the *cause* of nihilism. . . . Distress, whether of the soul, body, or intellect, cannot of itself give birth to nihilism (i.e. the radical repudiation of value, meaning, and desirability)—Such distress always permits a variety of interpretations. Rather: it is in one particular interpretation, the Christian-moral one, that nihilism is rooted.[5]

Would it be possible, then, to escape from the endless generation out of itself by metaphysics of nihilism, and the endless resubmission of nihilism to the metaphysics which defines it and is the condition of its existence? Is "deconstruction" this new way, a new threefold way out of the labyrinth of human history, which is the history of error, into the sunlit forum of truth and clarity, all ways made straight at last? Can semiotics, rhetoric, and tropology substitute for the old grammar, rhetoric, and logic? Would it be possible to be freed at last from the nightmare of an endless brother battle, Shem replacing Shaun, and Shaun Shem?

I do not think so. "Deconstruction" is neither nihilism nor metaphysics but simply interpretation as such, the untangling of the inherence of metaphysics in nihilism and of nihilism in metaphysics by way of the close reading of texts. This procedure, however, can in no way escape, in its own discourse, from the language of the passages it cites. This language is the expression of the inherence of nihilism in metaphysics and of metaphysics in nihilism. We have no other language. The language of criticism is subject to exactly the same limitations and blind alleys as the language of the works it reads. The most heroic effort to escape from the prisonhouse of language only builds the walls higher.

The deconstructive procedure, however, by reversing the relation of ghost and host, by playing on the play within language, may go beyond the repetitive generation of nihilism by metaphysics and of metaphysics by nihilism. It may reach something like that *fröhliche Wissenschaft* for which Nietzsche called. This would be interpretation as joyful wisdom, the greatest joy in the midst of the greatest suffering, an inhabitation of that gaiety of language which is our seigneur.

Deconstruction does not provide an escape from nihilism, nor from metaphysics, nor from their uncanny inherence in one another. There is no escape. It does, however, move back and forth within this inherence. It makes the inherence oscillate in such a way that one enters a strange borderland, a frontier region which seems to give the widest glimpse into the other land ("beyond metaphysics"), though this land may not by any means be entered and does not in fact exist for Western man. By this form of interpretation, however, the border zone itself may be made sensible, as quattrocento painting makes the Tuscan air visible in its invisibility. The zone may be appropriated in the torsion of the mind's expropriation, its experience of an inability to comprehend logically. This procedure is an attempt to reach clarity in a region where clarity is not possible. In the failure of that attempt, however, something moves, a limit is encountered. This encounter may be compared to the uncanny experience of reaching a frontier where there is no visible barrier, as when Wordsworth found he had crossed the Alps without knowing he was doing so. It is as if the "prisonhouse of language" were like that universe finite but unbounded which some modern cosmologies posit. One may move everywhere freely within this enclosure without ever encountering a wall, and yet it is limited. It is a prison, a milieu without origin or edge. Such a place is therefore all frontier zone without either peaceful homeland, in one direction, land of hosts and domesticity, nor, in the other direction, any alien land of hostile strangers, "beyond the line."

The place we inhabit, wherever we are, is always this in-between zone, place of host and parasite, neither inside nor outside. It is a region of the *Unheimlich,* beyond any formalism, which reforms itself wherever we are, if we know where we are. This "place" is where we are, in whatever text, in the most inclusive sense of that word, we happen to be living. This may be made to appear, however, only by an extreme interpretation of that text, going as far as one can with the terms the work provides. To this form of interpretation, which is interpretation as such, one name given at the moment is "deconstruction."

# III

As an "example" of the word "parasite" functioning parasitically within the "body" of work by one author, I turn now to an analysis of the word in Shelley.

The word "parasite" does not appear in *The Triumph of Life*. That poem, however, is structured throughout around the parasitical relationship. *The Triumph of Life* may be defined as an exploration of various forms of the parasitical relation. The poem is governed by the imagery of light and shadow, or of light differentiated within itself. The poem is a series of personifications and scenes each of which gives a figurative "shape" (Shelley's word) to a light which remains the "same" in all its personifications. The figurative shape makes the light a shadow. Any reading of the poem must thread its way through repeated configurations of the polarity of light and shadow. It must also identify the relation of one scene to the next which replaces it as sunlight puts out the morning star, and the star again the sun. That star is Lucifer, Venus, Vesper, all at once. The polarity constantly reforming itself within a light which turns into shadow in the presence of a novel light is the vehicle which carries, or is carried by, the structure of dream vision within dream vision and of person confronting or replacing precursor person. This structure is repeated throughout the poem. These repetitions make the poem a *mise en abîme* of reflections within reflections or a nest of Chinese boxes. This relation exists within the poem, for example, in the juxtaposition of the poet's vision and the prior vision which is narrated by Rousseau within the poet's vision. Rousseau's vision comes later in the linear sequence of the poem but earlier in "chronological" time. It puts early late, metaleptically, as late's explanatory predecessor. The relation in question also exists in the encapsulation in the poem of echoes and references to a long chain of previous texts in which the emblematic chariot or other figures of the poem have appeared: Ezekiel, Revelation, Virgil, Dante, Spenser, Milton, Rousseau, Wordsworth. Shelley's poem in its turn is echoed by Hardy, by Yeats, and by many others.

This relation inside the poem between one part of it and another, or the relation of the poem to previous and later texts, is a version of the relation of parasite to host. It exemplifies the undecidable oscillation of that relation. It is impossible to decide which element is parasite, which host, which commands or encloses the other. It is impossible to decide whether the series should be thought of as a sequence of elements each external to the next or according to some model of enclosure like that of the Chinese boxes. When the latter model is applied it is impossible to decide which element of any pair is outside, which is inside. In short, the distinction between inside and outside cannot be held to across that strange membrane, wall at once and copulating hymen, which stands between host and parasite. Each element is both exterior to the adjacent one and at the same time encloses and is enclosed by it.

One of the most striking "episodes" of *The Triumph of Life* is the scene of self-destructive erotic love. This scene matches a series of scenes elsewhere in Shelley's poetry in which the word "parasite" is present. The scene shows sexual attraction as one of the most deadly forms of the triumph of life. The triumph of life is in fact the triumph of language. For Shelley this takes the form of the subjection of each man or woman to illusory figures projected by his or her desire. Each of these figures is made of another substitutive shape of light which fades as it is grasped. It fades because it exists only as a transitory metaphor of light. It is a momentary lightbearer. Venus, star of evening, as the poem says, is only another disguise of Lucifer, fallen star of the morning. Vesper becomes Hesper by a change of initial consonant, masculine H for feminine V.

When the infatuated lovers of *The Triumph of Life* rush together, they annihilate one another, like particle and antiparticle, or, in the metaphors Shelley uses, like two thunderclouds colliding in a narrow valley, or like a great wave crashing on the shore. This annihilation, nevertheless, is not complete, since the violent collision leaves always a trace, a remnant, foam on the shore. This is Aphrodite's foam, seed or sperm which starts the cycle all over again in Shelley's drama of endless repetition. The darkest feature of the triumph of life, for Shelley, is that it may not even be ended by death. Life, for him, though it is a living death, may not die. It regenerates itself interminably in ever-new figures of light:

> . . . in their dance round her who dims the Sun
>
> Maidens & youths fling their wild arms in air
>     As their feet twinkle; they recede, and now
> Bending within each other's atmosphere
>
>     Kindle invisibly; and as they glow
> Like moths by light attracted & repelled,
>     Oft to new bright destruction come & go.
>
> Till like two clouds into one vale impelled
>     That shake the mountains when their lightnings mingle
> And die in rain,—the fiery band which held
>
>     Their natures, snaps . . . ere the shock cease to tingle
> One falls and then another in the path
>     Senseless, nor is the desolation single,
>
> Yet ere I can say *where* the chariot hath
>     Past over them; nor other trace I find
> But as of foam after the Ocean's wrath
>
>     Is spent upon the desert shore.
>
>                                         [ll. 148–64] [6]

This magnificent passage is the culmination of a series of passages writing and rewriting the same materials in a chain of repetitions beginning with *Queen Mab*. In the earlier versions the word "parasite" characteristically appears, like a discreet identifying mark woven into the texture of the verbal fabric. The word appears in *Queen Mab* and in the version of one episode of *Queen Mab* called *The Daemon of the World.* It appears then in *Alastor,* in *Laon and Cythna,* in *The Revolt of Islam,* in *Epipsychidion,* and in *The Sensitive Plant,* always with the same surrounding context of motifs and themes. These include narcissism and incest, the conflict of generations, struggles for political power, the motifs of the sun and the moon, the fountain, the brook, the caverned enclosure, ruined tower, or woodland dell, the dilapidation of man's constructions by nature, and the failure of the poetic quest.

That part of *Queen Mab* which Shelley reworked under the title *The Daemon of the World* contains the earliest version of the complex of elements (including the chariot from Ezekiel) which receives its final expression in *The Triumph of Life.* There Ianthe's "golden tresses shade / The bosom's stainless pride, / Twining like tendrils of the parasite / Around a marble column" (ll. 44–47).

In *Alastor* the doomed poet, like Narcissus searching for his lost twin sister, seeks the "veiled maid" (l. 151) who has come to him in dreams. He seeks her in a woodland glen with a "well / Dark, gleaming and of most translucent wave" (ll. 457–58), but he finds only his own eyes reflected there. These eyes, however, are doubled by "two eyes, / Two starry eyes" (ll. 489–90), which meet his eyes when his look rises. They are perhaps actual stars, perhaps the eyes of his evasive beloved. This play of eyes and looks had been prepared a few lines earlier in a description of "parasites, / Starred with ten thousand blossoms" (ll. 439–40), which twine around the trees of the dense forest hiding this well.

In Canto VI of *Laon and Cythna,* then again in the revised version, *The Revolt of Islam* (which veils the theme of incestuous love), Cythna rescues Laon from defeat in battle and takes him for a wild ride on a Tartar's courser to a ruined palace on a mountain top. There they make love, in another scene involving eyes, looks, stars, and Narcissus' well: "her dark and deepening eyes, / Which, as twin phantoms of one star that lies / O'er a dim well, move, though the Star reposes, / Swam in our mute and liquid ecstasies" (ll. 2624–28). This lovemaking takes place in a "natural couch of leaves" in a recess of the ruin. The recess is shaded in spring by "flowering parasites" which shed their "stars" on the dead leaves when the wandering wind blows (ll. 2578–84).

In *Epipsychidion,* the poet plans to take the lady Emily to an island with a ruined tower where, as he says, "We shall become the same, we shall be one / Spirit within two frames" (ll. 573–74). This ruin too is shaded by "parasite flowers" (l. 502), just as, in *The Sensitive Plant,* the garden which the lady personifies contains "parasite bowers" (l. 47) which die when winter comes.

A special version of the undecidable structure contained within the word "parasite" operates in all these passages. One could say either that the word contains the passages in miniature within itself or that the passages themselves are a dramatization of the word. The passages limit the word's meaning and expand it at the same time, tracing out one special design within the complex system of thought and figuration contained within the word.

These passages might be defined as an attempt to get a complicated group of themes to come out right. Their aim is magical or Promethean. They attempt to describe an act of Narcissistic self-begetting and self-possession which is at the same time an incestuous lovemaking between brother and sister. This lovemaking shortcircuits the differences of the sexes and the heterogeneity of families in an unlawful sexual coupling. At the same time this act is a breakdown of the barrier between man and nature. It is also a political act putting an end to a tyranny which is imaged as the familial domination of a bad father over his children and over his progeny in all succeeding generations. It is, finally, an act of poetry which will destroy the barriers between sign and signified. Such poetry will produce an apocalypse of immediacy in which no more poetry will be needed because no more figures will be needed, no metaphors, no substitutions or "standings for," no veils. Man will then stand in the presence of a universal present which will be all light. It will no longer require Luciferic shapes, persons, figures, or images from nature to bear that light and in the bearing hide it.

All these projects fail at once. They fail in a way which *The Triumph of Life* makes clearest in showing that the conjunction of lovers, clouds, wave and shore, or words both destroys what it conjoins and always leaves a remainder. This genetic trace starts the cycle of lovemaking, attempts by the self to possess itself, self-destructive political tyranny, and poetry-writing all over again. Shelley's poetry is the record of a perpetually renewed failure. It is a failure ever to get the right formula and so end the separate incomplete self, end lovemaking, end politics, and end poetry, all at once, in a performative apocalypse in which words will become the fire they have ignited and so vanish as words, in a universal light. The words, however, always remain, there on the page, as the unconsumed traces of each unsuccessful attempt to use words to end words. The attempt must therefore be repeated. The same scene, with the same elements in a slightly different arrangement, is written by Shelley over and over again from *Queen Mab* to *The Triumph of Life,* in a repetition ended only with his death. This repetition mimes the poet's failure ever to get it right and so end the necessity of trying once more with what remains.

The word "parasite," for Shelley, names the bridge, wall, or connecting membrane which at once makes this apocalyptic union possible, abolishing difference, and at the same time always remains as a barrier forbidding it. Like the thin line of Aphrodite's foam on the shore, this remnant starts the process all over again after the vanishing of the previous couple in their violent attempt to end the interminable chain. The parasite is, on the one hand, the barrier and marriage hymen between the horizontal elements which make some binary opposition. This opposition generates forms and generates also a narrative of their interaction. At the same time the parasite is the barrier and connecting screen between elements on different planes vertically, Earth and Heaven, this world and a spiritual one above it. The world above is the white radiance of eternity. This world's opposing pairs, male, for example, against female, both figure forth and hide that white fire.

Parasites for Shelley are always parasite *flowers.* They are vines

which twine themselves around the trees of a forest to climb to
light and air, or they grow on a ruined palace to cover its stone
and make fragrant bowers there. Parasitical flowering vines feed
on air and on what they can take from their hosts. Those hosts
they join with their stems. Shelley's parasites flower abundantly,
making a screen between sky and earth. This screen remains even
in winter as a lattice of dried vines.

A final ambiguity of Shelley's version of the system of parasite
and host is the impossibility of deciding whether the sister-
beloved in these poems is on the same plane as the desiring poet
or a transcendent spirit infinitely above him. She is both at once.
She is a sister to whom the protagonist might make love, inces-
tuously. At the same time she is an unattainable muse or mother
who governs all, as the spirit eyes Alastor pursues are those of no
earthly sister, or as the poet's love for Emily in *Epipsychidion* is
also an attempt, like that of Prometheus, to steal heavenly fire, or
as the scene of erotic love in *The Triumph of Life* is presided over
by the devouring female goddess, riding in her triumph, Life, or
as, in the first version of this pattern, the earthly Ianthe beloved
by Henry is doubled by the female Daemon of the World who
presides over their relation and who is present at the end of the
poem as the star repeating the heroine's eyes. These star-like eyes
are a constant symbol in Shelley of the unattainable transcendent
power in its relation to the earthly signs of it, but at the same
time they are no more than the beloved's eyes, and also, at the
same time, the protagonist's own eyes reflected back to him.


# IV


The motif of a relation between the generations in which one
generation is related parasitically to another, with the full ambiguity of that relation, appears in *Epipsychidion* in its most complete form. This version makes clearest the relation of this theme
to the system of parasite and host, to the theme in Shelley of a
repetition generated always by what is left over after an earlier cata-

clysmic self-destruction, to the political theme which is always present in these passages, to the relation of man's works to nature, and to the dramatization of the power of poetry which is always one of Shelley's themes.

The ruined tower in the Sporades to which the poet will take his Emily in *Epipsychidion* is said, in one of the drafts of the preface, somewhat prosaically, to be "a Saracenic castle which accident had preserved in some repair." In the poem itself this tower is a strange structure which has grown naturally, almost like a flower or stone, saxifrage and saxiform. At the same time it is almost supernatural. It is a house for a god and a goddess, or at any rate for a semi-divine Ocean-King and his sister-spouse. The building brackets the human level. It is above and below that level at once:

> But the chief marvel of the wilderness
> Is a lone dwelling, built by whom or how
> None of the rustic island-people know:
> 'Tis not a tower of strength, though with its height
> It overtops the woods; but, for delight,
> Some wise and tender Ocean-King, ere crime
> Had been invented, in the world's young prime,
> Reared it, a wonder of that simple time,
> An envy of the isles, a pleasure-house
> Made sacred to his sister and his spouse.
> It scarce seems now a wreck of human art,
> But, as it were Titanic; in the heart
> Of Earth having assumed its form, then grown
> Out of the mountains, from the living stone,
> Lifting itself in caverns light and high:
> For all the antique and learned imagery
> Has been erased, and in the place of it
> The ivy and the wild-vine interknit
> The volumes of their many-twining stems;
> Parasite flowers illume with dewy gems
> The lampless halls, and when they fade, the sky
> Peeps through their winter-woof of tracery
> With moonlight patches, or star atoms keen,

Or fragments of the day's intense serene;—
Working mosaic on their Parian floors.

[ll. 483–507]

An "Ocean-King" is, possibly, a human king of this ocean isle
and at the same time, possibly, a King of the Ocean, an Olym-
pian or a Titan. In any case, this dwelling was built "in the
world's young prime." It was built near the time of origin, when
the opposites were confounded or nearly confounded and when incest was not a crime, as it was not for those Egyptian pharaohs
who always mated with their sisters, only fit spouses for their
earthly divinity. In the same way, in that young time, nature and
culture were not opposed. The palace seems at once "Titanic," the
work of a superhuman strength, and at the same time human,
since it is, after all, "a wreck of human art," though it scarcely
seems so. At the same time it is natural, as though it had grown
from the rock, not been built by human art at all. Though the
building was once adorned with elaborate carved inscriptions and
images, those have been effaced by time. Its towers and facades
now seem once more natural rock, grown out of the mountains,
living stone. The natural, the supernatural, and the human were
reconciled in a union whose symbol was brother-sister incest, the
same mating with the same, so short-circuiting normal human
love with its production of new genetic lines. The prohibition
against incest, as Lévi-Strauss has argued, is both human and natural at once. It therefore breaks down the barrier between the
two. This breaking was doubly broken by the Ocean-King and
his sister. Their copulation kept crime from being invented. It
held nature, the supernatural, and the human together—mimick-
ing and maintaining that vision of unity which can be seen from
the palace. This seascape-landscape, two in one, makes the partic-
ulars of nature seem the ideal dream of a fulfilled sexuality between two great gods, Earth and Ocean:

And, day and night, aloof, from the high towers
And terraces, the Earth and Ocean seem

To sleep in one another's arms, and dream
Of waves, flowers, clouds, woods, rocks, and all that we
Read in their smiles, and call reality.      [ll. 508–12]

To this place the poet plans to bring his Emily, promising a
renewal of that ideal sexual union of the prime time. This renewal will magically renew the time itself. It will take them back
to a time prior to the invention of crime and reconcile once
more, in a performative embrace, nature, supernature, and man.

This performance, however, can never be performed. It remains at the end of *Epipsychidion* a proleptic hope which is forbidden by the words which express it. It can never be performed
because in fact this union never existed in the past. It is only a
projection backward from the present. It is a "seeming" created
by reading the signs or remnants still present in the present. The
Ocean-King, wise and tender though he may have been, was
human after all. The prohibition against incest precedes the com-
mitting of incest. It precedes the division between natural and
human while at the same time creating that division. The lovemaking of the Ocean-King and his spouse was itself the act which
"invented crime." Though it was a mating of the same with the
same, it did not put a stop to the difference of sexes, families,
and generations, as the peopling of the earth, the presence of political and paternal tyranny, the existence of the poet with his
unassuaged desire for Emily all demonstrate.

Moreover, the building only seemed to be natural, divine, and
human at once. Though its stone is natural enough, its shape was
in fact a product of human art, as is demonstrated by the presence
on it once of "antique and learnèd imagery." This imagery was
learned because it pointed back still further to a human tradition
already immemorial. The "volumes" of the ivy and the wild vine,
that screen of parasite flowers, the former making a hieroglyphic
pattern on the stone, the latter casting mosaic patterns in tracery
on the marble floors, are substitutes for that effaced writing. The
purely natural vines and parasites here paradoxically become a

kind of writing. They stand for the erased pattern of learned imagery carved in the stone by the Ocean-King's builders. They stand also by implication for writing in general, the writing for example of the poem itself which the reader is at that moment retracing. Yet the pattern of parasite vines is no legible language. It remains "in place of" the erased human language. In this "in place of" all the imaginary unity of "the world's young prime" breaks down. It is dispersed back into irreconcilable compartments separated by the dividing textured membrane which tries to bring them together. Male and female; divine, human, supernatural—all become separate realms. They are realms separated by language itself and by the dependence of language on figure, on the "in place of" of metaphor or allegorical substitution. Any attempt to cross the barrier and unify what have from all time been separated by the language which brings them together (that antique and learned imagery which was already there even for the wise and tender Ocean-King and his sister spouse), leads only to an exacerbation of the distance. It becomes a transgression which creates the barrier it attempts to efface or ignore. Incest cannot exist without kinship names and is "invented" as a crime not so much in sexual acts between brother and sister as in any imagery for them. This imagery, however, is always there, of immemorial antiquity. It joins nature and culture in what divides them, as the living stone is covered with carved images making it humanly significant, and as the parasite vines or rather the filigrees of their shadows are taken as signs.

In the same way the poet's attempt to repeat with Emily the pleasure of the Ocean-King and his sister only repeats the crime of illicit sexual relations, always at least implicitly incest for Shelley. "Would we two had been twins of the same mother!" (l. 45) says the protagonist to his Emily. The speaker's love only prolongs the divisions. His union with Emily remains always in the future, as is Henri's love in *The Daemon of the World,* or as is the hero's love in *Alastor,* and as the union of Laon and Cythna is paid for when they are burned at the stake. The lovemaking of Laon and Cythna does not in any case produce the political liberation of Islam. In the same way, the poet's attempt in *Epipsychidion* to express in words this union becomes itself the barrier forbidding it. It forbids also the poet's Promethean attempt to scale heaven and seize its fire through language and through erotic love. The passage is one of Shelley's grandest symphonic climaxes, but what it expresses is the failure of poetry and the failure of love. It expresses the destruction of the poet-lover in his attempt to escape his boundaries, the chains at once of selfhood and of language. This failure is Shelley's version of the parasite structure.

Who, however, is "Shelley"? To what does this word refer if any work signed with this name has no identifiable borders, and no interior walls either? It has no edges because it has been invaded from all sides as well as from within by other "names," other powers of writing—Rousseau, Dante, Ezekiel, and the whole host of others, phantom strangers who have crossed the thresholds of the poems, erasing their margins. Though the word "Shelley" may be printed on the cover of a book entitled *Poetical Works,* it must name something without identifiable bounds, since the book incorporates so much outside within its inside. The parasite structure obliterates the frontiers of the texts it enters. For "Shelley," then, the parasite is a communicating screen of figurative language which permanently divides what it would unify in a perpetual "in place of" forbidding union. This screen creates the shadow of that union as an effect of figure, a phantasmal "once was" and "might yet be," never "now" and "here":

> Our breath shall intermix, our bosoms bound,
> And our veins beat together; and our lips
> With other eloquence than words, eclipse
> The soul that burns between them, and the wells
> Which boil under our being's inmost cells,
> The fountains of our deepest life, shall be
> Confused in Passion's golden purity,
> As mountain-springs under the morning sun.
> We shall become the same, we shall be one

Spirit within two frames, oh! wherefore two?
One passion in twin-hearts, which grows and grew,
Till like two meteors of expanding flame,
Those spheres instinct with it become the same,
Touch, mingle, are transfigured; ever still
Burning, yet ever inconsumable:
In one another's substance finding food,
Like flames too pure and light and unimbued
To nourish their bright lives with baser prey,
Which point to Heaven and cannot pass away:
One hope within two wills, one will beneath
Two overshadowing minds, one life, one death,
One Heaven, one Hell, one immortality,
And one annihilation. Woe is me!
The wingèd words on which my soul would pierce
Into the height of Love's rare Universe,
Are chains of lead around its flight of fire—
I pant, I sink, I tremble, I expire!

{ll. 565–91]

No reader of these extraordinary lines can fail to feel that the poet here protests too much. Every repetition of the word "one" only adds another layer to the barrier forbidding oneness. The poet protests too much not only in the attempt in words to produce a union which these words themselves keep from happening, but even in the concluding outcry of woe. Not only does the poet not achieve union through words with his Emily and so climb to Love's fiery heights. He does not even "expire" through the failure of these magic performatives. Words do not make anything happen, nor does their failure to make anything happen either. Though the "Advertisement" to *Epipsychidion* tells the reader the poet died in Florence without ever reaching that isle, "one of wildest of the Sporades," the reader knows that words did not kill him, for "I pant, I sink, I tremble, I expire!" is followed by the relatively calm post-climax dedicatory lines beginning: "Weak Verses, go, kneel at your Sovereign's feet" (l. 591). The grand climactic passage itself is made of variations on the paradoxical parasite structure. The verbal signs for union necessarily rebuild the barrier they would obliterate. The more the poet says they will be one the more he makes them two by reaffirming the ways they are separated. The lips that speak with an eloquence other than words are doors which are also a liminal barrier between person and person. Those lips may eclipse the soul that burns between them, but they remain as a communicating medium which also is a barrier to union. The lips are the parasite structure once more. Moreover, the voice that speaks of an eloquence beyond words uses eloquent words to speak of this transverbal speech. By naming such speech it keeps the soul from being eclipsed. In the same way, the image of the deep wells reaffirms the notion of cellular enclosure, just as the clash of fire and water in the figure of the mountain-springs being "confused" under the morning sun tells the reader that only by evaporating as entities can lovers become one. The images of two frames with one spirit, the double meteors becoming one floating sphere, the pair each both eater and eaten ("in one another's substance finding food"), are the parasitical relation again. All play variations on "Shelley's" version of the parasite structure, the notion of a unity which yet remains double but in the figurative expression of that unity reveals the impossibility of two becoming one across a parasitic wall and yet remaining two.

This impossibility is mimed in the final *mise en abîme*. This is a cascade of expressions describing a twoness resting on the ground of a oneness which then subdivides once more to rest on a still deeper ground which ultimately reveals itself to be, if it exists at all, the abyss of "annihilation." The vertical wall between cell and cell, lover and beloved, is doubled by a horizontal veil between levels of being. Each veil when removed only reveals another veil, ad infinitum, unless the last veil exposes an emptiness. This would be the emptiness of that oneness which is implored into existence in the reiteration of "one," "one," "one," "one": "One hope within two wills, one will beneath / Two overshadowing minds, one life, one death / One Heaven, one Hell, one immortality, / And one annihilation. Woe is me!" The language

which tries to efface itself as language to give way to an unmediated union beyond language is itself the barrier which always
remains as the woe of an ineffaceable trace. Words are always
there as remnant, "chains of lead" which forbid the flight to fiery
union they invoke.

This does not mean that love-making and poetry-making are
the "same thing" or subject to the same impasses determining
their failure as performatives magically transforming the world.
In a sense they are antagonists, since lovemaking attempts to do
wordlessly what poetry attempts to do with words. No one can
doubt that Shelley believed sexual experience "occurs" or that he
"describes" it in his poetry, for example in *Laon and Cythna* and
in the great passage on erotic love in *The Triumph of Life*. Lovemaking and poetrymaking are not, however, stark opposites in
Shelley either. Each is, so to speak, the dramatization of the other
or the figure of it. This is an elliptical relation in which which-
ever of the two the reader focuses on reveals itself to be the metaphorical substitution for the other. The other, however, when the
reader moves to it, is not the "original" but a figure of what at
first seemed a figure for it. Lovemaking, as *The Triumph of Life*
shows, is a way to "experience," as incarnate suffering, the self-
destructive effects of signmaking, signprojecting, and sign-
interpretation. The wordlessness of lovemaking is only another way
of dwelling within signs after all, as is shown in *The Triumph of
Life* by the affirmed identity between Venus, evening star of love,
and Lucifer, star of morning, "light-bearer," personification of
personification and of all the other tropes, all the forms of the "in
place of."

Poetrymaking, on the other hand, is for Shelley always a figure
of, as well as figured by, the various forms of life—political,
religious, familial, and erotic. It does not have priority as an origin but can exist only embodied in one or another of the forms of
life it figures. There is, for Shelley, no "sign" without its material carrier, and so the play of substitutions in language can never
be a purely ideal interchange. This interchange is always contaminated by its necessary incarnation, the most dramatic form of

which is the bodies of lovers. On the other hand, lovemaking is never a purely wordless communion or intercourse. It is in its turn contaminated by language. Lovemaking is a way of living, in the flesh, the aporias of figure. It is also a way of experiencing the way language functions to forbid the perfect union of lovers. Language always remains, after they have exhausted or even annihilated themselves in an attempt to get it right, as the genetic trace starting the cycle all over again.

# V

Five times, or seven times if one counts *The Daemon of the World* and *The Revolt of Islam* as separate texts, seven times, or even more than seven if one includes other passages with the same elements where the word "parasite" does not appear—more than seven times, then, throughout his work, Shelley casts himself against the lips of the parasitical gate. Each time he falls back, having failed to make two into one without annihilating both. He falls back as himself the remainder, the power of language able to say "Woe is me!" and forced to try again to break the barrier only to fail once more, in repetitions which are terminated only by his death.

The critic, in his turn, like those poets, Browning, Hardy, Yeats, or Stevens who have been decisively "influenced" by Shelley, is a follower who repeats the pattern once again and once again fails to "get it right," just as Shelley repeats himself and repeats his precursors, and just as the poet and Emily follow the Ocean-King and his sister spouse.

The critic's version of the pattern proliferated in this chain of repetitions is as follows. The critic's attempt to untwist the elements in the texts he interprets only twists them up again in another place and leaves always a remnant of opacity, or an added opacity, as yet unraveled. The critic is caught in his own version of the interminable repetitions which determine the poet's career. The critic experiences this as his failure to get his poet right in a final decisive formulation which will allow him to have done with that poet, once and for all. Though each poet is different, each contains his own form of undecidability. This might be defined by saying that the critic can never show decisively whether or not the work of the writer is "decidable," whether or not it is capable of being definitively interpreted. The critic cannot unscramble the tangle of lines of meaning, comb its threads out so they shine clearly side by side. He can only retrace the text, set its elements in motion once more, in that experience of the failure of determinable reading which is decisive here.

The blank wall beyond which rational analysis cannot go arises from the copresence in any text in Western literature, inextricably intertwined, as host and parasite, of some version of logocentric metaphysics and its subversive counterpart. In Shelley's case these are, on the one hand, the "idealism" always present as one possible reading of his poems, even of *The Triumph of Life,* and on the other hand, the putting in question of this in Shelley's "scepticism" by a recognition of the role of projections in human life. This is that law of shadowing which deconstructs idealism. It is most explicitly formulated in *The Triumph of Life:*

> Figures ever new
> Rise on the bubble [of the phenomenal and historical world], paint
>     them how you may;
> We have but thrown, as those before us threw,
>
> Our shadows on it as it past away.
>
>                                      [ll. 248–51]

"The "deconstruction" of metaphysics by an appeal to the figurative nature of language always, however, contains its own impasse, whether this dismantling is performed within the writing of the author himself or in the following of that in repetitive retracing by the critic who comes after, as in my discussion here. This impasse is itself double. On the one hand, the poet and his shadow, the critic, can "deconstruct" metaphysics only with some tool of analysis which is capable of becoming another form of metaphysics in its turn. To put this another way, the differentiation between metaphysics and scepticism reforms itself as a new form of doubleness within "scepticism." Scepticism is not a firm and unequivocal machine of deconstruction. It carries within itself another form of the parasite structure, mirror image with the valences reversed of that within metaphysics itself.

The appeal to language from idealism is an admirable example of this. As is abundantly apparent in criticism at the present time, rhetorical analysis, "semiotics," "structuralism," "narratology," or the interpretation of tropes can freeze into a quasi-scientific discipline promising exhaustive rational certainty in the identification of meaning in a text and in the identification of the way that meaning is produced. The appeal to etymologies can become another archeology. It can become another way to be beguiled by the apparent explanatory power of seeming "origins" and the accompanying explanatory power of the apparently causally determined chains which emerge from a starting point in some "Indo-European root." Insofar as this move in contemporary criticism is motivated by an appeal to Freud's linguistic insights, such critics should perhaps remember Freud's demonstration, in *The Psychopathology of Everyday Life* and in *Jokes and the Unconscious,* of the way wordplay in all its forms is superficial. Wordplay is the repression of something more dangerous. This something, however, interweaves itself with that wordplay and forbids it to be merely verbal or merely play. Rhetorical analysis, the analysis of figure, and even an investigation of etymologies are necessary to put in question a heavily idealist reading of Shelley, but these must be dismantled in their turn in an interminable movement of interrogation which is the life of criticism. Criticism is a human activity which depends for its validity on never being at ease within a fixed "method." It must constantly put its own grounds in question. The critical text and the literary text are each parasite and host for the other, each feeding on the other and feeding it, destroying and being destroyed by it.

The dismantling of the linguistic assumptions necessary to dismantle Shelley's idealism must occur, however, not by a return to idealism, and not by the appeal to some "metalanguage" which will encompass both, but by a movement through rhetorical analysis, the analysis of tropes, and the appeal to etymologies, to something "beyond" language which can yet only be reached by recognition of the linguistic moment in its counter-momentum against idealism or against logocentric metaphysics. By "linguistic moment" I mean the moment in a work of literature when its own medium is put in question. This moment allows the critic to take what remains from the clashing of scepticism and idealism as a new starting place, for example by the recognition of a performative function of language which has entered into my discussion of Shelley. This again, in its reinstating of a new form of referentiality and in its formation of a new clashing, this time between rhetoric as tropes and rhetoric as performative words, must be interrogated in its turn, in a ceaseless movement of interpretation which Shelley himself has mimed in the sequence of episodes in *The Triumph of Life.*

This movement is not subject to dialectical synthesis, nor to any other closure. The undecidable, nevertheless, always has an impetus back into some covert form of dialectical movement, as in my terminology here of the "chain" and the "going beyond." This is constantly countered, however, by the experience of movement in place. The momentary always tends to generate a narrative, even if it is the narrative of the impossibility of narrative, the impossibility of getting from here to there by means of language. The tension between dialectic and undecidability is another way in which this form of criticism remains open, in the ceaseless movement of an "in place of" without resting place.

The word "deconstruction" is in one way a good one to name this movement. The word, like other words in "de," "decrepitude," for example, or "denotation," describes a paradoxical action which is negative and positive at once. In this it is like all words with a double antithetical prefix, words in "ana," like "analysis," or words in "para," like "parasite." These words tend to come in pairs which are not opposites, positive against negative. They are related in a systematic differentiation which requires a different analysis or untying in each case, but which in each case leads, in a different way each time, to the tying up of a double bind. This tying up is at the same time a loosening. It is a paralysis of thought in the face of what cannot be thought rationally: analysis, paralysis; solution, dissolution; composition, decomposition; construction, deconstruction; mantling, dismantling; canny, uncanny; competence, incompetence; apocalyptic, anacalyptic; constituting, deconstituting. Deconstructive criticism moves back and forth between the poles of these pairs, proving in its own activity, for example, that there is no deconstruction which is not at the same time constructive, affirmative. The word says this in juxtaposing "de" and "con."

At the same time, the word "deconstruction" has misleading overtones or implications. It suggests something a bit too external, a bit too masterful and muscular. It suggests the demolition of the helpless text with tools which are other than and stronger than what is demolished. The word "deconstruction" suggests that such criticism is an activity turning something unified back to detached fragments or parts. It suggests the image of a child taking apart his father's watch, reducing it back to useless parts, beyond any reconstitution. A deconstructionist is not a parasite but a parricide. He is a bad son demolishing beyond hope of repair the machine of Western metaphysics.

In fact, insofar as "deconstruction" names the use of rhetorical, etymological, or figurative analysis to demystify the mystifications of literary and philosophical language, this form of criticism is not outside but within. It is of the same nature as what it works against. Far from reducing the text back to detached fragments, it inevitably constructs again in a different form what it deconstructs. It does again as it undoes. It recrosses in one place what it uncrosses in another. Rather than surveying the text with sovereign command from outside, it remains caught within the activity in the text it retraces.

To the action of deconstruction with its implication of an irresistible power of the critic over the text must always be added, as a description of what happens in interpretation, the experience of the impossibility of exercising that power. The dismantler dismantles himself. Far from being a chain which moves deeper and deeper into the text, closer and closer to a definitive interpretation of it, the mode of criticism sometimes now called "deconstruction," which is analytic criticism as such, encounters always, if it is carried far enough, some mode of oscillation. In this oscillation two genuine insights into literature in general and into a given text in particular inhibit, subvert, and undercut one another. This inhibition makes it impossible for either insight to function as a firm resting place, the end point of analysis. My example here has been the co-presence in the parasite structure in Shelley of idealism and scepticism, of referentiality which only proleptically refers, in figure, therefore does not refer at all, and of performatives which do not perform. Analysis becomes paralysis, according to the strange necessity which makes these words, or the "experience," or the "procedure," they describe, turn into one another. Each crosses over into its apparent negation or opposite. If the word "deconstruction" names the procedure of criticism, and "oscillation" the impasse reached through that procedure, "undecidability" names the experience of a ceaseless dissatisfied movement in the relation of the critic to the text.

The ultimate justification for this mode of criticism, as of any conceivable mode, is that it works. It reveals hitherto unidentified meanings and ways of having meaning in major literary texts. The hypothesis of a possible heterogeneity in literary texts is more flexible, more open to a given work, than the assumption that a good work of literature is necessarily going to be "organically unified." The latter presupposition is one of the major factors inhibiting recognition of the possibly self-subversive complexity of meanings in a given work. Moreover, "deconstruction" finds in the text it interprets the double antithetical patterns it identifies, for example the relation of parasite and host. It does not claim them as universal explanatory structures, neither for the text in question nor for literature in general. Deconstruction attempts to resist the totalizing and totalitarian tendencies of criticism. It attempts to resist its own tendencies to come to rest in some sense of mastery over the work. It resists these in the name of an uneasy joy of interpretation, beyond nihilism, always in movement, a going beyond which remains in place, as the parasite is outside the door but also always already within, uncanniest of guests.

## NOTES

1. *Critical Inquiry,* II, 3 (Spring 1976), 457–58. The first phrase is quoted from Wayne Booth, "M. H. Abrams: Historian as Critic, Critic as Pluralist," *Critical Inquiry,* II, 3 (Spring 1976), 441. The opening pages of the present essay appeared in a preliminary form in *Critical Inquiry,* III, 3 (Spring 1977), 439–47, by permission of The University of Chicago Press.

2. All definitions and etymologies in this essay are taken from *The American Heritage Dictionary of the English Language,* William Morris, ed. (Boston: American Heritage Publishing Co., Inc. and Houghton Mifflin Company, 1969).

3. Walter Kaufmann and R. J. Hollingdale, trans., *The Will to Power* (New York: Vintage Books, 1968), p. 7; Friedrich Nietzsche, *Werke in Drei Bänden,* ed. Karl Schlechta, III (Munich: Carl Hanser Verlag, 1966), 881.

4. Jean T. Wilde and William Kluback, trans., *The Question of Being* [a bilingual text] (New Haven, Conn.: College & University Press, 1958), pp. 36–39.

5. Kaufmann and Hollingdale, p. 7; Schlechta, III, 881.

6. *The Triumph of Life* is cited from the text established by Donald H. Reiman in *Shelley's "The Triumph of Life": A Critical Study* (Urbana, Ill.: The University of Illinois Press, 1965). All other citations from Shelley are taken from *Poetical Works,* ed. Thomas Hutchinson, corrected by G. M. Matthews (London, Oxford, New York: Oxford University Press, 1973).

# Contributors

HAROLD BLOOM is Professor of Humanities at Yale University. His recent books include a tetralogy of critical studies on "poetic misprision": *The Anxiety of Influence* (1973), *A Map of Misreading* (1975), *Kabbalah and Criticism* (1975), *Poetry and Repression* (1976). Since then he has published a collection of essays, *Figures of Capable Imagination* (1976); a full-scale study, *Wallace Stevens: The Poems of Our Climate* (1977); and a visionary novel, *The Flight to Lucifer: A Gnostic Fantasy* (1979).

PAUL DE MAN is Chester D. Tripp Professor of Humanities at Yale University and Chairman of the Department of Comparative Literature. He is the author of *Blindness and Insight: Studies in the Rhetoric of Contemporary Criticism* (1971). A new book of his, *Allegories of Reading: Figural Language in Rousseau, Nietzsche, Rilke and Proust,* will appear in 1979.

JACQUES DERRIDA teaches philosophy and the history of philosophy at the École Normale Supérieure (Paris) and, since 1975, has been Visiting Professor of Humanities at Yale University. He is known in the English-speaking world for *"Speech and Phenomena" and Other Essays on Husserl's Theory of Signs* (1973), *Of Grammatology* (1976), *Edmund Husserl's "Origin of Geometry": An Introduction* (1978), *Writing and Difference* (1978), and *Spurs: Nietzsche's Styles* (1979). Among his other works are *La dissémination* (1972), *Marges—de la philosophie* (1972), *Positions* (1972), *L'archéologie du frivole* (1973), *Glas* (1974), and *La vérité en peinture* (1978).

GEOFFREY H. HARTMAN is Karl Young Professor of English and Comparative Literature at Yale University. He is the author of *The Unmediated Vision* (1954), *André Malraux* (1960), and *Wordsworth's Poetry* (1964); two collections of critical essays, *Beyond Formalism* (1970) and *The Fate of Reading* (1975); and a volume of poems, *Akiba's Children* (1978). He is also the editor of *Psychoanalysis and the Question of the Text* (1978). A new book, *Criticism in the Wilderness,* is scheduled to appear in 1980.

J. HILLIS MILLER is Frederick W. Hilles Professor of English at Yale. He is the author of a number of books on nineteenth- and twentieth-century English literature, among them *The Disappearance of God* (1963), *Poets of Reality* (1965), and *Thomas Hardy: Distance and Desire* (1970). He is at present completing three books: "Fiction and Repetition," on nineteenth- and twentieth-century English fiction; "The Linguistic Moment," on English and American Poetry of the same period; and "Ariadne's Thread," on narrative theory.